T0330435

Institutions and Wage Formation in the New Europe

Institutions and Wage Formation in the New Europe

Edited by

Gabriel Fagan

Head of Econometric Modelling Division, Directorate General Research, European Central Bank, Germany

Francesco Paolo Mongelli

Adviser, Directorate General Economics, European Central Bank, Germany

Julian Morgan

Senior Economist, Directorate General Research, European Central Bank, Germany

Edward Elgar
Cheltenham, UK • Northampton, MA, USA

Published by
Edward Elgar Publishing Limited
Glensanda House
Montpellier Parade
Cheltenham
Glos GL50 1UA
UK

Edward Elgar Publishing, Inc.
136 West Street
Suite 202
Northampton
Massachusetts 01060
USA

A catalogue record for this book
is available from the British Library

Library of Congress Cataloguing in Publication Data

Institutions and wage formation in the new Europe/edited by Gabriel Fagan,
    Francesco Paolo Mongelli, and Julian Morgan.
        p. cm.
    Papers from a workshop held at the European Central Bank in Frankfurt, 2001.
        1. Wages, Europe—Congresses. 2. Labor market—Europe—Congresses. 3.
    Europe—Economic integration—Congresses. I. Fagan, Gabriel, 1961– II.
    Mongelli, Francesco P. III. Morgan, Julian, 1966–   IV. European Central Bank.
    HD5014.I57 2004
    331.2'94—dc22

                                                                        2003047223

ISBN 1 84376 432 6

Typeset by Cambrian Typesetters, Frimley, Surrey
Printed and bound in Great Britain by MPG Books Ltd, Bodmin, Cornwall

Contents

Abbreviations

ALMP	active labour market policies
ANFC	Acuerdo Nacional de Formación Continua (National Agreement on Continuing Training – Spain)
AUT	Association of University Teachers (UK)
BHPS	British Household Panel Survey
BIS	Bank of International Settlements
CEPR	Centre for Economic Policy Research (UK)
CPI	Consumer Price Index
CPS	Current Population Survey
DG ECFIN	EU Commission DG for Economic and Financial Affairs
DTI	Department of Trade and Industry (UK)
ECB	European Central Bank
EIRO	European Industrial Relations Observatory
EIRR	European Industrial Relations Review
EMU	Economic and Monetary Union
ESRC	Economic and Social Research Council
ETUC	European Trade Union Confederation
ETUI	European Trade Union Institute
Eurostat	Statistical Office of the European Communities
FE	fixed-effects (model)
FLC	firm-level contract
GDP	gross domestic product
GLS	generalized least squares
GSOEP	German Socio-Economic Panel
ICT	information and communication technology
ILO	International Labour Organization
IMF	International Monetary Fund
IRAP	Imposta Regionale sull' Attività Produttiva
JER	Joint Employment Report
JSA	job search assistance
LDC	less developed country
LO	Landsorganisationen i Sverige (Swedish workers' organization)
MAE	mean absolute error
MEI	main economic indicators

NAIRU	non-accelerating inflation rate of unemployment
NAP	National Action Plan for Employment
NBER	National Bureau of Economic Research (USA)
NDYP	New Deal for Young People
NESP	New Earnings Survey Panel
NI	national insurance
NLSY	National Longitudinal Survey of Youth
NUTEK	Verket för Näringslivsutveckling (Swedish National Board for Industrial and Technical Development)
OECD	Organisation for Economic Co-operation and Development
OLS	ordinary least squares
ONS	Office of National Statistics
OWW	Occupational Wages around the World
PES	Public Employment Services
PPP	purchasing power parity
PSID	Panel Study of Income Dynamics
QNA	Quarterly National Accounts
RAE	Research Assessment Exercise (UK)
RE	random-effects (model)
RES	Royal Economic Society (UK)
RMSE	root mean square error
SAF	Svenska Arbetsgivareföreningen (Swedish employers' organization)
SIC	Standard Industrial Classification
SIM	Survey on Investment in Manufacturing (Italy)
SME	small and medium-sized enterprise
SNC	sectoral national contract
SOC	Standard Occupational Classification
SURE	seemingly unrelated regression estimation
TQM	total quality management
TUC	Trades Union Congress
VAR	vector auto regression
YTS	Youth Training Scheme

Contributors

Leandro Arozamena, Assistant Professor, Universidad Torcuato Di Tella, Buenos Aires

Alison L. Booth, Professor of Economics, Australian National University Canberra and University of Essex

Piero Casadio, Economist, Research Department, Bank of Italy, Rome

Mário Centeno, Economist, Research Department, Banco de Portugal, and Instituto Superior de Economia e Gestão, Universidade Técnica de Lisboa

Silvia Fabiani, Economist, Research Department, Bank of Italy, Rome

Gabriel Fagan, Head of Econometric Modelling Division, Directorate General Research, European Central Bank, Frankfurt/Main

Marco Francesconi, Principal Research Officer, Institute for Social and Economic Research, University of Essex

Jeff Frank, Professor of Economics, Royal Holloway College, University of London

Richard B. Freeman, Herbert Ascherman Chair in Economics, Harvard University; Director, Labor Studies Program, National Bureau of Economic Research, Cambridge, MA; Co-Director, Centre for Economic Performance, London School of Economics, Co-Director Labor and Work life program, Harvard Law School; Visiting Professor at the London School of Economics

Véronique Genre, Economist, Directorate General Economics, European Central Bank, Frankfurt/Main

Nadine Leiner-Killinger, Economist, Directorate General Economics, European Central Bank, Frankfurt/Main

Assar Lindbeck, Professor of International Economics, Institute for International Economic Studies, University of Stockholm; Research Fellow, Research Institute for Industrial Economics, Stockholm

Francesco Paolo Mongelli, Adviser, Directorate General Economics, European Central Bank, Frankfurt/Main

Julian Morgan, Senior Economist, Directorate General Research, European Central Bank, Frankfurt/Main

Annabelle Mourougane, Economist, Economics Department, Organisation for Economic Co-operation and Development, Paris

Gilles Mourre, Economist, Directorate General Economics, European Central Bank, Frankfurt/Main

Remco H. Oostendorp, Senior Researcher, Free University, Amsterdam

Karl Pichelmann, Research Adviser, Directorate General for Economic and Financial Affairs, European Commission, Brussels; Associate Professor, Institute d'Études Européennes, Université Libre de Bruxelles

Eswar S. Prasad, Division Chief (China Division), Asia and Pacific Department, International Monetary Fund, Washington DC; Research Fellow, Institute for the Study of Labor, Bonn

Ramón Gómez Salvador, Economist, Directorate General Economics, European Central Bank, Frankfurt/Main

Mark E. Schweitzer, Economic Advisor, Federal Reserve Bank of Cleveland

Dennis J. Snower, Professor of Economics, Birbeck College, University of London; Research Fellow, Centre for Economic Policy Research, London; Research Fellow, Program Director 'Welfare State and Labor Market', Institute for the Study of Labor, Bonn

Acknowledgements

We are grateful to the large number of people who made the ECB workshop 'How are Wages Determined in Europe' possible. In addition to the authors we wish to acknowledge the contributions made by the discussants: Michael Burda, Oliver de Bandt, Philip Du Caju, Jörg DeCressin, Florentino Felgueroso, Véronique Genre, Juan Francisco Jimeno, Julian Messina, Ricardo Mestre, Marga Peters, Ilmo Pyyhtiä and Eva Uddén Sonnegård. The following people also played an important role in the planning and organization of the workshop: Juan Angel García, Ramón Gómez Salvador, Ana Lamo, Nadine Leiner-Killinger, Gilles Mourre, Diego Rodríguez Palenzuela, Jarkko Turunen and Melanie Ward-Warmedinger. Excellent administrative assistance was provided by Christina Brandt and Birgitte Ilving. Last, and certainly not least, we wish to acknowledge the very important contribution of our editorial assistant, Annette Hochberger, whose careful attention to detail helped to smooth the publication process.

Gabriel Fagan, Francesco Paolo Mongelli and Julian Morgan

Introduction

Gabriel Fagan, Francesco P. Mongelli and Julian Morgan

This volume stems from a workshop entitled 'How are Wages Determined in Europe?' which took place at the European Central Bank in Frankfurt on 10–11 December 2001. The aim of the workshop was to analyse several features of European wage determination and how it has changed in recent years. This topic is particularly relevant at the present juncture in view of the possible effects of the introduction of the euro, the continuing implementation of the Single Market Programme and increasing economic integration. Such reforms, and changes in the economic environment, are unlikely to leave wage determination processes unaffected. The precise nature of these effects will depend crucially on labour market institutions and structures. Hence, a common theme linking the contributions in this volume is the role institutions and labour market structures are playing in wage formation. Moreover, European economic integration may itself feed back onto labour market institutions. Institutions are endogenous[1] and therefore can adapt to changing economic and social circumstances. A number of chapters in this volume seek to shed some light on how ongoing economic integration and new business practices may be leading to changes in institutions.

The chapters in this volume offer, *inter alia*, some new and interesting insights into the impact of trade unions and the nature of collective bargaining, unemployment benefits, minimum wages, employment protection legislation and the use of atypical forms of employment.[2] Under the general heading of Institutions and Wage Formation in Europe, three distinct broad themes emerged at the workshop. The first was the role of institutions in affecting the dispersion of wages across occupational, age, skill, industry and employment contract categories. The second was the explanation for recent wage moderation in Europe and the role of bargaining systems. The third was the extent to which institutions are evolving within Europe in the light of EMU and other economic and commercial factors. These themes are addressed either at the general European level or by investigating developments within some selected European countries.

INSTITUTIONS AND WAGE DISPERSION

Many labour market institutions that play a relatively significant role in European countries – for example trade unions, minimum wages and unemployment benefits – have been associated with the more compressed wage distribution seen in many European countries when compared with the United States. Issues surrounding wage dispersion and relative wages are at the forefront of the first four chapters of this volume.

In Chapter 1, 'Is European wage-setting different? Evidence from the Occupational Wages around the World data file', Richard Freeman and Remco Oostendorp shed light on the role that European wage-setting institutions play in affecting occupational wage formation. An important innovation of this study is the use of occupational wage data drawn from the ILO's data set 'Occupational Wages around the World' (OWW). In order to make these data usable, the authors needed to undertake a large calibration and standardization exercise. They then use these data to examine the extent to which wage patterns and wage determinants differ between advanced European countries and other advanced economies and less developed countries. The authors find substantially different wage patterns between advanced European countries, other advanced economies and less developed countries. In particular it appears that higher GDP per capita is associated with a more compressed distribution of occupational pay in advanced European economies than for other countries. The authors' interpretation of this observation is that the greater impact of growth on wage dispersion in Europe reflects the influence of European wage-setting institutions. It is also found that institutional factors – trade unionism and measures of economic freedom – have different impacts on European wage-setting compared with other countries.

In Chapter 2, 'What determines the reservation wages of unemployed workers? New evidence from German micro data', Eswar Prasad examines the effects of unemployment benefits and the minimum wage on the lower end of the wage distribution in Germany. A key element of both these institutions is that they can affect the reservation wage in wage bargaining models. Prasad constructs a simple theoretical model that relates the reservation wage of unemployed workers to macroeconomic factors (both cyclical and structural) and individual characteristics (for example proxies for human capital). The predictions of the model are tested with data drawn from the German Socio-Economic Panel (GSOEP). This panel of individual data is well suited for such analysis as it explicitly asks unemployed workers for their reservation wage and includes a rich subset of individual and household specific characteristics. A particularly interesting finding of this chapter is a negative relationship between the reservation wage ratio (ratio of reservation to offer wages) and skill levels. In other words, the reservation wage is relatively high in relation to the available offers for those at the low end of the wage distribution. The tentative conclusion drawn from this finding is that there appear to be significant labour supply rigidities at the low end of the German skill/wage distribution, which may in part be attributable to the unemployment benefit system. The author argues that these point to the need for comprehensive policy reforms which allow for more flexibility in the dispersion of wages and also reduce the disincentives for seeking employment for those at the low end of the wage distribution.

The next contribution considers the effects of temporary contracts, including the relative wages of those on temporary and permanent contracts. In Chapter 3, 'Labour as a buffer: Do temporary workers suffer?', Alison Booth, Marco Francesconi and Jeff Frank examine this issue with data from the UK. They consider whether fixed-term workers are disproportionately female or from other 'equal opportunities' groups, and whether such workers receive less pay than comparably qualified permanent workers. To address these questions, the authors develop a buffer-stock model which provides a number of reasons why ethnic minorities and women may be more likely to be on fixed-term contracts than comparable white males and why those on fixed-term contracts may receive lower pay. These findings are tested empirically using three data sources relating to the UK: the British Household Panel Survey, data on academic economists and data on university employees. In the raw data they find evidence that women (but not ethnic minorities) are more likely to be employed on a fixed-term basis and that there is a positive wage differential favouring permanent employees over fixed-term ones. After controlling for a wide range of individual and workplace characteristics, the evidence on representation in fixed-term work by gender is less clear, although the existence of a wage differential between fixed-term and permanent employment remains. The authors argue that the existence of such a differential combined with a greater prevalence of women in fixed-term employment – even if explainable by observed characteristics – means that there is an important equal opportunities dimension to regulating equal pay and conditions for such work. However, these regulations need to be considered in tandem with any adverse effects on total employment as indicated by the authors' buffer-stock model.

Leandro Arozamena and Mário Centeno study the effect of increasing tenure on the relationship between wages and external labour market conditions in Chapter 4, 'Moving from the external to an internal labour market: Job tenure, cycle and wage determination'. The authors use a matching model that incorporates learning about job quality while employed and introduce business cycle effects by allowing both the expectation of the quality of new matches and the value a match to vary with the cycle. They show that as job-specific human capital is accumulated, the wage received by the worker is protected from cyclical variation in the external labour market. Arozamena and Centeno test this implication of the model by evaluating the effect of tenure on the elasticity of wages to unemployment using data from the United States. They find that the elasticity is lower for workers with more tenure, thus supporting a key finding of the theoretical model.

CAN BARGAINING SYSTEMS EXPLAIN WAGE MODERATION IN EUROPE?

Three chapters in this volume seek to shed some light on the factors behind the wage moderation that has been seen in many European countries in the run-up to, and early years of, EMU. In Chapter 5, 'Wage developments in the early years of EMU', Karl Pichelmann opens this debate with an examination of the recent evolution of wages in euro area countries and a discussion of possible causal factors. Pichelmann reviews the evidence on wage and unit labour cost developments, which reveals a marked slowdown in both measures in recent years. However, labour costs are growing more rapidly in some EMU member states and there was a pick-up – albeit modest by historical standards – in aggregate unit labour costs in 2001. The role of several possible explanatory factors for the slowdown in wage growth, including reforms to labour and product markets – and the monetary-union process itself – is discussed. The author argues that, while these factors are likely to have played a role in restraining wage growth, there is also likely to have been a role for 'informal incomes policies' in a number of countries. As such policies tend to be 'inherently fragile', this factor cannot be relied upon to sustain moderation in the future.

Piero Casadio analyses the main effects of the 1992–93 Italian income policy agreement in Chapter 6, 'Wage formation in the Italian private sector after the 1992–93 Income Policy Agreements'. Consistent with Pichelmann's finding, Casadio argues that these agreements were a crucial ingredient of the wage moderation at this time. In his view, they facilitated employment growth, fiscal consolidation and the participation in the first wave of EMU. Casadio also suggests that in the Italian case such policies cannot be relied upon to sustain wage moderation in the near future. In the longer term he is more sanguine, arguing that overall wage moderation seems not to be at risk. However, he suggests that firm level flexible arrangements – relating for instance to wage differentials and temporary contracts – may be more vulnerable.

In Chapter 7, 'A widening scope for non-wage components in collective bargaining in the EU?', Véronique Genre, Ramón Gómez Salvador, Nadine Leiner-Killinger and Gilles Mourre note that collective bargaining is increasingly taking place against the background of a growing importance of non-wage elements. They find such elements to be in four main areas: training and life-long learning, health and safety at work, reconciling work and private life and, lastly, working time. Although there are no direct indicators for non-wage components in collective bargaining in most EU countries, it seems that the number of agreements actually covering these non-wage-labour-related aspects, albeit still limited in some countries, has increased in the latter part of the 1990s. It is possible to interpret the bargaining on these non-wage components as beneficial for both workers and firms. On the one hand, employees obtain a compensation in exchange for moderate wage developments. On the other hand, factors such as training and working-time flexibility can increase workers' productivity. Thus, the emergence of non-wage components in wage bargaining may have contributed to a slower growth in wages than would otherwise have been the case.

THE EXTENT TO WHICH INSTITUTIONS ARE EVOLVING IN EUROPE

As indicated at the start of this introduction, a number of chapters examine the changing role of institutions. Stemming both from autonomous private sector responses to the economic environment as well as the impacts of public policies, these ongoing changes raise issues such as whether labour markets are becoming more flexible, the prospects for ongoing wage moderation and the future of centralized bargaining. However, before considering such questions it is useful to take stock and consider how much wage formation differs across euro area countries. This is particularly relevant as it is sometimes argued that EMU will tend to encourage some sort of convergence in labour markets across the euro area.

A problem for labour market analysts since the start of EMU has been to what extent they should focus on trying to understand aggregate euro area developments as opposed to aiming to understand national developments. In Chapter 8, 'Aggregation and euro area Phillips curves', Silvia Fabiani and Julian Morgan address this issue by considering the extent to which the relationship between wage growth, inflation and the tightness of the labour market is similar in the large euro area countries. Their analysis – using a wage–price Phillips relationship – suggests that freely estimated national equations do generate different estimates of the impact of the rate of unemployment on wage formation. However, when considered as a part of a system, some of these differences do not prove to be statistically significant, and it is possible to impose a common unemployment effect on wage growth across countries.

Fabiani and Morgan also consider the potential gains and losses from pursuing aggregate as opposed to country-level analysis of such relationships. Although the statistical properties of the euro area-wide equation were quite good overall, its standard error was higher than the aggregated standard errors from the national equations, estimated both independently and as a system. The authors also examined the forecast performance of the aggregate and national equations and found that short-term aggregate wage growth (that is, one to two quarters ahead) would have been better predicted if the national approach had been adopted and the results aggregated. Overall, the results point to some advantages from estimating national wage-based Phillips curves rather than conducting the analysis at the euro area-wide level. None the less, the results also suggest that – at least at the macro level – differences in wage formation across euro area countries are less pronounced than is usually supposed.

Moving to the country level, it is widely believed that the labour market reforms implemented in the 1980s and 1990s have led to greater flexibility in the UK. In Chapter 9, 'Wage flexibility in Britain: Some micro and macro evidence', Mark Schweitzer addresses this question using data from the New Earnings Survey (1975 to 2000). He considers alternative macro- and micro-economic methods of measuring wage flexibility and investigates whether wages in Britain have become more flexible in recent years. Evidence from macroeconomic wage equations suggests that, although the relationship between wages and employment has changed over time, there has been no significant increase in wage flexibility as the responsiveness of wages to unemployment has declined in the 1990s. The microeconomic tests find that the prevalence of nominal rigidities has not declined, except for weak evidence for the most recent years. Real rigidities are also shown to be statis-tically significant and overall, the microeconomic evidence points to an increase rather than a decline in real rigidities in recent years. Hence, the evidence that the author finds is not supportive of the view that UK labour markets have become more flexible.

In Chapter 10, 'Centralized bargaining and reorganized work: Are they compatible?' by Assar Lindbeck and Dennis Snower, the future of centralized wage bargaining is considered. The authors argue that new information and production technologies are encouraging firms to flatten their hierarchies of control and responsibility, allowing for greater decentralization of decision-making. This means that the new forms of work are often organized around small, customer-oriented teams, rather than large functional departments, with considerable discretion both for the teams and individual workers. With such an organization of work there is a move away from occupational specializa-tion towards multi-tasking. The authors show that, with such new forms of organization, centralized bargaining becomes increasingly inefficient and detrimental to firms' profit opportunities as it prevents them from offering their employees adequate incentives to perform the required mix of tasks. Centralized bargaining is also shown to inhibit firms from using wages to encourage workers to learn how to use their experience drawn from one set of tasks to improve their performance at other tasks. They argue that these factors may help explain the increasing resistance to centralized bargaining in many advanced market economies.

While changes in private sector behaviours are likely to impact on wage formation and employment patterns, government interventions are also expected to play a prominent role in influencing labour markets. In recent years, there has been a growing policy focus on active labour market policies (ALMPs). Such measures have the potential to affect labour supply, and in some cases also labour demand, and thereby would be expected to have a bearing on wage pressures. The effects of these policies are analysed in Chapter 11 by Julian Morgan and Annabelle Mourougane entitled 'The impact of active labour market policies in Europe'. This chapter highlights the policy measures that are being undertaken in the European Union, reviews the literature on the effectiveness of such interventions and draws some general conclusions on their likely impact on unemployment and wage formation. The analysis indicates important differences in the effects of different types of ALMPs (for instance, training or subsidized employment schemes) and that key elements in scheme design (for instance, whether the training is classroom based or provided by potential employers) can have a major bearing on its effectiveness.

To sum up, the chapters in this volume address the role played by institutional factors in wage formation. Under this general heading, there are three distinct broad themes. The first emphasizes the role of institutions in affecting the dispersion of wages across occupational, age, skill, industry and employment contract categories. The contributions make clear the profound effect that European institutions can have in influencing, and in most cases compressing, such pay differentials with consequent implications for the employment prospects of certain segments of the labour force. The second theme is the explanation for recent wage moderation in Europe. The contributions here emphasize the role of developments in the bargaining systems of European countries and the presence of a number of temporary or specific factors which have helped to bring about wage moderation. The third, and final, broad theme is the extent to which institutions are changing within Europe in the light of EMU and the adoption of new business practices.

NOTES

1. As emphasized by Saint-Paul (2002).
2. Morgan and Mourougane (2001) provide a brief review of the likely effects of these institutions on wage bargaining.

REFERENCES

Morgan, J. and A. Mourougane (2001), *What can changes in structural factors tell us about unemployment in Europe*, ECB Working Paper No. 81.

Saint-Paul, G. (2002), 'The political economy of employment protection', *Journal of Political Economy*, June **110** (3), 672–704.

1. Is European wage-setting different? Evidence from the Occupational Wages around the World data file

Richard B. Freeman and Remco H. Oostendorp

1 INTRODUCTION

To what extent does the pattern of wage outcomes and determinants of wages differ between advanced countries, particularly those in the European Union, and less developed countries? Do the same labour market measures and tools of analysis apply equally to countries with very different levels of economic development, or do wage outcomes differ so much between countries as to put differences in institutional wage-setting at the heart of labour market analysis?

The Washington consensus view of the world economy gives little scope for differences in institutions and levels of economic development to affect outcomes, once countries accept markets as the main allocative device for labour. After all, 'markets are market are markets', with the same modes of operation across countries. From this perspective, globalization should reduce differences in wages and wage structures across countries, with the global labour market replacing national markets to a considerable extent over the long run.[1] By contrast, institutionally oriented economists assume that labour markets differ depending on institutional factors. They expect that labour markets with the 'social partnership' arrangements and related thick institutions of most European countries would operate differently from those in other countries, yielding different wage outcomes and different relations to wage-determining factors.

To what extent do wage patterns and the determinants of wages differ between advanced European countries and the less developed countries which make up the bulk of the world's working population and between European and other advanced countries?

This chapter uses the newly developed Occupational Wages around the World (OWW) data file to examine these questions. It contrasts wage inequality by occupation and wage levels in common currency units by occupation between advanced European countries and the rest of the world. Section 2 gives a brief description of the OWW data file and describes its strengths and weaknesses for comparing wages across countries. Section 3 compares the dispersion of wages by occupation in advanced Europe with the dispersion of wages in other parts of the world. Section 4 looks at the cross-country difference in wages for the same occupations, focusing on the clustering of wages by level of economic development. Section 5 examines the relation between measures of market institutions and the level of wages between advanced European economies and other economies.

2   THE OWW DATA FILE[2]

Since 1924, as part of its October Inquiry investigation of living conditions around the world the ILO has sent an annual questionnaire to national governments asking for data on wages in detailed occupations. To ensure comparability of occupational definitions across the countries, the ILO specifies in great detail the work involved in each occupation. To get a flavour of the specificity consider the following description of a clicker cutter in the footwear industry:

> Clicker cutter (machine). Operates press machine which cuts out upper parts of footwear; lays material on the table of machine; selects cutting dies; arranges dies on material to cut it economically and avoid weaknesses; cuts out show part by lowering press onto dies; removes cut-out parts from material.

Or this (abbreviated) description of an accountant in a bank:

> Accountant. Plans and administers accounting services and examines, analyses, interprets and evaluates accounting records for the purpose of giving advice on accountancy problems or preparing statements and installing or advising on systems of recording costs or other financial and budgetary data: . . . keeps record of all taxes, fees, etc. to be paid by the bank . . . conducts financial investigations on suspected fraud . . . prepares and certifies financial statements for presentation to the board of directors, executives, shareholders . . .

The scope of the October Inquiry data has expanded over time from data on male earners in 18 occupations in 15 countries in 1924 to wage statistics on 161 occupations for 158 countries in at least one year and up to 76 countries in any given year from 1983 to 1999.[3] In the 1983–99 period there were 17 high-income European countries, including one former communist country – Slovenia. Germany provided the most consistent and detailed data while by contrast France provided no data.

If each country obtained wages from a nationally representative survey based on ILO definitions, the October Inquiry would be the ideal source for comparing the pay of comparable labour across countries. Clicker cutters, accountants, economists, whoever – from Pakistan or Romania or Germany or the USA – would have interchangeable skills, so that one would truly be comparing equivalent labour. But the October Inquiry data fall short of ideal. To the contrary, the Inquiry data have so many problems that the survey is one of the least-used sources of cross-country data in the world.

The principal reason for the problem is that countries report data from different national sources rather than conducting special surveys to answer the ILO request. Some countries report wages paid in an occupation from an establishment survey. Other countries report legislated minimum wages for some occupations. Yet others, such as Germany, report minimum wage rates based on collective agreements on hourly, daily, weekly and monthly wage rates, depending on the occupation. Moreover, the sources of the data change over time. For example, up to 1985 the USA reported wage rates from trade unions and earnings from Industry Wage Surveys. From 1986 to 1997 the USA reported median usual weekly earnings from the Current Population Survey. Since 1997 the USA has reported median wage rates from an employer-based survey. Some countries give wages for men in some occupations. Others report wages for men and women, while others report wages for women in some occupations, and so on.

Countries also do not report consistently from year to year. In the 1983–99 period 158 countries reported wages in at least one year, but just five countries reported wages 17 times (every year), 40 reported 10–16 times, 51 reported five to nine times, 43 reported two to four times, and 19 reported just once. Looking across the years, in 1983, 56 countries reported wages; in 1985, 71 reported wages; in 1990, 72 reported; in 1992, 60 reported; in 1995, 76 reported; in 1997, 66 reported; and finally, in 1999, 45 countries reported wages.

Table 1.1 gives a detailed description of information in the Inquiry files from the 1983–99 period on which we focus. Panel A gives information on the size of the sample. The first column gives data from the entire file, including observations that the ILO statistics office regards as being of poor or lower quality. We report these data because the published versions of the October Inquiry data contain this information and because for some analyses even data of dubious quality may be preferable to no data at all. The second column records the number of observations from sources which the ILO statistics office regards as acceptable or better. The third column gives figures for all high-income European economies.

The row labelled 'maximum conceivable observations' shows the number of observations that the Inquiry would contain if each country reported a single wage statistic for each occupation yearly: over 432 000 pieces of data.[4] The actual number of observations is smaller, largely because most countries

Table 1.1   Observations in the 1983–99 October Inquiry computer files

A.   Sample size

	All data	Acceptable data	Europe data[5]
Maximum conceivable observations	432 446	369 495	46 529
Observations missing because country did not report in given year	255 990	211 393	14 007
Observations missing because occupation missing in year country reported	93 913	83 008	16 505
Actual year–country–occupation observation	82 543	75 094	16 017
Observations with multiple figures	38 107	34 117	8 168
multiple figures	54 969	50 219	12 668
Total, including all multiple observations	137 512	125 313	28 685

B.   Countries and occupations with at least one reported wage statistic

Countries with reported wage statistic for different numbers of occupations

No. of occupations	All data, no. of countries (total: 158)	Acceptable data, no. of countries (total: 135)	Europe data, no. of countries (total: 17)
<30	8	6	–
30–59	21	17	4
60–79	21	18	3
80–99	21	18	1
100–119	32	27	2
120–139	20	20	3
140+	35	29	4

Occupations with one reported wage statistic for different numbers of countries

No. of countries reporting on occupation	All data	Acceptable data, no. of occupations (total: 161)	Europe data
<59	15	22	161
60–79	25	42	
80–99	38	44	
100–119	47	48	
120+	36	5	

C.   Actual observations

	All data	Acceptable data	Europe
Pay concept			
Wages (142 countries)	88 453	82 251	17 059
Earnings (95 countries)	49 059	43 062	11 626

Table 1.1 continued

	All data	Acceptable data	Europe
Averaging concept			
Mean	95 221	85 255	20 249
Minimum	30 060	28 902	7 541
Maximum	4 202	4 023	649
Average of min–max	336	330	89
Prevailing	4 491	3 748	157
Median	2 542	2 434	
Other	13	13	
Missing	647	638	
Period concept			
Monthly	86 906	79 173	16 263
Hourly[a]	23 471	22 931	8 863
Weekly	15 987	13 883	2 886
Daily	7 220	6 562	399
Annual	2 529	2 308	274
Fortnight	1 253	439	
Other	146	17	
Gender			
Males	58 555	51 783	11 830
Both	49 294	46 861	9 710
Females	29 663	26 669	7 145

Note: [a]The hourly figures include a small number for whom the data tell us that they relate to hours paid for and another small number for whom the wages relate to hours worked.

Source: Tabulated from ILO October Inquiry files, 1983–99. All data include observations where the ILO statistics office judged the data to be of poor or lower quality. The acceptable data include only observations of acceptable/good or excellent quality. See Table 1.2.

do not report statistics in many years. On average, countries report wages for 6.9 years out of 17 possible years. As a result over a quarter of a million (255 990) of the potential observations are missing because countries did not report data in particular years. In addition, countries do not report data for every occupation in the years when they do report, and some of the data come from sources that the ILO labels of poor quality. The bottom line is that there are 75 094 actual year–country–occupation observations of acceptable or better quality and 16 017 data points for the high-income European countries on which we focus.

There is a further complication that gives us a handle on the diversity of data. Many countries report more than one wage for a single occupation. Some give hourly wage rates *and* average earnings. Others give wages for men *and* wages for women. Others give wages for one gender *and* for both genders. Nearly half of the observations (46.2 per cent) in the first column contain multiple wage figures. Having multiple figures for the same occupation makes the raw data difficult to use in cross-country comparisons – particularly since different countries report pay differently – but allows us to calibrate the data to a single form, using standard statistical techniques. Including multiple wages, we have 125 313 pieces of data of acceptable or better quality, and 28 685 pieces of data for advanced European economies.

Panel B of Table 1.1 shows the frequency distribution of countries by the number of occupations they report, and the frequency distribution of occupations by the number of countries that report statistics on them. The distribution of countries by number of occupations shows that in most countries there are a sufficient number of occupations with wage data to get a good measure of the overall wage structure. In addition, however, these data show that different countries report on different numbers of occupations, which creates problems in comparing wage structures across countries. The distribution of occupations by country shows that many occupations have wage data for large numbers of countries, which will allow us to contrast labour costs and living standards for workers in the same occupation around the world.

Panel C shows the diverse way in which countries report wages. Most countries report wage rates from employer surveys or collective bargaining contracts or legislated pay schedules. However, many report earnings, largely from employer surveys, though some report earnings from household surveys. Most give statistics in the form of averages[6] but 22 per cent report minimum wages, some from collective bargaining contracts. Some countries report maximum wages. Others give prevailing wages. The time period to which the pay refers also varies. The most common period is the month, followed by the hour, but some countries report weekly pay, others give daily rates for some occupations and so on. There is also variation by gender. A total of 43 per cent of the observations relate to male workers, 36 per cent to all workers and 21 per cent to female workers. Combining all of these different variants, the vast majority of the Inquiry statistics are non-comparable. Just 5.7 per cent relate simultaneously to the most common pay concept (wages), use the most common averaging concept (mean), cover the most common time span (monthly) and relate to the most common gender (male).[7]

Despite these and other problems described in detail in Freeman and Oostendorp (2001),[8] the October Inquiry data remain a potentially valuable – indeed a unique – source of information on wages by occupation around the world.[9] Accordingly we undertook a massive standardization exercise to make the data useful for research. Our goal was to transform each observation, however reported, into a standard rate based on the most common form of data

in the Inquiry – monthly average wages for male workers. To see how we standardized the data, consider each observation W to be the sum of a standard rate
W^* and an adjustment for the way the data are reported, W^a, where the super-
script a reflects the deviation of the observed wage from the most common
form, and an error term, v:

$$W(i,j,o,t) = W^*(j,o,t) + W^a (i,j,o,t) + v(i,j,o,t) \qquad (1.1)$$

where i measures the data type,[10] j refers to the country, o is the occupation,
and t is the time period.

The calibration problem is to estimate W^* for observations where data are
reported in non-standard form – that is, to find adjustment coefficients that
measure how non-standard forms of data diverge from W^* for different countries, occupations and time periods. Let $X (i,j,o,t)$ be a row vector of dummies
for data type, which takes the value one if the observation is of the particular
data type and $B(i,j,o,t)$ be a column vector of deviations of a particular type of
data from the normal. Then we write (1.1) as:

$$W(i,j,o,t) = W^*(j,o,t) + X(i,j,o,t) B(i,j,o,t) + v(i,j,o,t) \qquad (1.2)$$

The key to the adjustment process is finding B coefficients by which to assess
how much a given observation must be changed to reach the standard form.
Given the data we have, the natural way to estimate the B coefficients is to regress
the $W(i,j,o,t)$ on $W^*(j,o,t)$ and the dummy variables using the observations in
which there are data for both the standard form and the non-standard form:

$$W(i,j,o,t) = W^*(j,o,t) + X(i,j,o,t) B(i,j,o,t) + v(i,j,o,t) \qquad (1.3)$$

where the observations (i,j,o,t) are those for which we have both standard and
non-standard wages and where v is a residual term with $E(v) = 0$.

Given the estimated Bs, we can predict W^* for observations that did not
have both types from the following equation:

$$PW^*(j,o,t) = W(i,j,o,t) – X^a(i,j,o,t) PB(i,j,o,t) \qquad (1.4)$$

where P before a term reflects the predicted or estimated value.[11]

To see what this means in practice, consider a situation in which the standard form is specified as male monthly mean wages (because this is the most
frequently reported form). Then, an observation which gives mean monthly
wages for females would require one adjustment, for gender. If we know the
impact of gender on wages for the specific occupation or country, this would
require one adjustment in the reported wage. For example, the reported mean
wage for cloth weavers in China in the 1990 data is 171 yuan per month for
women. Under our base calibration we estimate that this wage should be raised

to 201 yuan per month to be on a male basis. Fifty per cent of our calibrations involve the addition of one adjustment factor, 46 per cent involve the addition of two adjustment factors, 4 per cent require three adjustments, and there are sporadic cases where four adjustments are necessary.

The result of our exercise is a huge country–occupation–time file on pay in 161 occupations in over 150 countries from 1983 to 1999, where pay is defined consistently for a particular reference group, albeit with many missing elements. We use it to examine differences in the structure and determinants of pay between advanced European countries and the rest of the world.

3   OCCUPATIONAL EARNINGS INEQUALITY ACROSS COUNTRIES

To obtain manageable and comprehensible statistics on occupational earnings differentials from the OWW matrix, we calculated for every country the standard deviation of the log of pay and the ratio of the wages in the occupation in the 90th percentile of the occupation wage distribution to the wages in the occupation in the 10th percentile of the distribution for *all of the occupations* reported in a given period. These comparisons use the maximum amount of data but are based on different numbers of occupations across countries which could affect the measured spread of wages.[12] The most natural way to deal with this problem is to compute measures of skill differences for exactly the same occupations for all countries. But countries give wages for different occupations, so that this least common denominator strategy would greatly reduce the sample size. Instead we treat observations as samples from the distribution of occupational wages for each country rather than as estimates of wages for a specific occupation. We then compute the decile distribution of wages by occupation and calculate measures of dispersion from this distribution. Specifically we ordered occupations by their wage in each country time period, divided the ordering into deciles and took the median wage in each decile as that decile's wage in the country.[13] This gives us ten decile wages for each country, from which we calculate measures of dispersion. For instance, if the top 10 per cent paying occupations in the USA consisted of eight occupations, we would use the median wage among those eight to represent the top decile in the USA, whereas if the top 10 per cent in India had wages only for three occupations, we would use those three wages to estimate the top decile in India. It turns out that the measures of dispersion of pay based on this decile analysis and measures using all of the data are highly correlated, which implies that the number of occupations does not create a serious problem in our data. Accordingly we report results from analysis of the maximum number of occupational data points, though limiting our sample to countries that report on 30 or more occupations.[14]

Table 1.2   Measures of the occupational wage structure within countries, 1989–92

High-income economies	No. of occupations	Sd Ln W		p90/p10	
		All	Decile	All	Decile
European countries		0.28	0.26	2.01	2.06
AT – Austria	144	0.33	0.33	2.18	2.47
BE – Belgium	42	0.17	0.17	1.49	1.52
CY – Cyprus	112	0.44	0.40	2.94	2.85
DE – Germany	159	0.37	0.35	2.52	2.60
DK – Denmark	57	0.19	0.19	1.57	1.67
FI – Finland	124	0.25	0.26	1.83	1.98
GB – United Kingdom	50	0.28	0.26	2.04	2.01
GI – Gibraltar	32	0.28	0.26	1.91	2.00
IE – Ireland (1984)	46	0.33	0.32	2.22	2.29
IS – Iceland	<30	–	–	–	–
IT – Italy	144	0.27	0.25	1.76	1.92
LU – Luxembourg (1995)	74	0.28	0.27	1.87	2.02
NL – Netherlands	70	0.22	0.22	1.62	1.75
NO – Norway	31	0.18	0.17	1.69	1.55
PT – Portugal	<30	–	–	–	–
SE – Sweden	130	0.20	0.17	1.53	1.57
SI – Slovenia	57	0.35	0.35	2.93	2.65
Other high-income countries		0.41	0.39	2.70	2.88
AN – Netherlands Antilles	47	0.40	0.37	2.70	2.82
AU – Australia	149	0.24	0.26	1.80	1.99
BM – Bermuda	46	0.41	0.39	2.10	2.60
CA – Canada (1985)	76	0.27	0.27	2.07	2.10
GU – Guam (1987)	90	0.47	0.46	3.30	3.51
HK – Hong Kong	52	0.44	0.41	2.53	2.97
JP – Japan	43	0.35	0.31	1.96	2.31
MO – Macau	<30	–	–	–	–
NC – New Caledonia (1983)	65	0.56	0.56	4.25	4.27
NZ – New Zealand	136	0.35	0.31	2.25	2.30
PF – Polynesia, French	87	0.46	0.44	3.40	3.22
PM – Saint-Pierre-et-Miquelon	67	0.30	0.32	2.10	2.40
SG – Singapore	121	0.54	0.51	3.66	3.94
US – United States	86	0.34	0.35	2.31	2.46
VG – Virgin Islands (British) (1985)	55	0.59	0.45	2.99	3.39
VI – Virgin Islands (US)	70	0.40	0.39	3.15	2.93

Table 1.2   continued

High-income economies		Sd Ln W		p90/p10	
	No. of occupations	All	Decile	All	Decile
Upper middle income (9)		0.47	0.44	3.42	3.53
Lower middle income (9)		0.44	0.41	3.30	3.48
Low-income (18)		0.58	0.57	4.44	4.93
IN – India	92	0.58	0.50	4.51	3.47
Small populations* (9)		0.46	0.45	3.10	3.45
Communist and ex-communist* (6)		0.29	0.28	2.03	2.18
CN – China	82	0.28	0.27	1.88	1.97

Note: In some tabulations we allocate the small economies or communist economies to their appropriate income class. *Except the high-income countries already listed.

Table 1.2 presents our measures of the dispersion of wages by occupation for the mid-period in our data, 1989–92, for the advanced European countries and for other advanced countries and for all other countries in the file, by the level of development of countries. As measures of dispersion we use the standard deviation of the logarithm of wages (SD in wage) and the ratio of the 90th and 10th percentile of the wage distribution within a country (p90/p10). To obtain the maximum number of comparisons over this period, we report the figures for the year in the interval which gave the most data. Columns 2 and 4 give the statistics based on all of the occupations reporting in the peak year, while columns 3 and 5 give the statistics based on our estimated decile earnings in the occupation–earnings distribution. Both calculations show that wage inequality is smaller in the more advanced countries, particularly the European advanced economies, and is particularly small in the communist countries.

Figure 1.1 shows the inverse relation between skill differentials and level of economic development in a somewhat different way. It graphs the standard deviation of ln wages by occupation in a country against the level of GDP per capita in the country for the year for which the highest number of occupations was reported (GDP per capita in constant PPP). While there is considerable variation in occupational wage inequality for countries with the same level of GDP per capita – for instance the USA has a high level of inequality for advanced countries – the scatter diagram shows clearly the inverse relation between income per head and the spread of wages among occupations. An inverse relation between earnings inequality and GDP per capita has been found in other data sets, albeit none with the same extent of coverage across countries and occupation as in the OWW, so there is no 'news' in this figure. But the richness of the OWW allows us to examine the GDP–inequality relationship in greater detail.

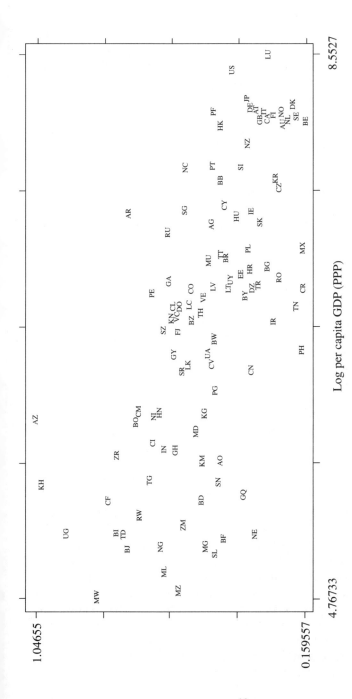

Key: Countries included are: AO – Angola; AG – Antigua and Barbuda; AR – Argentina; AT – Austria; AU – Australia; AZ – Azerbaijan; BB – Barbados; BD – Bangladesh; BE – Belgium; BF – Burkina Faso; BG – Bulgaria; BI – Burundi; BJ – Benin; BO – Bolivia; BR – Brazil; BW – Botswana; BY – Belarus; BZ – Belize; CA – Canada; CF – Central African Republic; CI – Côte d'Ivoire; CL – Chile; CM – Cameroon; CN – China; CO – Colombia; CR – Costa Rica; CV – Cape Verde; CY – Cyprus; CZ – Czech Republic; DE – Germany; DK – Denmark; DO – Dominican Republic; DZ – Algeria; EE – Estonia; ER – Eritrea; FI – Finland; FJ – Fiji; GA – Gabon; GB – United Kingdom; GH – Ghana; GQ – Guinea Equatorial; GY – Guyana; HK – Hong Kong; HN – Honduras; HR – Croatia; HU – Hungary; IE – Ireland; IN – India; IR – Iran, Islamic Rep. of; IT – Italy; JP – Japan; KG – Kyrgyzstan; KH – Cambodia; KM – Comoros; KN – Saint Kitts and Nevis; KR – Korea, Rep. of; LC – St Lucia; LK – Sri Lanka; LT – Lithuania; LU – Luxembourg; LV – Latvia; MD – Moldova; MG – Madagascar; ML – Mali; MU – Mauritius; MW – Malawi; MX – Mexico; MZ – Mozambique; NC – New Caledonia; NE – Niger; NG – Nigeria; NI – Nicaragua; NL – Netherlands; NO – Norway; NZ – New Zealand; PE – Peru; PF – French Polynesia; PG – Papua New Guinea; PH – Philippines; PK – Pakistan; PL – Poland; PT – Portugal; RO – Romania; RU – Russian Federation; RW – Rwanda; SE – Sweden; SG – Singapore; SI – Slovenia; SK – Slovakia; SL – Sierra Leone; SN – Senegal; SR – Suriname; SZ – Swaziland; TD – Chad; TG – Togo; TH – Thailand; TN – Tunisia; TR – Turkey; TT – Trinidad and Tobago; UG – Uganda; US – United States; UY – Uruguay; VC – St Vincent and the Grenadines; VE – Venezuela; ZM – Zambia; ZR – Zaire.

Figure 1.1 Standard deviation of ln occupational wages vs log GDP per capita (PPP), by country

Table 1.3 presents the result of regressing the level of dispersion in occupational wages on the log of GDP per capita measured in constant PPP units or in constant US 1995 dollars (which gives us a slightly larger sample due to absence of PPP adjustment for some countries in some years) for the advanced European countries, other advanced countries and for the rest of the world – the less developed countries. In addition to GDP per capita, the independent variables include a dummy variable for countries that had communist regimes in the year covered by the observation. Inclusion of year dummies eliminates variation in dispersion over time that is common to countries, so that the coefficients on log of GDP per capita simply reflect the cross-country variation in the data. The estimated coefficients on log of GDP per capita show a much greater impact of the GDP on inequality for advanced European countries than for other advanced countries or for the rest of the economies in the world. For whatever reason – mode of wage-setting, the strength of unions and employer federations, the social welfare floor on earnings or the educational system – GDP per capita reduces inequality more in advanced Europe than elsewhere. This is despite the fact that the variation in levels of GDP per capita is much greater among LDC than among advanced European countries.

The cross-section calculation does not, however, tell us how *changes* in GDP per capita in a given country affect skill differentials. To identify the effect of changes in GDP over time on inequality within a country, we estimated a fixed-effects model in which we added country dummies to the regression of the standard deviation of ln wages on ln GDP per capita. Table 1.4 gives the results of these calculations. Since this calculation includes controls for both country and time, it estimates the effect within the same country of increased GDP on inequality. For the advanced European countries the estimated coefficients on GDP per capita are comparable between Tables 1.3 and 1.4, but the estimated coefficients for the other countries show greater divergences. Using GDP per capita in PPP units, there is no impact of growth on inequality on LDCs and a much smaller impact of growth on inequality for other advanced countries. Using GDP in constant dollar units, the estimated fixed-effect impact of GDP per capita on inequality for LDCs is insignificant while that for other advanced countries is a bit higher than in Table 1.3. Overall, however, the key finding is that in the fixed-effects as in the cross-section analysis, the level of GDP per capita has a greater impact in reducing occupational pay inequality in advanced Europe than elsewhere in the world.

There is one additional way in which we can probe this generalization with our data. As noted before, countries often do not report the same (number of) occupations across time, leading us to calculate the inequality measure in our analysis for different sets of occupations. Although it is not clear in which direction this may bias the results in Tables 1.3 and 1.4, we used a pair-wise regression method to correct for possible bias. For each country we formed

Table 1.3   Cross-section regression estimates of the effect of per capita income on standard deviation of log occupational wages (standard errors in parentheses), European countries vs Other countries

	With GDP in PPP			With GDP in constant US$ (1995)		
	European	Other adv.	LDCs	European	Other adv.	LDCs
Log GDP per capita	-0.36	-0.23	-0.09	-0.14	-0.06	-0.07
	(0.08)	(0.13)	(0.02)	(0.04)	(0.08)	(0.01)
Communist	-0.09	–	18	-0.05	–	-0.22
(1 = comm. years)	(0.04)		(0.02)	(0.03)		(0.02)
Year dummies	X	X	X	X	X	X
Constant	X	X	X	X	X	X
Observations	144	85	475	151	87	490
R^2	0.408	0.291	0.293	0.350	0.108	0.278

Note: These regressions used dispersions based on raw data for countries on 30 or more occupations. Standard errors are corrected for clustering.

Table 1.4 Fixed-effects regression estimates of the effect of per capita income on standard deviation of log occupational wages (standard errors in parentheses), European countries vs other countries

	With GDP in PPP			With GDP in constant US$ (1995)		
	European	Other adv.	LDCs	European	Other adv.	LDCs
Log GDP per capita	-0.29	-0.09	-0.02	-0.26	-0.11	-0.05
	(0.16)	(0.07)	(0.04)	(0.14)	(0.06)	(0.04)
Communist	0.02	–	-0.23	0.01	–	-0.26
(1 = comm. years)	(0.09)	–	(0.05)	(0.09)	–	(0.05)
Year dummies	X	X	X	X	X	X
Country dummies	X	X	X	X	X	X
Constant	X	X	X	X	X	X
Observations	144	85	475	151	87	490
R^2	0.393	0.161	0.175	0.131	0.046	0.255

Note: These regressions used dispersions based on raw data for countries on 30 or more occupations. Standard errors are corrected for clustering.

matched pairs of adjacent years reported, and we calculated for each matched pair the wage inequality for the set of occupations reported by the country in *both* years. Next we used these paired observations in the regression and included for each country pair a random effect to control for the actual set of occupations used in the calculation of the inequality measure.[15] Table 1.5 summarizes the results in this case. Here we find a huge difference between the effect of GDP per capita on inequality for both the European and other advanced countries (larger in the PPP analysis than in the exchange rate analysis) compared to the less developed countries, but obtain comparable coefficients on the impact of GDP per capita on inequality in the European and other advanced economies. However, if we control for differences in schooling and wage-setting institutions, we still find a larger coefficient for European advanced countries than for non-European advanced countries (this is discussed in Section 5 and reported in Table 1.7).[16]

In sum, the OWW data file shows that the relation between GDP per capita and inequality is greater among advanced European countries than among other countries, particularly less developed countries. One interpretation is that the greater impact of growth on inequality in Europe reflects the distinct influence of European wage-setting institutions. If that is correct, then without such institutions, developing countries will not experience as much reduction in inequality with economic growth as Europe has.

4   COST OF LABOUR DIFFERENCES ACROSS COUNTRIES

Globalization is supposed to create pressures for wages to converge across countries. If two workers in the same occupation can perform the same work, why should they be paid any differently in a world with free trade or capital flows and some (more limited) immigration? Almost any theory of globalization will predict a fall in the variation in the cost of the same skills across countries, particularly measured by exchange rate. Has the past decade of globalization done this?

To analyse differences in the cost of skills across countries, we have deflated the wages for each country–year–occupation by exchange rates for the US dollar. The resulting dollar measure shows great variation across countries in the cost of labour. A carpenter in construction in India, for example, earns $52 per month while one in Sweden earns $2474 per month and one in Argentina earns $223 per month on average in the 1989–92 period. Even among the advanced countries there are considerable differences in labour costs: on average over the 1989–92 period a kindergarten teacher earned $1775 per month in Italy, $1536 per month in the USA, $1256 in Japan and $2468 in Germany.

Table 1.5 *Pair-wise random effects GLS regression estimates of the effect of per capita income on standard deviation of log occupational wages (standard errors in parentheses), European countries vs other countries*

	With GDP in PPP			With GDP in constant US$ (1995)		
	European	Other adv.	LDCs	European	Other adv.	LDCs
Log GDP per capita	-0.32	-0.32	-0.09	-0.12	-0.14	-0.06
	(0.06)	(0.07)	(0.01)	(0.03)	(0.06)	(0.01)
Communist	-0.03	–	-0.20	-0.02	–	-0.23
(1 = comm. years)	(0.08)		(0.05)	(0.08)		(0.05)
Year dummies	X	X	X	X	X	X
Country dummies	X	X	X	X	X	X
Constant	X	X	X	X	X	X
Observations	148	78	433	155	80	442
R²	0.301	0.378	0.282	0.267	0.123	0.267

Note: These regressions used dispersions based on raw data for countries on 30 or more occupations. Standard errors are corrected for clustering.

Figure 1.2 displays the variation in pay across countries for five occupations in the 1983–99 period: a high-wage occupation (general physician), a low-wage occupation (logger), a white-collar occupation (insurance agent), a blue-collar occupation (clicker cutter) and a high-tech occupation (programmer). For ease of presentation we have standardized the wages relative to the highest wage in the category. That is, the wage in the highest-wage country in a given occupation is scaled as 1.0 and the wages of workers in that occupation in other countries are fractions between zero and one. The frequency distribution shows the number of countries with given wages relative to the highest-paying country in each occupation.

We calculated two statistics to measure the spread of wages across the world in the same occupation. The first is the standard deviation of the ln wage in the occupation: the higher the standard deviation in an occupation, the greater is the inequality in wages across the world in that occupation. The second statistic is the ratio of the wage in the median country in the distribution of wages relative to the wage in the country with the highest wage for a given occupation. This is not a common measure of dispersion, but it is an easily interpreted statistic: the higher the maximum wage relative to the median wage, the greater is the dispersion above the median.

To see if the increased globalization and the spread of technology of the 1990s reduced differences in wages across occupations, we compare these two measures of the dispersion of occupational pay for the same countries over time. With countries reporting observations in some years and not others, the most natural way to do this is to group the data into 'early' (1983–88) and 'late' (1992–99) years. We use the earliest reported pay for the 1983–88 years and the latest reported pay for the 1992–99 years to maximize the time period. We then regress the measures of dispersion of pay on a dummy variable for the most recent period and individual occupation dummy variables to eliminate cross-occupation variation in dispersion. Only countries in the regression which report in both periods are included. The coefficients on the dummy variable on period measure the change over time in the inequality.

Table 1.6 presents estimates of these trend effects for both of our measures of inequality of pay across countries for all countries, for all advanced countries and for LDCs. In the columns listed under standard deviation of ln wage, a positive coefficient on the period dummy variable indicates that inequality of occupational wages rose across countries. In the columns listed under median/max. wage a negative coefficient on the period dummy variable indicates that inequality rose (that is, the median fell further behind the maximum country wage). While there are enough European advanced countries to do a separate analysis, there are not enough non-European advanced countries for the analysis. Since the separate European analysis gave similar results to the analysis for all advanced countries, we report those statistics here.

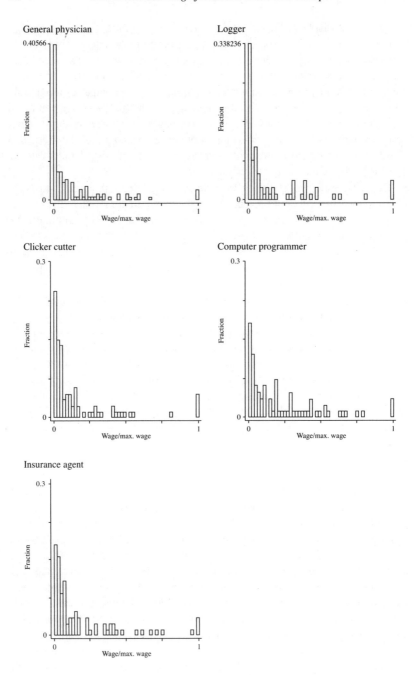

Figure 1.2   Variation in wages around the world for five occupations

Table 1.6   Estimates of differences in wages in occupations across countries in two different time periods (using exchange rates), 1983–88 to 1992–99

	Standard deviation in wage			Median/max. wage		
	All	Advanced	LDCS	All	Advanced	LDCs
Dummy on later	0.11	−0.13	−0.08	−0.038	0.016	0.015
Period	(0.01)	(0.01)	(0.01)	(0.005)	(0.005)	(0.006)
Occupational dummies	X	X	X	X	X	X
Constant	X	X	X	X	X	X
R^2	0.82	0.87	0.72	0.85	0.65	0.70
Number of occupations	312	126	290	312	126	290

Note: Standard errors are corrected for clustering.

The regressions with both measures of the within-occupation variation in earnings across countries tell the same story. Overall, for all countries there has been a *divergence* in the variation in wages across countries – the opposite of what one would expect on the basis of a more global economy. But the regressions for the advanced countries and LDCs separately show the opposite: convergence within the two groups. Put differently, there was a convergence in wage costs for workers in given occupations among the advanced countries and a convergence in wage costs for workers in given occupations among the less developed countries, at the same time that wage costs diverged between the two groups. One possible explanation for this 'twin peaks' pattern is that the two groupings are specializing in very different industries with the advanced countries dominating the higher-productivity sectors in a non-Hecksher/Ohlin world.[17] Another possible explanation is that the advent of China and Russia into the world trading system has adversely affected wages in developing countries, while the advanced countries have not experienced the rise of major new competitors.

5   INSTITUTIONAL ARRANGEMENTS AND PATTERNS OF PAY

To what extent can we relate the different relationships between GDP per capita and pay inequality between advanced European and other countries to different institutional modes of pay-setting?

We examine this question in two steps. First we have regressed the standard

Table 1.7 Regression coefficients and standard errors for factors that affect the standard deviation of ln wages, European countries vs other countries

	Cross-section			Pair-wise regression		
	European	Other adv.	LDCs	European	Other adv.	LDCs
Economy-wide						
GDP per capita (constant US$)	-0.217	-0.050	-0.019	-0.170	-0.081	-0.042
	(0.033)	(0.027)	(0.046)	(0.057)	(0.042)	(0.027)
Years of schooling	0.009	-0.003	-0.044	-0.001	-0.002	-0.032
	(0.014)	(0.003)	(0.025)	(0.010)	(0.007)	(0.014)
Communist			-0.183			-0.233
			(0.050)			(0.071)
Wage-setting						
Union	0.125	-0.160	-0.544	0.084	-0.176	0.609
	(0.068)	(0.029)	(0.518)	(0.068)	(0.047)	(0.229)
Wage–price regulations	-0.014	-0.098	-0.078	-0.002	-0.119	0.102
	(0.015)	(0.015)	(0.030)	(0.029)	(0.050)	(0.020)
Year dummies	X	X	X	X	X	X
R^2	0.40	0.83	0.38	0.31	0.81	0.45
Number of observations	146	82	204	151	76	186

Note: Standard errors are corrected for clustering in pooled cross-section regressions. Random effects are included in the pair-wise regressions.

deviation of ln occupational wages on indicators of education and wage-setting institutions in a pooled cross-section analysis over all the years for which we have country data.[18] The number of observations in the various regressions differs somewhat due to the availability of measures for particular countries. Since the explanatory variables are from single years, we include year dummies in each regression and report robust standard errors that take account of the clustering of observations. For our measures of wage determinants we use:

1. Years of schooling in 1985 from the Barro–Lee data set.[19]
2. Union density for 1990–95 from Visser (1997), where we have adjusted density for collective bargaining coverage in countries, as described in Freeman and Oostendorp (2000).[20]
3. A measure of the degrees of wage-price regulations from the Heritage Foundation, also described in Freeman and Oostendorp (2000).

The results in Table 1.7 show that with the addition of measures for years of schooling, unionization and a measure of the use of wage and price regulations, GDP per capita continues to have a larger impact on pay inequality in advanced European countries than in other countries. The implication is that the relationship between GDP and inequality operates through mechanisms beyond these. This is also the case if we use the pair-wise regression technique of Table 1.5. In addition, whereas years of schooling reduces inequality in LDCs, it has little or no effect on inequality in European and other advanced countries. The indicators of wage-setting institutions also show a difference in impacts, with unionization associated with higher inequality in European countries (but insignificant in the pair-wise regression), possibly because this measure is too crude to allow for the extensive institutional differences in wage-setting or because extensive unionization increases pay differences across occupations while reducing disparity of pay within occupations. By contrast, unionization reduces inequality in other countries. Similarly the indicator for wage and price regulations has little effect in European countries but reduces inequality in other countries.

6   CONCLUSIONS

To sum up, we have used the Occupational Wages around the World data file that we developed to examine occupational wage structures and wages of comparably skilled workers across the world. The OWW data file gives consistent pay in 161 occupations in over 150 countries from 1983 to 1999 and thus is potentially the best source of data by skill around the world. Our analysis shows substantially different wage patterns between advanced European countries, other advanced economies and less developed countries. GDP has a greater impact on wage inequality in advanced European economies than in other economies, particularly less developed economies. Institutional factors – unionism and measures of market economic freedoms – also have different relations to wages among European economies than among other economies. We also find that wages for comparable work diverged between advanced and less advanced countries while wages for comparable work narrowed within both groupings. We conclude that European wage-setting is indeed different.

NOTES

1. Only in some cases can trade accomplish this by itself. But with free capital flows, immigration and the flow of technology across national boundaries, it is hard to find 'pure' market reasons for wages and wage structures to diverge around the world.
2. This section is derived from Freeman and Oostendorp (2001); also see http://www.nber. org/oww.
3. The ILO actually asks for information on 159 occupations but it differentiates occupation 139, executives in the government into three sectors: national, regional or provincial and local governments.
4. The maximum is the multiplicand of the number of countries (158) times the number of occupations (161) times the number of years (17).
5. Here Europe includes all high-income European countries (World Bank, 2001). Only acceptable data are included, but only six data points of dubious quality needed to be discarded.
6. In a few cases the wages are in the form of ranges. We found the midpoint of the range and report it as the wage for the category.
7. The situation is not quite as dire as this statistic indicates because we can obtain some greater comparability by taking account of the natural time dimensions, such as turning yearly earnings into monthly figures by dividing by 12, turning weekly wages into monthly by multiplying by 4.3 or by multiplying hourly pay by hours worked reported in the survey. But even if we standardize using these procedures, only 15.7 per cent of the reported figures are directly comparable.
8. One other problem is the failure to cover all supplementary labour costs. The ILO asks that countries include cost-of-living adjustments and other guaranteed and regularly paid allowances and paid vacation and holidays as well in earnings. But the Inquiry excludes employer contributions to social security, pension funds, severance pay, irregular bonuses, including such important payments as the annual or bi-annual bonuses paid in Japan and some other Asian countries, and contributions to health insurance.
9. The most comparable data set is from the Union Bank of Switzerland, *Prices and Earnings around the Globe, 2000 edition* (18 August 2000): http://www.ubs.com/e/index/about/ research/pcc/ublications.html.
10. The different data types are formed by different combinations of pay concepts, averaging concepts, gender concepts and period concepts (in so far as these cannot be standardized by dimensional analysis).
11. The extent of variation in the Inquiry data makes the standardization exercise more complicated, however. The big problem is that there are many different types of data. There are two types of earnings, three types of data by gender, three forms of data by time span that cannot be standardized by dimensional analysis, and five distinct forms of averaging. This gives us 90 (= $2 \times 3 \times 3 \times 5$) different potential combinations of data types. For the ways in which we deal with this problem see Freeman and Oostendorp (2000), especially the appendix.
12. Obviously with just one occupation, the standard deviation is zero; with just two occupations drawn from a normal distribution, the standard deviation will be higher. The likely relation

between numbers of occupations and the measures of dispersion depends on the underlying distribution of wages by occupation.

13. This procedure keeps the vast bulk of our country–year data since virtually all countries report on some occupations in a given grouping. Out of 982 country–year data points, 949 have information on each decile.

14. The sample was limited to those countries which report at least 30 occupations because it makes the standardization procedure more robust (see appendix in Freeman and Oostendorp, 2000).

15. The Hausman test for fixed versus random effects is in virtually all circumstances rejected.

16. The use of controls makes the sample slightly smaller as not information on all countries is available, but this does not explain the difference between Table 1.5 and (last three columns of) Table 1.7.

17. See Quah (1996).

18. These measures are all weak ones subject to considerable measurement error. See Freeman and Oostendorp (2000).

19. This is downloadable from the World Bank: http://www.worldbank.org/research/growth/ddbarle2.htm

20. See Visser (1997) and ILO (1997).

REFERENCES

Barro, R. and J.W. Lee (1996), 'International measures of schooling years and schooling quality', *AER Papers and Proceedings*, **86** (2), 218–23.

Freeman, R.B. and R. Oostendorp (2000), *Wages around the World: Pay across Occupations and Countries*, NBER Working Paper No. 8058.

Freeman, R.B. and R. Oostendorp (2001), 'The Occupational Wages around the World data file', *International Labor Review*, **140** (4), 379–401.

ILO (1997), *World Labour Report 1997–98*, Geneva: ILO.

Quah, D.T. (1996). 'Twin Peaks: growth and convergence in models of distribution dynamics', *Economic Journal*, **106**, 1045–55.

Visser, J. (1997), *Global Trends in Unionization*, Geneva: ILO.

World Bank (2001), *World Development Report 2001: Attacking Poverty*, New York: Oxford University Press.

2. What determines the reservation wages of unemployed workers? New evidence from German micro data

Eswar S. Prasad[*]

INTRODUCTION

The reservation wage is an important concept for modelling certain key aspects of labour market dynamics. In particular the theory of optimal job search typically implies the reservation wage property in the context of structural models of job search behaviour. The reservation wage is also a concept that has relevance for modelling labour supply decisions, through its influence on transitions from non-employment to employment. Understanding the factors, both microeconomic and macroeconomic, that influence the reservation wage is therefore of considerable importance from both analytical and policy perspectives.

In this chapter I provide an empirical analysis of the determinants of reservation wages using individual data from the German Socio-Economic Panel (GSOEP). One of the questions included in the survey explicitly asks unemployed workers what wage rate would have to be offered in order for them to consider accepting a job, that is, their reservation wage. In addition, the GSOEP is particularly well suited to the analysis of reservation wages since it includes a rich set of individual- and household-specific characteristics. In this chapter I also exploit another strength of the GSOEP, which is the availability in each survey wave of detailed retrospective information on employment and income histories for individual workers. For the purposes of analysing reservation wages, this data set is unique in that the longitudinal aspect enables direct comparisons of reservation wages with accepted wages in future periods and can also be used to examine changes in reservation wages over time. Earlier studies of reservation wages typically had access to only one year's worth of data on reservation wages and, to the best of my knowledge, none had access to both past wages and future accepted wages. Thus, unlike in earlier studies, this data set permits a direct validation of the quality of the reservation wage data, a perennial concern that cannot be addressed in most other data sets that contain reservation wage data.

Previous studies of reservation wages have been based on far less comprehensive information and have generally been limited to either making indirect inferences about reservation wages (for example Kiefer and Neumann, 1979; Blau, 1991) or using one or two years of data, sometimes with little retrospective information about employment or income histories (for example Franz, 1982; Lancaster and Chesher, 1983; Feldstein and Poterba, 1984; Jones, 1988, 1989; Hui, 1991; Schmidt and Winkelmann, 1993).

The results in this chapter are of analytical interest from a number of different perspectives. Understanding the determinants of reservation wages could shed light on various aspects of labour supply and job search behaviour. Theoretical models of job search also typically have strong implications regarding the relationships between reservation wages and variables such as unemployment duration. Rather than test a particular structural model, however, in this chapter my strategy is to estimate reduced-form equations in order to model the determinants of reservation wages, thereby providing indirect evidence on the empirical relevance of some of these theoretical models.

The analysis presented here is of considerable policy relevance as well. In the final part of the chapter I develop an empirical procedure that enables me to use the reservation wage data to shed some light on one of the main problems facing the West German labour market – the high rate of non-employment among low-skilled workers. In particular a comparison of the ratio of reservation wages to market offer wages at different points of the skill distribution suggests that there exist labour supply rigidities at the low end of the skill/wage distribution. In tandem with the results of an earlier paper (Prasad, 2000), I argue that the results indicate the need for comprehensive reforms to influence both labour demand and labour supply at the low end of the skill/wage distribution in order to solve the German unemployment problem.[1]

THEORETICAL FRAMEWORK

In this section I discuss the main elements of a simple theoretical framework that is relevant for the analysis of reservation wages. Standard (and somewhat stripped-down) models of job search imply that the reservation wage is a function of the offer-wage distribution, the arrival rate of job offers and search costs. Search costs could of course be determined by individual-specific factors as well as institutional factors such as the features of the unemployment compensation (UC) system.[2] The availability of detailed individual- and household-specific information is thus crucial for analysing the determinants of reservation wages. For instance, conditional on other characteristics, an agent with alternative sources of income and/or other employed family members would tend to have lower search costs. Furthermore, agents in households with higher levels of wealth might have better access to financial instruments to insure against labour income risk and would therefore tend to have higher reservation wages.

Macroeconomic determinants are likely to play a role as well in determining reservation wages. Aggregate demand conditions (and hence the derived demand for labour) could influence both the overall offer-wage distribution and the arrival rate of job offers and therefore affect reservation wages. The general equilibrium effects are, however, unclear. For instance, a higher local unemployment rate could drive down reservation wages as job offers become scarcer. On the other hand, since it presumably implies a lower real wage (if real wages are procyclical) and a lower probability of employment for workers with low levels of human capital, a drop in job search intensity could result from such workers' intertemporal optimization decisions. Workers at the margin might then drop out of job search altogether, driving up the observed distribution of reservation wages among workers engaged in active job search.

Another potential determinant of the reservation wage is unemployment duration. As discussed in more detail below, one would expect the reservation wage to decline over time on account of wealth effects and human capital depreciation. However, a problem that complicates estimation with the unemployment duration variable is that the reservation wage and the duration of unemployment could be endogenously determined. Optimal search theory, under the assumption of a stationary reservation wage, predicts a *positive* correlation between these variables. That is, workers with higher reservation wages tend to have longer unemployment spells. To test this prediction and to obviate the problem of endogeneity, I use a reduced-form instrumental variables estimation approach suggested by Jones (1988) to study the relationship between reservation wages and unemployment duration.

DATA

This section contains a brief description of the data used in the empirical analysis. The data set is the public-use version of the German Socio-Economic Panel (GSOEP). I restrict my analysis to residents of West Germany between the ages of 17 and 55 who, at the time of the survey, were non-employed and reported that they were looking for a full-time job.[3] The distinction between non-employment and unemployment is of course an important one and will be considered carefully in the analysis below.

The survey question that is intended to elicit the reservation wage is: 'How much would the net pay have to be for you to consider accepting a job that was offered to you now?' The possible responses are a figure for 'DM per month' or 'Don't know, it depends'. Note that the reservation wage concept here is net monthly earnings.[4] Although my data set includes data from the 1984–97 survey waves, the reservation wage question was included in the survey only in the years 1987–89, 1992–94 and 1996–97. Observations with left-censored unemployment spells were excluded from the analysis. It should also be noted that the unemployment duration variable reflects an ongoing rather than completed spell of unemployment as of the date of the interview. All nominal variables are deflated by the CPI (1992Q4 = 100) for West Germany.

Summary statistics for the main variables used in the analysis are shown in Table 2.1. The sample has a total of 2372 observations, of which about 60 per cent are men. Note that the sample tends to have a higher proportion of younger workers in the 17–25 and 26–35 age ranges. Net household income is adjusted by a simple equivalence scale, where each adult gets a weight of one and each child under 17 gets a weight of 0.5. Although it was possible to construct a dummy variable to capture receipt of unemployment compensation, data on the actual level of benefits were available for only about one-third of the sample.

A potential concern is the high survey non-response rate for the reservation wage question, which could indicate that respondents have trouble understanding or interpreting this question. For instance, the non-response rate on this question among those registered as unemployed was about 25 per cent. This could influence the analysis in this chapter if there were a systematic pattern in the non-response rates, that is, if non-response was correlated with any of the individual-specific characteristics. To examine this I took the sample of unemployed workers and generated a dummy variable for non-response to the reservation wage question. I then estimated simple probit regressions (separately for men and women) of this dummy on a vector of individual-specific characteristics. The regressions had very low explanatory power (pseudo-R^2 of about 0.01) and none of the estimated coefficients was statistically significant at conventional levels of significance. Thus I conclude that, although the high rate of non-response to the reservation wage question is a potential concern, there is at least no obvious relationship between observed characteristics and the pattern of non-response.[5]

One interesting issue is whether the reported reservation wage data bear any relationship to actual economic behaviour. For instance, are accepted wage offers correlated with stated reservation wages in a reasonable manner? A unique feature of the GSOEP is that, unlike previous data sets that have been used to analyse reservation wages, the panel aspect of this data set provides a means for answering this question.[6] For workers who report earnings on a full-time job in the year after a reservation wage observation, I compute the differential between accepted (time $t + 1$) and reservation wages (time t) (both variables are deflated by the CPI). The top panel of Figure 2.1 plots this differential as a percentage

Table 2.1   Summary statistics

	All workers		Men		Women	
	Mean	Std dev.	Mean	Std dev	Mean	Std dev.
Log reservation wage	7.60	0.40	7.71	0.36	7.43	0.40
Unemployment duration (months)	34.92	33.21	33.36	33.35	37.33	32.85
General schooling	0.55	0.50	0.53	0.50	0.59	0.49
Apprenticeship	0.29	0.45	0.32	0.47	0.23	0.42
Vocational training	0.12	0.32	0.11	0.31	0.14	0.34
University degree	0.05	0.21	0.05	0.22	0.05	0.21
Age 17–25	0.46	0.50	0.44	0.50	0.49	0.50
Age 26–35	0.30	0.46	0.31	0.46	0.27	0.44
Age 36–45	0.13	0.33	0.12	0.32	0.14	0.35
Age 46–55	0.12	0.32	0.13	0.34	0.10	0.30
Male	0.62	0.49	–	–	–	–
Married	0.36	0.48	0.33	0.47	0.40	0.49
Household head	0.39	0.49	0.47	0.50	0.27	0.45
Children	0.42	0.49	0.37	0.48	0.50	0.50
Home ownership	0.27	0.45	0.29	0.45	0.25	0.43
Other employed person in household	0.62	0.49	0.57	0.49	0.70	0.46
Citizen	0.63	0.48	0.66	0.47	0.59	0.49
Log net household income	2.26	0.45	2.25	0.45	2.29	0.44
UI benefits/assistance (dummy)	0.32	0.47	0.37	0.48	0.25	0.43
Log unemployment compensation	6.94	0.52	7.01	0.54	6.78	0.45

Number of observations:			
1987	386	232	154
1988	388	237	151
1989	302	203	99
1992	283	162	121
1993	283	180	103
1994	281	178	103
1996	219	133	86
1997	230	145	85
Totals	2372	1470	902

Notes: The reservation wage is defined in terms of real net monthly earnings. Net household income is adjusted by a simple equivalence scale where each adult gets a weight of 1 and each child under 17 gets a weight of 0.5. Data on amounts of unemployment compensation were available only for 704 observations (500 men, 204 women). All nominal variables were deflated by the CPI (1992Q4 = 100) for West Germany.

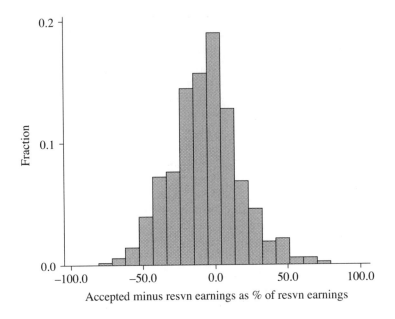

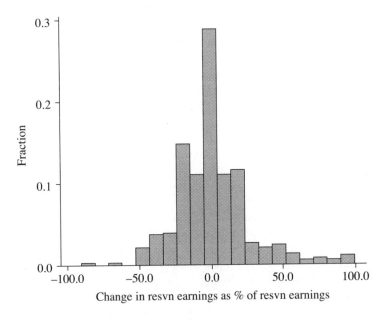

Figure 2.1   Validating the reservation wage

of the time *t* reservation wage. Although the distribution of this variable has a fairly large variance, it is comforting that a majority of the observations are clustered around zero. Observations that have a positive differential – to the right of the zero line – indicate accepted wage offers that are greater than stated reservation wages. As for the observations in the left tail of the distribution, a negative differential can be rationalized on the grounds of a declining reservation wage over time for a given individual.

To examine whether reservation wages change over time, I analyse those individuals for whom the data set contains two consecutive observations on the reservation wage.[7] This change, expressed as a percentage of the first reservation wage observation, is shown in the bottom panel of Figure 2.1. Whether reservation wages would be expected to increase or decrease over time is of course far from obvious. On the one hand wealth effects and the cost of depreciating human capital should drive down the reservation wage over time. On the other hand the reservation wage could actually increase over time simply as a result of increases in overall wage (offer) levels. Furthermore, increasing knowledge over time about the true offer wage distribution could result in changes in the reservation wage. Nevertheless one would not a priori expect to see substantial changes in reservation wages from year to year for a given individual. Indeed, although there are a few observations with large increases or decreases, most of the mass of the distribution is around zero. But note that this plot does not appear to provide strong evidence in favour of the hypothesis of stationary reservation wages: as discussed below, this has important implications for the analysis that follows.[8]

Overall I interpret the results in this section as indicating that the reservation wage data in the GSOEP are reliable and have the potential to provide a reasonable means of testing the determinants of reservation wages and, by extension, to shed light on certain aspects of labour supply among workers in the West German labour market.

MAIN RESULTS

I first examine the determinants of reservation wages using a set of reduced-form specifications that relate each individual's reservation wage to a vector of individual-specific and macroeconomic characteristics. For this part of the analysis the data are treated as a repeated set of cross-sections.[9] OLS estimates are presented in Table 2.2. The excluded education dummy is 'general schooling'. Rather than restrict the age effects to take a quadratic form, I have explicitly created four age groups. In these regressions the excluded age category is AGE2536.

Table 2.2 *Determinants of the reservation wage: OLS regressions;*
dependent variable: log reservation wage

	(1)	(2)	(3)	(4)
Apprenticeship	0.002	–0.006	0.047*	0.013
	(0.019)	(0.019)	(0.021)	(0.023)
Vocational training	0.025	0.028	0.074*	0.052*
	(0.021)	(0.021)	(0.022)	(0.026)
University degree	0.161*	0.156*	0.315*	0.254*
	(0.039)	(0.040)	(0.047)	(0.051)
Age 17–25	–0.112*	–0.105*	–0.089*	–0.074*
	(0.020)	(0.020)	(0.026)	(0.027)
Age 36–45	–0.097*	–0.083*	–0.017	–0.032
	(0.021)	(0.021)	(0.023)	(0.025)
Age 46–55	–0.125*	–0.111*	–0.029*	–0.013
	(0.024)	(0.024)	(0.024)	(0.027)
Male	0.213*	0.217*	0.131*	–0.152*
	(0.025)	(0.025)	(0.026)	(0.031)
Married	–0.051	–0.045	–0.068*	–0.092*
	(0.029)	(0.029)	(0.034)	(0.038)
Male* married	0.201*	0.198*	0.203*	0.128*
	(0.035)	(0.034)	(0.038)	(0.040)
Children	–0.004	–0.002	0.059*	0.047*
	(0.020)	(0.020)	(0.021)	(0.023)
Other emp. person(s) in household	–0.115*	–0.104*	–0.104*	–0.066*
	(0.019)	(0.019)	(0.021)	(0.021)
Home ownership	0.085*	0.087*	0.008	–0.008
	(0.022)	(0.022)	(0.022)	(0.026)
Log net household income	0.195*	0.184*	0.096*	0.058*
	(0.022)	(0.022)	(0.027)	(0.027)
Citizen	–0.004	0.004	–0.026	–0.045*
	(0.02)	(0.021)	(0.023)	(0.022)
UC dummy	–0.082*	–0.095*	0.038*	–
	(0.015)	(0.015)	(0.018)	
Log UC benefits	–	–	–	0.094*
				(0.021)
Log past wage	–	–	–	0.178*
				(0.030)
Unemployment rate	–0.006	–	–0.002	–0.010
	(0.006)		(0.006)	(0.007)
Regional unemployment rate	–0.003	–	–0.003	0.003
	(0.004)		(0.004)	(0.004)
Year dummies	–	included	–	–
Adj. R^2	0.227	0.244	0.333	0.500
No. of observations	2371	2371	1073	547

Notes: Columns (1) and (2) include the full sample. Column (3) is limited to workers who are officially registered as unemployed. Column (4) is restricted to registered unemployed workers for whom data on amounts of unemployment compensation are available. The excluded education dummy in all regressions is 'general schooling'. The excluded age dummy is AGE2635. Robust standard errors are reported in parentheses below coefficient estimates.
* Statistical significance at the 5% level.

Results from the baseline specification are presented in column (1) of Table 2.2. For workers with a university degree reservation wages are about 15 per cent higher than for workers with only general schooling, controlling for other characteristics. For workers with an apprenticeship or vocational training, however, reservation wages are statistically similar to those of workers with only general schooling. Relative to workers in the 26–35 age group, reservation wages are lower for workers in both younger and older age groups. Male workers have much higher reservation wages, although in large part this probably just reflects the male age premium that exists in Germany. Interestingly, marital status and the presence of children in the household have little effect on reservation wages, although married men do have significantly higher reservation wages than married women. The presence of other employed persons in the household exerts a negative influence on reservation wages, suggesting 'peer' effects within the household on employment search.

Individuals who live in households with higher net household income are more likely to be able to afford to wait and search for jobs with higher wages and would therefore be expected to have higher reservation wages. Indeed, variables that proxy for alternative sources of income and wealth, including total net household income and a dummy for home ownership, are positively correlated with reservation wages. One somewhat odd result is that the dummy for receipt of unemployment compensation is negatively correlated with the reservation wage. I investigate this further below.

Aggregate and regional unemployment rates (the latter expressed as a deviation from the aggregate unemployment rate) are not significantly correlated with the reservation wage.[10] Entering unemployment rates in the regression implies a particular and possibly restrictive assumption about the effects of the overall macroeconomic environment on reservation wages. A simple alternative is to replace unemployment rates with time dummies. Although the estimated time effects do not have an economic interpretation, they should in principle soak up all the time-specific variation in reservation wages that are common to all individuals in a given time period. Column (2) of Table 2.2 reports the estimated specification with the time dummies (which were barely jointly significant at the 10 per cent level). In this more general specification the coefficients on the individual-specific variables remain very similar to those in column (1). Since the time dummies do not seem to make much of a difference, I retain the use of the unemployment rates in further regressions since they have a more obvious economic interpretation.

Table 2.2 (column (3)) also reports results restricted to the subsample of workers who, in the month of the interview, report that they are registered with the unemployment office and are also actively engaged in job search. This sample of workers excludes those non-employed who may have weaker attachment to the labour market and whose reservation wages may therefore be less relevant in determining labour market outcomes. The reservation wage is presumably a more meaningful concept for those actively engaged in job search.

Many of the results are stronger for this subsample. In particular, reservation wages monotonically increase by education level, although age effects are now less significant for older labour force participants relative to those in the 26–35 age group. One important difference relative to the previous results is that the coefficient on the dummy for receipt of unemployment compensation now turns significantly positive. This result appears more reasonable than those in columns (1) and (2) since one would expect UC and other alternative income sources to increase reservation wages.

In column (4) of Table 2.2 I present results for those workers for whom data on the level of unemployment compensation benefits as well as information on earnings in the last job are available. The results on the other coefficients are generally similar to those in column (3). Both the past wage and the level of unemployment compensation clearly exert a strong positive effect on reservation wages. However, it should be noted that the implied elasticity of the reservation wage to unemployment compensation, although statistically significant, is not very large in economic terms.[11]

Table 2.3 shows results from the sample used for the fourth regression in Table 2.2, but with the results now broken down by gender. There are some notable differences between men and women in terms of the determinants of reservation wages. The presence of children raises the reservation wage of men but has no effect on that of women. For men the presence of other employed persons in the household reduces reservation wages by almost 7 per cent – perhaps a strong peer (or 'macho') effect for men who do not want to sit idly at home while others in their household are employed and are therefore willing to accept lower wages in order to find a job!

For both men and women, the levels of UC benefits and wages on the last job are positively associated with reservation wages. However, one key difference is that the elasticity of reservation wages with respect to unemployment benefits is more than twice as large for women (0.161) than it is for men (0.069). While the statistical significance of these parameter estimates clearly indicates the disincentive effects of the UC system in terms of engendering higher reservation wages, it should again be emphasized that these estimates suggest that the quantitative impact of UC benefits on reservation wages is not very large, at least in these regression results.

Unemployment Duration and the Reservation Wage

As discussed earlier, the duration of unemployment spell is likely to be correlated with the reservation wage, although different theories have different

Table 2.3   Determinants of reservation wage, by gender: OLS regressions; dependent variable: log reservation wage

	Men	Women
Apprenticeship	0.022	0.007
	(0.027)	(0.051)
Vocational training	0.074*	0.016
	(0.029)	(0.054)
University degree	0.213*	0.290*
	(0.073)	(0.075)
Age 17–25	–0.066*	–0.089
	(0.032)	(0.052)
Age 36–45	0.001	–0.100*
	(0.031)	(0.047)
Age 46–55	–0.007	–0.004
	(0.032)	(0.072)
Married	0.031	–0.074
	(0.027)	(0.053)
Children	0.082*	–0.013
	(0.027)	(0.042)
Other emp. person(s) in hpusehold	–0.070*	–0.067
	(0.024)	(0.044)
Home ownership	–0.007	–0.016
	(0.033)	(0.048)
Log net household income	0.092*	–0.030
	(0.032)	(0.057)
Citizen	–0.033	–0.081
	(0.025)	(0.044)
UC dummy	–	–
Log UC benefits	0.069*	0.161*
	(0.022)	(0.044)
Log past wage	0.170*	0.178*
	(0.036)	(0.061)
Unemployment rate	–0.005	–0.015
	(0.008)	(0.016)
Regional unemployment rate	0.003	0.003
	(0.005)	(0.007)
Adj. R^2	0.333	0.461
No. of observations	394	153

Notes: The regressions reported above were restricted to registered unemployed workers for whom data on amounts of unemployment compensation are available. The excluded education dummy in all regressions is 'general schooling'. The excluded age dummy is AGE2635. Robust standard errors are reported in parentheses below coefficient estimates.
  * Statistical significance at the 5% level.

predictions about the sign of this relationship. Hazard models are generally preferable to linear regression models when analysing unemployment duration. However, one problem in this context is that the unemployment spell duration is measured as of the interview date and, by construction, there are no exits into employment in the period when the reservation wage is observed. Hence I first estimate reduced-form OLS regressions for unemployment duration with the reservation wage as a dependent variable.[12]

The OLS estimates are presented in the first two columns of Table 2.4. The first regression includes the aggregate and regional unemployment rates as

Table 2.4   Unemployment duration and reservation wages; dependent variable: log unemployment duration (months)

	OLS	OLS	IV	IV
Log reservation wage	−0.083	−0.059	4.431*	3.359*
	(0.117)	(0.119)	(1.985)	(1.484)
Apprenticeship	−0.408*	−0.398*	−0.776*	−0.645*
	(0.111)	(0.112)	(0.221)	(0.169)
Vocational training	−0.219	−0.238	−0.529*	−0.467*
	(0.123)	(0.124)	(0.220)	(0.182)
University degree	0.067	0.070	−9.18	−0.659
	(0.185)	(0.181)	(0.526)	(0.410)
Age 17–25	−0.088	−0.092	0.775	0.523
	(0.112)	(0.114)	(0.407)	(0.295)
Age 36–45	−0.255	−0.271	0.074	−0.071
	(0.153)	(0.1530	(0.236)	(0.194)
Age 46–55	−0.072	−0.085	0.369	0.190
	(0.143)	(0.145)	(0.289)	(0.220)
Male	−0.227*	−0.226*	−1.373*	−1.092*
	(0.098)	(0.098)	(0.515)	(0.388)
Citizen	0.000	0.013	−0.114	−0.111
	(0.098)	(0.098)	(0.156)	(0.137)
Unemployment rate	−0.020	–	0.041	–
	(0.035)		(0.058)	
Regional unemployment rate	0.047*	–	0.053	–
	(0.019)		(0.028)	
Year dummies	–	included	–	included
Adj. R^2	0.041	0.041	–	–
No. of observations	1151	1151	1151	1151

Notes: In the IV regressions, the (log) reservation wage is instrumented using dummies for receipt of unemployment compensation, marital status, presence of children and home ownership. Robust standard errors are reported in parentheses.
* Statistical significance at the 5% level.

regressors while the second regression uses time dummies to capture a broader range of macroeconomic influences. In these regressions the conditional correlation between the reservation wage and unemployment duration appears to be essentially zero. In fact, although not statistically significant, the parameter estimates are slightly negative. At an intuitive level this might seem reasonable, since for the reasons cited earlier one might expect the reservation wage to decline as the non-employment spell duration lengthens.

As noted by Jones (1988), however, the reservation wage and unemployment duration are endogenously determined. One way to obviate this problem is to instrument for the reservation wage using variables that, except through their effects on search costs and hence on the reservation wage, are unlikely to have *additional* effects on unemployment duration. Jones (1988) uses unemployment insurance benefits as an instrument. Since the GSOEP is a richer data set than the one used by Jones, I have a number of potential instruments available. Following some preliminary analysis for instrument relevance, I chose a small set of instruments that worked best – dummies for marital status, presence of children and receipt of unemployment compensation.

The results from IV regressions are presented in the third column of Table 2.4. Remarkably the coefficient on the log reservation wage now turns positive and significant. Again, using time dummies rather than aggregate and regional unemployment rates makes little difference to the results (column 4). The results were quite similar across alternative choices of instrument sets. Interestingly, the pattern of the switch of the sign in coefficients when going from OLS to IV estimates and the actual magnitudes of the coefficients on the reservation wage variable are quite similar to those found by Jones (1988), who uses a one-year cross-sectional sample of data from the United Kingdom.

However, it should be noted that the positive correlation found here is predicted by optimal search theory under the assumption of a stationary reservation wage. The evidence in the previous section suggested that this assumption is not necessarily borne out in the data. Hence the interpretation of the positive correlation between reservation wages and unemployment duration as being consistent with optimal search theory requires some caution and deserves further scrutiny in future work.

THE RELATIONSHIP BETWEEN SKILL LEVELS AND RESERVATION WAGES

In this section I examine further the relationship between imputed skill levels and reservation wages. This analysis can be interpreted as providing some indirect evidence on labour supply, based on reservation wage data, at different points of the skill/wage distribution. This is of particular relevance for shedding light on potential determinants of rigidities in labour supply at the low end of the skill/wage distribution that could have implications for understanding the German unemployment problem.

The approach I adopt can be broken down into the following steps: (i) estimate annual selection-corrected Mincerian wage equations for full-time employed workers; (ii) based on those estimates, generate a predicted offer wage for each unemployed worker conditional on observed characteristics; and (iii) construct the reservation wage ratio – which is the ratio of reservation to (predicted) offer wages – for each worker who reports a reservation wage.

Net monthly earnings deflated by the CPI for West Germany are used as the dependent variable in the regression for the first step. Wage regressions were estimated separately for each year for which reservation wage data are available. The regressors included education dummies, experience and its square, dummies for citizenship and gender and a full set of interactions of these two dummies with the other variables. Since the observed wage distribution could be a biased measure of the offer wage distribution – an issue of particular importance for this analysis – an expanded sample including non-employed workers was used to estimate and correct for selectivity bias using Heckman's (1979) two-step procedure. Instruments used for the selection correction were dummies for marital status and the presence of children. Other instruments (for example home ownership) seemed to add little to this limited set.

The coefficients in the selection-corrected wage regressions appeared quite stable over time, consistent with other evidence that returns to observed skill attributes have been remarkably stable in West Germany over the last decade and a half (for example Prasad, 2000). To conserve space, the results of these wage regressions are not reported here but are available from the author upon request. In the discussion below it should be kept in mind that in these annual wage regressions observed worker characteristics explain only about 30–40 per cent of the cross-sectional variation in wages.[13]

In Figure 2.2 I plot the reservation wage ratio against the offer wage which may be considered a comprehensive measure of skill level. The top panel pools observations across all years. The vertical line shows the median real wage across all years for which the reservation wage data are available. As noted earlier, all wage variables including imputed ones correspond to net measures of real monthly earnings.

The interesting observation from Figure 2.2 is that there appears to be a negative relationship between the reservation–offer wage ratio and skill level. For most highly skilled workers in the sample – those whose offer wages lie to the right of the median – the reservation – wage ratio is below one. For these workers the value of employment is apparently high enough that they are willing to accept employment even slightly below their market offer wage. This could be because of the much greater value of skilled workers' human capital

All workers

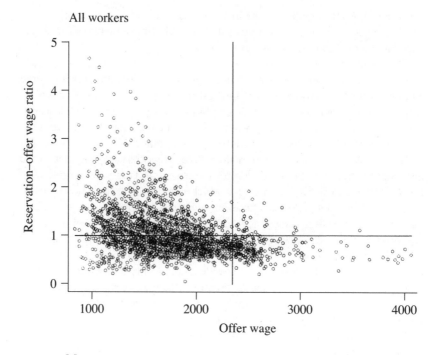

Men

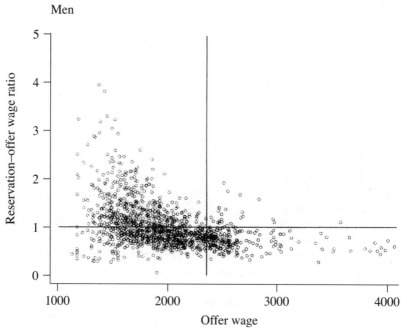

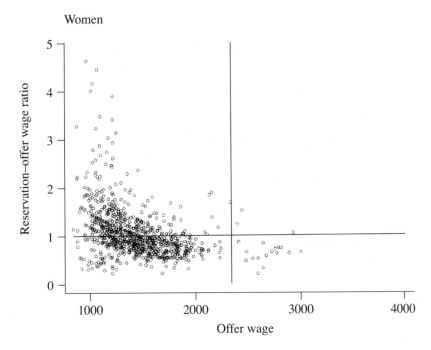

Figure 2.2   Reservation wage ratios and offer wages

investments and the associated higher absolute amount of depreciation of that capital as unemployment duration increases. By contrast, for a large fraction of low-skill workers reservation wages appear significantly higher than market offer wages, and this relationship is stronger at lower skill levels.

The lower panels of Figure 2.2 plot reservation–wage ratios against offer wages for men and women separately.[14] The positive male–female wage differential, conditional on observed worker characteristics, is apparent as one can infer from these panels that (for the sample of unemployed workers) the distributions of both offer and reservation wages for women are to the left of the corresponding distributions for men. But the negative relationship between the reservation–wage ratio and the composite measure of skills proxied by the offer wage holds for both men and women. I also redid the plots separately for each year and found that the negative relationship between the reservation–wage ratio and the offer wage was present in every year taken individually. Limiting the sample to workers engaged in active job search at the time of the survey revealed a similar result.

In interpreting this evidence an important underlying assumption concerns the unobserved worker characteristics that could affect the conditional offer wage distribution facing a worker. The comparison of reservation and offer wages is based on the assumption that the effect of unobserved characteristics on reservation wages is uncorrelated with residuals from the estimated wage equations; these residuals could partly be driven by some of those same unobserved characteristics. Even if this assumption were not true, however, there is no a priori reason why the magnitude of this correlation should be systematically related to observed skill level. Hence, while the levels of the reservation–wage ratios must be interpreted with caution, systematic relationships between reservation–wage ratios and observed worker characteristics cannot simply be ascribed to this correlation.

I now turn to a discussion of the implications of these findings for interpreting labour market outcomes and for labour market policies in (West) Germany to address the unemployment problem.

Implications for Labour Market Policies

In an earlier paper (Prasad, 2000) I have argued that the inability of the German wage structure to adjust to an increase in the relative demand for skilled labour has led to substitution of capital and skilled labour for unskilled labour and consequently rising non-employment rates for unskilled workers in Germany. A possible concern with that analysis is that the offer-wage distribution could in fact be truncated from below on account of high reservation wages. Thus the apparent rigidity of the wage structure might be reflective not of institutional constraints imposed by the wage bargaining structure, but rigidities in labour supply caused perhaps by other factors, such as the UC system.

The cluster of reservation–wage ratios for labour force participants below the median wage and even close to the left tail of the skill distribution suggests that this issue is not of great empirical relevance. There appear to be enough low-skill workers willing to work at wages below their market offer wages if jobs are available. Thus labour demand is apparently one of the problems inhibiting better employment outcomes for low-skill workers. Nevertheless the large number of observations with reservation–wage ratios above unity suggests that labour supply is also a problem at the low end of the skill distribution and that measures to influence labour demand alone would have a relatively small effect since a large number of unskilled workers are not willing to work at the going wage.

Regression results (not reported here) confirmed the existence of a strong negative relationship between the reservation–offer wage ratio and education level.[15] This differential initially declines with age but then turns around at about 47 years of age. The differential is positively related to household net income and, more importantly, to the availability of unemployment compensation. This latter result suggests that the system of unemployment compensation appears to play a role in driving up the reservation wages of many low-skill workers and in limiting their incentives to accept job offers at their respective conditional offer wages. Of course the disincentive effects of the UC system could be compounded by other aspects of the social benefits system as well as the tax system. This is an interesting topic that is left for future research.[16]

CONCLUSIONS

This chapter has used a unique and rich data set – the German Socio-Economic Panel – to provide a detailed empirical analysis of the determinants of reservation wages among unemployed workers in West Germany. This data set is unique in that the (limited) longitudinal aspect enables direct comparisons of reservation wages with accepted wages in future periods and can also be used to examine changes in reservation wages over time. Earlier studies of reservation wages have typically had access to only one year's worth of data on reservation wages and none have had access to both past and future accepted wages. Thus, unlike in earlier studies, this data set permits a direct validation of the quality of the reservation wage data, a perennial concern that cannot be addressed in most other data sets that contain reservation wage data.

In the sample of West German unemployed workers analysed here, reservation wage levels are found to be positively correlated with observed attributes of general human capital (education level), are generally higher for men and appear to be significantly influenced by the availability of unemployment compensation. The chapter also included an analysis of the reservation–wage ratio, defined as the ratio of the stated reservation wage to the market offer wage, the latter variable being defined as the predicted wage from estimated wage equations that account for sample selectivity effects. The reservation–wage ratio was found to be negatively correlated with observed measures of skill level.

An interesting although tentative implication of these results is that there appear to be significant labour supply rigidities at the low end of the German skill/wage distribution, attributable in part to the generous UC system (and perhaps also to other factors such as high effective marginal tax rates). A key policy conclusion that emerges from this and my previous work is that comprehensive reforms that influence both labour demand (by allowing for more flexibility in the dispersion of wages) and labour supply (by changing the disincentives for seeking employment) at the low end of the skill/wage distribution could be crucial for solving the structural problem of high non-employment rates for low-skill workers in West Germany.

NOTES

*   I have benefited from discussions with John Haisken-DeNew, Jennifer Hunt, Astrid Kunze, Jean-Marc Robin, Axel Schimmelpfennig and numerous other colleagues and from the comments of participants at the GSOEP 2000 Conference, the World Congress of the Econometric Society, the CEPR European Summer Symposium in Labour Economics, the European Central Bank's Labour Market Workshop and seminars in the European and Research Departments of the IMF. I am grateful to John Haisken-DeNew and Jürgen Schupp for assistance with the data. The views expressed in this paper are those of the author and do not necessarily reflect those of the IMF.

1.   Freeman and Schettkat (2000) by contrast argue that the German unemployment problem is mainly a consequence of deficient aggregate demand.

2.   The UC system in Germany has two components. The first (Arbeitslosengeld) has the characteristics of a traditional unemployment insurance system, with a well-defined termination period and a replacement rate determined by earnings on the last job. The second component (Arbeitslosenhilfe), which follows after unemployment insurance benefits have expired, is unemployment assistance. This component involves a lower replacement rate, is means-tested and is of longer duration. For the purposes of the analysis in this chapter, I do not draw a distinction between these components unless explicitly stated otherwise.

3.   For workers older than 55, the reservation wage may be determined by strategic considerations about the timing of retirement and exit from the labour force that are difficult to capture in the reduced-form framework used in this chapter. For recent entrants into the labour market, reported reservation wages might also be less reliable, especially for first-time job applicants who may have very limited knowledge about the offer-wage distribution. Below I examine the sensitivity of the results in this chapter to the exclusion of younger workers.

4.   An important issue here is whether, as suggested by this question, job offers stipulate both the hourly wage and a contracted number of hours per month. An alternative possibility is that employers offer an hourly wage and workers then decide how much labour in terms of hours per week or month they want to supply at that wage rate. It seems more plausible, especially in the German context, that job offers take the form of a combined package of wages and hours that determines total monthly earnings.

5.   Needless to say, there could still be a correlation between *unobserved* individual-specific characteristics and the non-response pattern. It is worth noting that the non-response rate here is substantially lower than that reported in most previous studies that have used survey data on reservation wages.

6.   Lancaster and Chesher (1983) and Gorter and Gorter (1993) test the predictions of stationary search models using data sets that contain information for unemployed workers on the reservation wage as well as the conditional *expected* wage in the next employment. The data set used by Jones (1988) also has both of those questions but he finds that, in this data set, the responses to the two questions are not in general mutually consistent. The availability of data on actual *accepted* wage offers obviates many of the problems associated with the interpretation of the expected wage variable.

7.   If reservation wage data are available for an individual in three consecutive years, this results in two observations for the purposes of this exercise.

8.   I regressed the change in the (log) reservation wage on a variety of individual-specific characteristics, duration of unemployment spell and total and regional unemployment rates but could not detect any systematic relationships between any of these variables and changes in the reservation wage. Kiefer and Neumann (1979) find (indirect) evidence that reservation wages decline significantly with duration.

9.   Unfortunately the fact that there are breaks in the availability of the reservation wage data makes it difficult to exploit fully the panel aspect of the data set to control for unobserved individual-specific heterogeneity. Furthermore, on account of sample attrition, attempts to construct a longitudinal data set implied a substantially smaller number of observations than in the cross-sectional approach adopted here.

10. The aggregate unemployment referred to here is for West Germany only. Note that in general equilibrium higher reservation wages and higher unemployment would tend to be positively correlated. The reduced-form specification used here can be viewed as being motivated by a partial equilibrium framework in which an individual worker takes total and regional unemployment rates as given.

11. It would be interesting to analyse in more detail how reservation wages are correlated with past earnings (see for example Kaspar, 1967). In future work I intend to examine the sensitivity of these results to the industry and other characteristics related to each worker's last employment preceding the current spell of unemployment.

12. For a more detailed analysis of unemployment durations in Germany using the GSOEP data set, see Hunt (1995).

13. This fraction is quite similar across data sets for many industrial countries and appears to be almost a law of nature.

14. As noted earlier, these results are based on estimates of selection-corrected wage equations for the sample including both men and women. Re-estimating the wage equations separately for men and women and recomputing the reservation–wage ratios based on those estimates made little qualitative difference to the results.

15. The regression results reported in this section were based on OLS specifications (for the sample of unemployed workers who report a reservation wage) with the reservation–offer wage ratio as the dependent variable and a set of regressors that included education dummies, age and its square, real household net income, year dummies and dummies for gender, citizenship and receipt of unemployment compensation.

16. Jaeger (1999) has also argued that the high effective marginal tax rates faced by workers at low income levels deter the acceptance of job offers in low earnings ranges.

REFERENCES

Blau, D.M. (1991), 'Search for nonwage job characteristics: a test of the reservation wage hypothesis', *Journal of Labor Economics*, **9**, 186–205.

Feldstein, M. and J. Poterba (1984), 'Unemployment insurance and reservation wages', *Journal of Public Economics*, **23**, 141–67.

Franz, W. (1982), 'The reservation wage of unemployed persons in the Federal Republic of Germany: theory and empirical tests', *Zeitschrift für Wirtschafts- und Sozialwissenschaften*, **102**, 29–51.

Freeman, R.B. and R. Schettkat (2000), *The Role of Wage and Skill Differences in US–German Employment Differences*, NBER Working Paper No. 7474.

Gorter, D. and C. Gorter (1993), 'The relation between unemployment benefits, the reservation wage and search duration', *Oxford Bulletin of Economics and Statistics*, **55**, 199–214.

Heckman, J.J. (1989), 'Sample selection bias as a specification error', *Econometrica*, **47**, 153–61.

Hui, W.-T. (1991), 'Reservation wage analysis of unemployed youths in Australia', *Applied Economics*, **23**, 134–50.

Hunt, J. (1995), 'The effect of unemployment compensation on unemployment duration in Germany', *Journal of Labor Economics*, **13** (1), 88–120.

Jaeger, A. (1999), 'Institutional Change and Economic Performance in Germany: A Fifty Year Perspective', Manuscript, IMF.

Jones, S.R.G. (1988), 'The relationship between unemployment spells and reservation wages as a test of search theory', *Quarterly Journal of Economics*, **103**, 741–65.

Jones, S.R.G. (1989), 'Reservation wages and the cost of unemployment', *Economica*, **56**, 225–46.

Kaspar, H. (1967), 'The asking price of labor and the duration of unemployment', *Review of Economics and Statistics*, **49**, 165–72.

Kiefer, N.M. and G.R. Neumann (1979), 'An empirical job-search model, with a test of the constant reservation-wage hypothesis', *Journal of Political Economy*, **87** (1), 89–107.

Lancaster, T. and A. Chesher (1983), 'An econometric analysis of reservation wages', *Econometrica*, **51**, 1661–76.

Prasad, E.S. (2000), *The Unbearable Stability of the German Wage Structure: Evidence and Interpretation*, IMF Working Paper No. 00/20.

Schmidt, C.M. and R. Winkelmann (1993), 'Reservation wages, wage offer distribution and accepted wages', in H. Bunzel, P. Jensen and N. Westergård-Nielsen (eds), *Panel Data and Labor Market Dynamics*, Amsterdam: North-Holland.

3. Labour as a buffer: Do temporary workers suffer?*

Alison L. Booth, Marco Francesconi and Jeff Frank

Under a European directive put into force in the UK in October 2002, firms are required to offer fixed-term workers the same treatment with regard to pay and benefits (including, for example, holiday pay and maternity benefits) as permanent workers, along with the same rights to be protected against discrimination. After a year fixed-term workers also gain redundancy and unfair dismissal rights. The Commission has now proposed (March 2002) that equal treatment be extended to agency workers as well. The UK government Department of Trade and Industry (DTI) estimates that there are perhaps 700 000 agency workers in the UK. One possible rationale for these extensions of employment rights is that fixed-term and agency workers (as well as part-time workers, also covered by European directives) are predominantly women. Differential pay and benefits for fixed-term and agency workers might therefore be viewed as a form of gender discrimination, *ceteris paribus*. Another rationale for employment rights is to improve the training of temporary workers. The DTI consultative document on agency workers estimates a productivity gain from improved training (required by the directive) of between £98 million and £272 million per year.

In this chapter we investigate two issues. First, are fixed-term workers disproportionately female or from other 'equal opportunities' groups such as ethnic minorities? Second, do fixed-term workers receive less pay than comparably qualified permanent workers? To answer these questions, we use three data sets: a representative panel survey spanning ten years and two cross-sectional surveys specifically addressed to eliciting information about (un)equal opportunities. The British Household Panel Survey (BHPS) is a representative survey of British households and we use information from the first ten waves collected over the period 1991–2000. These data allow us to examine temporary work across the entire economy, covering the range of experience from that of casual and seasonal low-skilled workers to highly-educated consultants in information technology. The other two data sets are from the UK university sector. One was collected by the Royal Economic

Society (RES) Working Party on Ethnic and Other Minority Representation. By restricting attention to a relatively homogeneous group – academic economists – we are able to gain good measures of ability and productivity to see if earnings effects can be explained by these objective factors. The final data set was collected by the Association of University Teachers (AUT) Equal Opportunities Committee. These data include university employees from both the academic and administrative side, and also include workers in all disciplines. As with the Royal Economic Society data, the AUT survey provides relatively good measures on individuals (although – since all disciplines are covered – productivity measures are less clear), but over a broader span of university workers. Importantly, we can compare individuals holding similar posts (for example, university lecturer) but under a different form of contract (fixed-term or permanent). A further interest in using university data is that this sector is generally perceived to be enlightened, in the sense that higher education promotes rationality, and rationality and discrimination make unlikely bedfellows. Thus discrimination in who holds fixed-term contracts, and in the terms and conditions of those contracts, is arguably relatively low in this market.[1] Estimated effects might therefore be expected to represent a lower bound for the economy as a whole.

Section 1 of the chapter outlines a simple theoretical model to inform our analysis of the data. We are interested in investigating the conditions under which certain groups (such as women or ethnic minorities) are more likely to hold fixed-term jobs and if these jobs pay less than permanent posts. Section 2 examines the evidence from our three surveys about who holds these jobs. In particular we investigate whether or not fixed-term jobs are disproportionately held by women and by ethnic minorities. Section 3 examines the pay obtained in these jobs. Are these low paid relative to comparable permanent jobs and does the pay differ by gender or ethnic group? Section 4 extends the analysis to types of temporary employment other than fixed-term jobs, such as agency temping, and compares the wages in such jobs to the wages earned in full-time and part-time jobs. Section 5 draws our main conclusions.

1 A 'BUFFER-STOCK' MODEL OF TEMPORARY JOBS, WAGES AND REGULATIONS

In this section we develop a model of temporary jobs to guide our empirical analysis. Temporary workers can serve as a buffer stock of employees to be discharged in adverse economic environments.[2] Recognizing that these workers are more likely to be laid off, the firm will invest less in their training. In so far as training has a general as well as specific component, temporary workers will have fewer outside opportunities, and hence will be paid a lower wage.

We construct this model and consider its implications for gender and ethnic minority discrimination, as well as the effects of regulation.

There is an *ex ante* hiring cost h per worker and, for analytical convenience, we assume that there are no firing costs.[3] Permanent and temporary workers differ only *ex post*, in that the firm provides permanent workers with training at a cost c in an instantaneously short training period. There is a specific human capital component to this training that raises the worker's productivity by $s > 1$. There is also a general human capital component to the training. Without training, workers who are hired by the firm and then separate (either by quitting or by redundancy) have an opportunity wage w; with training, their opportunity wage is gw where $s > g > 1$. That is, the training has a large specific component and a smaller general component. Thus permanent and temporary workers are substitutes in production but the former are characterized by higher *ex post* productivity through their acquisition of work-related training. The number of workers hired *ex ante* forms a pool of potential workers who can be employed *ex post* once the market state is revealed. This assumption captures in a simple fashion the fact that, in the real world, hiring takes time and thus the firm wants its workforce in place before the state is revealed. Note that in this model there is no legislated difference between permanent and temporary workers. The difference arises only in so far as the firm chooses to train some of its workers (permanent workers) and not others (temporary workers), and then chooses to treat them differently in wages and in redundancy in adverse market environments.

Output at the firm is $m_i Q(sN_p^i + N_t^i)$ where m_i represents the market environment (state i having probability π_i) and N_p^i and N_t^i are the permanent and temporary workers employed *ex post* in market state i. The production function $Q(\cdot)$ is strictly concave. The firm chooses *ex ante* how many workers to hire on each contract, $\hat{N}_p$ and $\hat{N}_t$, and how many of each type to make costlessly redundant ($\hat{N}_j - \hat{N}_{ij} \geq 0_j, j = p, t$) in different market environments i. Although the firm in principle chooses how much to pay each type of worker, the outside opportunity levels w and gw effectively determine the wage rates for temporary and permanent workers.[4] There is no incentive for the firm to pay more in any market state, and – if it paid less – all the workers would quit.

The firm chooses *ex ante* hires $\hat{N}_p$, $\hat{N}_t$ and state-dependent *ex post* employment levels to maximize expected profits:

$$\sum_i [m_i Q(sN_p^i + N_t^i) - gwN_p^i - wN_t^i - c\hat{N}_p - (\hat{N}_p + \hat{N}_t)]\pi_i$$

subject to the constraints: $\hat{N}_p \geq N_p^i$ and $\hat{N}_t \geq N_t^i$.

Writing the multipliers λ_p^i and λ_t^i on these constraints, we have first-order conditions:

$$\partial L/\partial \hat{N}_p = -c - h + \sum_i \lambda_p^i \pi_i = 0 \qquad (3.1)$$

$$\partial L/\partial \hat{N}_t = -h + \sum_i \lambda_t^i \pi_i = 0 \qquad (3.2)$$

$$\partial L/\partial N_p^i = m_i sQ'(\cdot) - gw - \lambda_p^i = 0 \qquad (3.3)$$

$$\partial L/\partial N_t^i = m_i Q'(\cdot) - w - \lambda_t^i = 0 \qquad (3.4)$$

From (3.3) and (3.4), the firm will retain all of its permanent workers (if m_i is sufficiently large) before employing any of its temporary workers, even in the absence of any regulatory firing costs. This is because $s > g$, so that the firm makes a greater *ex post* gain on its permanent workers – the difference in productivity between trained permanent workers and untrained temporary workers exceeds the wage differential. It retains its permanent workers to the point where the marginal product equals the wage and – if these are fully employed – retains temporary workers to the point where their (lower) marginal product equals their (lower) wage.[5]

To determine the numbers of workers hired under each type of contract, substitute from (3.3) and (3.4) into (3.1) and (3.2):

$$-c - h + \sum_i [m_i sQ'(\cdot) - gw] \pi_i = 0 \qquad (3.5)$$

$$-h + \sum_i [m_i Q'(\cdot) - w] \pi_i = 0 \qquad (3.6)$$

Suppose the firm only hired permanent workers. Then, by (3.5), it would hire them to the point where the expected marginal product, net of the wage, equalled the hiring and training costs. The expression inside the summation (the marginal product net of wage) is strictly positive in market states where the firm would like to employ more workers than the number originally hired. It is for these states that the firm keeps a buffer stock of temporary workers who are retained if a high m_i is drawn and otherwise discharged. Even though the expression inside the summation is larger for permanent workers, temporary workers will still be hired if c is relatively high (so there are not that many permanent workers) and h is relatively low (so that it is not costly to build the buffer stock of temporary workers). Indeed, if hiring costs are very low, the firm will hold a very large buffer stock of temporary workers (such that $m_i Q'(\cdot) - w \sim 0$ in every state).

This simple framework allows us to isolate three reasons why women might be disproportionately in temporary jobs. The first is similar to that in Lazear and Rosen (1990). Some women may have better non-market outside opportunities than men. Suppose that there is an exogenous probability δ that a woman will leave for non-market work after the firm incurs hiring and (in the case of permanent workers) training costs. Then the firm loses the expected value $\delta\Sigma_i[m_i s Q'(\cdot) - gw]\pi_i = \delta(c + h)$ if the firm trains a woman rather than a man, and the smaller sum $\delta\Sigma_i[m_i s Q'(\cdot) - w]\pi_i = \delta h$ if the woman is untrained.[6] The firm will find it profitable to offer women temporary contracts rather than make the investment c in training.

Women are also offered temporary rather than permanent contracts if alternatively firms have a taste for discrimination. As described in the context of promotion by Booth, Francesconi and Frank (2003), this can be viewed as the firm treating women as if they had a lower productivity than men by the factor d. If the taste for discrimination is specific to the firm (so that outside wages are the same for men and women), the firm loses the expected value $d\Sigma_i m_i s Q'(\cdot)\pi_i\eta_i^p$ if it trains a woman rather than a man, and the smaller value $d\Sigma_i m_i s Q'(\cdot)\pi_i\eta_i^t$ if it hires a woman rather than a man to a temporary post, where η_i^j, $j = p, t$ is the proportion of permanent or temporary workers employed by the firm in market state i.[7] Note that $\eta_i^p \geq \eta_i^t$ since the firm (for reasons discussed above) retains all permanent workers before retaining any temporary ones.

The third reason why women may be disproportionately allocated to temporary contracts is due to a different form of a taste for discrimination. Trained permanent workers gain rents in this model. Although they do not contribute to the cost of training, their wage rises by the factor g since the firm pays them more for retention purposes. Even if the firm believes that women (or ethnic minorities, for example) are just as productive as men, managers can choose without cost the recipients of these rents, and may discriminate in favour of white males.

What would happen if legislation – as in the European directives – required equal treatment in wages between temporary and permanent workers? Unless the firm moved to having only temporary workers,[8] it would have to pay gw to its temporary workers as well as to its permanent ones. In any given state, by (3.4) but replacing w by gw, the firm employs *ex post* fewer of the originally hired temporary workers. From (3.6), the firm would also hire *ex ante* fewer temporary workers. However, because of this, the expected marginal product of permanent workers in (3.5) rises, and the firm hires *ex ante* more permanent workers. Note that it typically still pays to hire some temporary workers as a buffer stock (even though they have to be paid the same wages if employed as permanent, more productive workers) for very good market states, since the firm avoids the training cost c. The imposition of equal pay regulations entails that, while total expected employment goes down, temporary workers receive higher wages, and there is some substitution of the hiring of additional trained permanent workers in place of untrained temporary workers.

2   THE DATA

From our 'buffer-stock' model outlined above, temporary workers have lower human capital than permanent workers and, as a consequence, lower wages. Temporary jobs are, in this sense, bad jobs. There may therefore be a social interest in encouraging the substitution of permanent jobs by requiring equal wages and conditions of work. Further, either because of a taste for discrimination or because it is believed that some women will find better non-market opportunities than men, these jobs will be held disproportionately by women. A taste for discrimination would also explain why these jobs might be held disproportionately by ethnic minorities. We now investigate these bases for intervention by using our three data sources. Are temporary jobs disproportionately held by women and ethnic minorities? Are they poorly paid?

The British Household Panel Survey (BHPS) is a nationally representative random sample. We use the first ten waves (1991–2000) and have a longitudinal sub-sample of 3122 male and 3401 female workers.[9] The precise form of the question in waves one to eight of the BHPS is as follows: 'Is your current job: A permanent job; A seasonal, temporary or casual job; Or a job done under contract or for a fixed period of time?' These data are discussed in greater detail in Booth, Francesconi and Frank (2002).[10] From wave nine onwards, this question was expanded to include an additional question on agency workers. This information will be exploited in Section 4 of this chapter, while Section 3 will specifically focus on fixed-term contracts. Note that, because of the small representation of ethnic minorities, and the heterogeneity of jobs, we cannot use these data to investigate the relationship between temporary work and ethnicity in great detail.[11]

In 1999, the Royal Economic Society (RES) Working Party on the Representation of Ethnic and Other Minorities in the Economics Profession surveyed 516 UK academic economists holding full-time posts in universities. These cross-sectional data cover a homogeneous group and, in particular, allow us to measure productivity across academics. These data are discussed in greater detail in Blackaby and Frank (2000). Respondents are asked 'What is your current rank?' and choose from a number of alternatives, including 'Fixed-term lecturer', 'Senior researcher, fixed-term' and 'Researcher, fixed-term'. These three options are viewed as fixed-term contracts, while the other posts are viewed as permanent.[12]

The Association of University Teachers (AUT) Equal Opportunities Committee surveyed 813 university employees in 2000/2001 in six representative English universities. The six universities are a mix of traditional and new universities, in different regions of the country. In contrast to the RES survey, these data include academics across different disciplines as well as employees on the administrative side of the universities. These data are discussed in greater detail in Frank (2002). Respondents were asked 'What type of contract do you have?' and asked to choose from 'Fixed-term' and 'Permanent'.

What do the raw data tell us about who holds temporary jobs rather than permanent jobs? The top panel of Table 3.1 (panel A) shows that women are significantly more likely to hold fixed-term contracts than are men in the academic data, but not in the BHPS data on the British economy as a whole. There is no significant difference between ethnic minorities and white employees.

Now consider wages, reported in the bottom panel (panel B) of Table 3.1. With the exception of women in the BHPS data, where there is a significant negative relationship (and the BHPS and RES ethnic minorities where there is no significant relationship), permanent workers are paid significantly more than temporary workers, at significance levels shown in note (c) to the table. Interestingly, this wage gap is greater for men than for women from all three data sources, although – as shown by the asterisks within the body of the table – this is not significant for the RES data.

Table 3.1 Percentage holding fixed-term contracts and wage differences

	Men	Women	Ethnic minorities	White
A. Percentage holding fixed-term contracts				
BHPS	3.3	3.4	4.0	3.3
RES	7.1**	19.8**	8.2	9.5
AUT				
Researchers	96.1	98.6	100	97.4
Other posts	27.9	40.8	41.7	34.2
B. Percentage wage differences between permanent and fixed-term workers				
BHPS	18.5**	–8.3**	–4.6	6.0**
RES	37.4	31.4	14.5*	41.4*
AUT	37.1*	24.6*	38.5	34.0

Notes:
(a) The BHPS data are for fixed-term contracts (and not for seasonal and casual workers) and refer to waves one through ten (1991–2000). The number of person–wave observations are: 18 349 (men), 21 273 (women). There are 513 observations in the RES data and 813 in the AUT.
(b) We test for significant differences (in the first two columns) between the percentages for men and women and (in the last two columns) between ethnic minorities and whites. This is shown by: ** significantly different at the 1% level, * significantly different at the 5% level.
(c) The following coefficients are significantly different from 0 and therefore show a significant difference between permanent and fixed-term workers within the data set: BHPS, RES and AUT men and women (1%), BHPS white workers, RES white worker, and AUT white and ethnic minority workers (5%).

3   WAGES, GENDER AND ETHNICITY

Do the raw data results hold when we add controls for individual characteristics such as age and education and workplace characteristics? Each of the data sets has different variables, but none the less it is instructive to compare the results.

The top panel (panel A) of Table 3.2 shows estimated marginal effects obtained from estimation of a simple probit model of the determinants of the probability of being on a fixed-term contract.[13] Men and women and all ethnic groups are pooled, for each data set, so that we can estimate the impact of gender and ethnicity on the fixed-term contract probability. The additional explanatory variables used for each data set are reported in notes to the table. From these estimations, there is evidence that, after controls, women in the RES sample are more likely to hold fixed-term posts, although this is not confirmed in the BHPS, where in fact men are about 1 per cent more likely to be observed in a fixed-term job. There is no evidence that ethnic minorities are more likely to be on fixed-term contracts.

What about wages? The bottom panel of Table 3.2 reports the estimated coefficient to the fixed-term contract variable included as an exogenous regressor obtained from ordinary least squares (OLS) estimation of the natural logarithm of hourly wages (BHPS) or annual salary (RES and AUT).[14] This time, each data set was stratified into two groups – men and women. There is evidence that being on a fixed-term contract lowers wages for both men and women, although tests do not show a differential effect between men and women, except in the case of the BHPS where the more negative effects for men are statistically different than those for women ($p < 0.01$).

In summary, the estimated results support the idea – consistent with the buffer-stock model – that fixed-term jobs are poorly paid.[15] Regulations to require equal pay across types of contract, fixed-term or permanent, will clearly have an effect. However, there is no clear evidence that – having accounted for individual and workplace characteristics – women or ethnic minorities suffer disproportionately from fixed-term contracts.

4   TYPES OF TEMPORARY WORK

A new European directive requires the extension of equal terms and benefits to agency workers, as well as employees holding a fixed-term contract at the firm where they are actually working. This extension is important since it potentially limits the extent to which firms can substitute low-paid agency workers for low-paid fixed-term contract workers, now covered by new regulations. While earlier waves of the BHPS only distinguish between fixed-term

Table 3.2   Gender, ethnicity, fixed-term contracts and wages

	BHPS	RES	AUT (all)	AUT (acad.)
A. Probability of being on a fixed-term contract (%)[a]				
Men	0.007**	–0.038**	–0.007	–0.065
	(3.08)	(–2.96)	(–0.17)	(–1.10)
White	–0.001	0.002	–0.053	–0.137
	(–0.30)	(0.47)	(–0.59)	(–1.00)
Pseudo R^2	0.113	0.552	0.229	0.32
N	36 850	320	756	409
B. The effect of fixed-term contracts on wages[b]				
Men	–0.147**	–0.160**	–0.235**	–0.321**
	(–8.18)	(–3.59)	(–5.43)	(–6.53)
R^2	0.544	0.620	0.410	0.438
N	16 646	291	345	205
Women	–0.076**	–0.174**	–0.170**	–0.208**
	(–4.82)	(–2.88)	(–4.95)	(–4.28)
R^2	0.527	0.778	0.398	0.403
N	19 278	60	386	192

Notes:

[a] Additional controls included in the BHPS data analysis are: age, labour market experience in part-time and full-time employment, part-time status, number of children by age group, marital status, disability status, housing tenure, education, cohort of entry in the labour market, industry (1-digit SIC), occupation (1-digit SOC), employing sector, trade union coverage, firm size, local unemployment-to-vacancy ratio. Additional controls included in the RES data analysis are: marital status, age, degree class, PhD, publications, research, teaching, RAE (Research Assessment Exercise) scores, region, old or new university, career break. Additional controls included in the AUT data analysis are: age, experience, region, degree class, PhD.

[b] Additional controls included in the BHPS data analysis are: non-white ethnicity, labour market experience in part-time and full-time employment, part-time status, number of children by age group, marital status, disability status, housing tenure, education, industry (1-digit SIC), occupation (1-digit SOC), employing sector, trade union coverage, firm size, local unemployment-to-vacancy ratio. For the RES and AUT data, the same controls are used as in (a).

The difference in sample size in the AUT data arises since not all respondents reported their salary. The *z*- and *t*-statistics are reported in parentheses. In the regressions that use BHPS data, these statistics have been computed with robust standard errors.

* significant at 5% level; ** significant at 1% level.

contract workers and seasonal/casual workers, the latest waves nine and ten include a separate category of agency work. In this section, we examine – using the BHPS data – differences in gender representation and wages across the types of temporary work. Note that none of the regulations requiring equal treatment for fixed-term contract workers, much less agency workers, were in place during the sample period. The other data sources do not distinguish between types of temporary workers, so they are not used in this section. Due to small sample sizes, there are no meaningful results for workers of different ethnicity across the different types of temporary work, so issues of ethnicity are not examined in this section. However, we do investigate the incidence and wages of part-time work compared to full-time. Equal treatment of part-time work is also covered by European directives, and it is interesting to see whether there is a greater or lesser disparity along that dimension than in comparing temporary to permanent jobs.

Table 3.3 shows the raw data proportions of men and women in each type of temporary work, and the average hourly pay associated with that type of

Table 3.3   Worker distribution (proportion) and gross hourly wages (£) by contract type, employment status, and gender, BHPS data

	Men		Women	
	Proportion	Hourly pay	Proportion	Hourly pay
Contract				
Permanent	0.941	9.557	0.916	7.465
Seasonal/casual	0.022	6.095	0.033	7.610
Fixed-term contract	0.020	7.770	0.027	8.434
Agency temping	0.017	5.962	0.025	6.061
Equality tests by gender (male–female):				
Permanent (proportion; £)	0.026 (*t*-stat 4.603); 2.092 (*t*-stat 17.021)			
Seasonal/casual (proportion; £)	–0.011 (*t*-stat –2.965); –1.515 (*t*-stat –0.395)			
Fixed-term contract				
(proportion; £)	–0.007 (*t*-stat –2.241) ; –0.664 (*t*-stat –0.695)			
Agency temping (proportion; £)	–0.008 (*t*-stat –2.539); –0.099 (*t*-stat –0.047)			
N	3715		4224	
Employment status				
Part-time	0.048	6.179	0.267	5.802
Full-time	0.952	9.069	0.733	7.519
Equality tests by gender (male–female):				
Part-time (proportion; £)	–0.219 (*t*-stat –69.935); 0.377 (*t*-stat 1.806)			
Full-time (proportion; £)	0.219 (*t*-stat 69.935); 1.550 (*t*-stat 25.996)			
N	18 389		21 273	

Notes: Figures for 'Contract' are from waves nine and ten (1999 and 2000) of the British Household Panel Survey. Figures for 'Employment status' are from waves one to ten (1991 to 2000). N = number of person–wave observations. Gross hourly wages are in constant (2000) prices.

contract, using the data from waves nine and ten only. The table also reports standard equality tests by gender to detect the presence of any significant differences in representation or wages between men and women. The data and gender equality tests for part-time working use the full set of BHPS data from 1991 to 2000.[16]

As seen from the table, men are significantly more likely than women to hold a permanent contract, and significantly less likely to have any of the three types of temporary contracts.[17] These differences, however, are small compared to the large difference in representation of men and women in part-time work. As in our earlier analysis, there are also major differences in wages. The differences by gender emerge quite strikingly among permanent workers, with permanent men earning about £2 per hour more than women do, as well as among full-timers, with men earning £1.55 per hour more than women do. Interestingly there is no significant gender pay gap among workers on any of the three types of temporary contracts. Men on temporary contracts earn significantly less than men on permanent contracts, while women on fixed-term contracts actually earn significantly more than women on permanent contracts. In contrast there is a significant gender pay gap favouring men among part-time workers.

Do these differences in wages hold after controlling for other characteristics? Table 3.4 presents wage estimates from the BHPS using waves nine and ten. For both men and women, there are significant differences – in either the OLS or RE estimates – between permanent workers and seasonal/casual workers, and between permanent workers and agency temping workers. For example, compared to their permanent counterparts, men in seasonal/casual jobs earn at least 16 per cent lower wages, while the wage penalty for male agency workers is of the order of 18–20 per cent. The pay differentials for women are smaller but still sizeable and significant. In contrast, for both men and women, we cannot detect any significant difference in pay between permanent workers and workers on fixed-term contracts. Part-time women suffer a significant wage penalty compared to full-time women. Part-time men suffer a significant wage penalty compared to full-time men using the random effects estimator, but not under OLS.

The results in this section are consistent with those in Sections 2 and 3. Recall that (with respect to temporary contracts) there is a smaller sample here, since there are only two waves of data, but that there is greater detail as to the actual form of temporary contract held by workers (and thus less measurement error). As with the earlier BHPS results, men suffer a greater wage penalty than do women when holding temporary jobs. There are differences in results with respect to representation by gender in temporary jobs. While the raw BHPS data in Section 2 show an (insignificantly) higher representation of women in fixed-term contracts, the breakdown into types of

Table 3.4   Estimations of log gross hourly wages

	Men		Women	
	OLS	RE	OLS	RE
Contract				
Seasonal/casual	-0.160**	–0.188*	–0.041*	–0.071*
	(0.049)	(0.087)	(0.020)	(0.028)
Fixed-term contract	–0.034	–0.051	–0.010	–0.018
	(0.058)	(0.040)	(0.039)	(0.037)
Agency temping	–0.206**	–0.182*	–0.075**	–0.040*
	(0.057)	(0.084)	(0.027)	(0.018)
Employment status				
Part-time	–0.006	–0.065*	–0.041*	–0.033*
	(0.035)	(0.032)	(0.016)	(0.017)
R^2	0.543	0.535	0.489	0.488
N	3715		4224	

Notes: Figures are estimates obtained from ordinary least squares (OLS) and random-effects (RE) models. The base for contract type is permanent employment. Other controls are: education, marital status, number of children by age group, full-time and part-time work experience, housing tenure, industry, occupation, employing sector, firm size, local unemployment/vacancy ratio, trade union coverage, and a constant. Robust standard errors in parentheses.
** significant at 1% level; * significant at 5% level.

contracts in waves nine and ten leads to *significantly* higher representation of women in each type. Recall that in Table 3.2 men were actually more likely than women to hold fixed-term contracts in the BHPS data, after controlling for individual and workplace characteristics. We have estimated relative risk ratios, using waves nine and ten, of holding each of the three types of temporary jobs relative to holding a permanent job, by gender, using the same controls as in Table 3.2.[18] The estimated coefficients (*t*-statistics) for the effect of being male is: fixed-term contract, 1.037 (0.21), seasonal/casual job, 0.814 (–2.12) and agency temping, 1.022 (1.11). Only the coefficient on seasonal/casual is significant (at the 5 per cent level), and it shows that men are less likely to hold these jobs. These results – which are more in line with the other data sets – may arise because of the more accurate assignment of workers to type of contract in the later waves, or because there has been a shift over time in representation.

Our main interest in this section was to try to compare the importance of equal treatment regulations for different types of contracts and employment status.[19] While there is a similar gender difference in representation across the three types of temporary contracts, the large gender difference concerns part-time working. The major wage gaps concern seasonal/casual work, agency temping and part-time work. There is no significant difference, for either men or women, in pay estimations for fixed-term contracts compared to permanent jobs. Indeed the biggest gaps concern agency temping, suggesting the importance of extending equal treatment regulations to that class of workers. Recall that this result holds in these data collected before regulations were in effect for fixed-term workers. Therefore it is not a product of any improvement in wages for fixed-term workers subsequent to regulation. The gap between fixed-term workers and agency temps can be expected to have increased as fixed-term workers came under the directive which effectively treats them in a comparable way to permanent workers.

5   CONCLUSIONS

In this chapter we have presented a buffer-stock model of temporary workers. Even if – as in the model – all workers are *ex ante* identical, it is still optimal for the firm to offer some of its new hires permanent contracts with high training, and to offer others temporary contracts with low training. Permanent workers receive higher wages in light of their additional training. The model also suggests a number of reasons why ethnic minorities and women may be more likely to be on fixed-term contracts than comparable white males. For both groups discrimination may lead to an under-evaluation of their productivity and a disincentive to invest in their training. Alternatively discrimination may take the form of allocating rents (received by permanent workers) to preferred groups such as white males. A further reason for allocating female workers to temporary jobs is the possibility that they will leave for non-market opportunities.

We examined empirically the contract types offered by gender and ethnicity, and the wage differentials associated with temporary work in Britain. We used three different sources of data: the BHPS panel data on a random representative selection of households, the RES data on academic economists and the AUT data on university employees, covering all disciplines and both academic and administrative workers. The BHPS data give a broader picture of the prevalence and wage implications of temporary work in Britain, while the other data sources allow us to focus on more homogeneous groups of workers to isolate gender, ethnicity and wage effects. For comparative purposes we use the full set of waves of the BHPS – along with the RES and AUT data – for an initial examination of gender, ethnicity and wage effects of fixed-term contracts. As a further exercise we use the last two waves of the BHPS to examine more closely different types of temporary work, since these are the only waves that distinguish agency temping from other forms of temporary work.

We find – in the raw data – evidence that women (but not ethnic minorities) are more likely to be employed on a fixed-term basis. We find generally that there is a positive wage differential favouring permanent employees over fixed-term ones, although – interestingly – this differential seems to be greater for male than for female workers. Indeed, in the BHPS data (but not the RES and AUT data) there is a negative differential for permanent female employees over fixed-term female employees.

After controlling in the different data sets for a wide range of individual and workplace characteristics, the evidence on representation in fixed-term work by gender is less clear. In the RES data women are significantly more likely to hold fixed-term posts, while there is an insignificant relationship of the same sign in the AUT data. In the BHPS men are actually significantly more likely to hold fixed-term posts. As with the raw data, there is no evidence that ethnic minorities are either more or less likely to hold temporary jobs. We find strong support for the existence of a positive wage differential favouring permanent employees over fixed-term ones. The effect is larger for men than for women. Finally from the last two waves of the BHPS, we find that agency temping work has the largest negative estimated impact on wages of any of the forms of temporary jobs.

From the raw data on representation by gender in temporary jobs it is clear that there is an important equal opportunities dimension to regulating equal pay and conditions for temporary work. This holds even if – as in the BHPS data – the higher representation of women in fixed-term posts can be explained by observable individual and workplace characteristics. There is clear evidence in our results that there is a pay gap – allowing for individual and workplace characteristics – between temporary and permanent jobs, so effective regulation will have a positive impact in this respect. However, it must not be forgotten that the imposition of equal pay regulations has a negative effect on total expected employment, as shown by our buffer-stock model. Our empirical results also show the importance of considering extending the regulation to agency temping, since these are the jobs with the highest pay gap. This pay gap and the use of agency workers is likely to increase as fixed-term posts (but not yet agency work) becomes covered by equal treatment rules.

NOTES

*   A related version of this chapter was presented at the European Central Bank Labour Market Workshop: 'How are Wages Determined in Europe?', 10–11 December 2001, Frankfurt/Main, Germany. Comments by participants are gratefully acknowledged. Marco Francesconi is also grateful to the ESRC for financial support.
1.   This is not to say that there is no discrimination in the academic labour market and – while there are no comparative studies of discrimination across all sectors of the labour market – the available evidence for academia suggests that pay and promotion discrimination is fairly

widespread; see for example Ginther and Hayes (1999); Booth and Burton, with Mumford (2000); Booth, Frank and Blackaby (2002), and references therein.

2. Booth, Dolado and Frank (2002: F182) suggest that in principle there are at least three types of temporary work: (i) employment under probation where the temporary contract is by way of a period of probation, (ii) replacement contracts for workers who are on leave; and (iii) fixed-term contracts that may provide a 'buffer stock' of workers (allowing the firm to adjust to changes in the business environment owing to seasonal and/or other transitory causes). It is the third type that we consider in the model developed in this chapter. We use the term 'buffer stock' of workers in a different way to Keynesian analysts such as Mitchell (1988), who advocates that governments should in recessions become an employer of last resort – hence the term 'buffer-stock employment'.

3. In the absence of hiring or firing costs for temporary workers, the firm would have an infinitely large buffer stock. Firing costs for either permanent or temporary workers, or both, would not change the conclusions of the model, and are ignored for simplicity. In the usual way, firing costs would lead to fewer redundancies but also fewer initial hires.

4. In a more complicated model, both permanent and temporary workers might draw from a distribution of outside offers, as in Booth, Frank and Blackaby (2002). Even if the distribution were the same for both types, the firm would offer permanent workers a higher wage given the greater loss in productivity if they were to quit.

5. If there were firing costs for permanent workers, then the firm would retain workers until the marginal product plus firing cost equals the wage. Fewer permanent workers would be made redundant in those very bad states of nature where all temporary workers were laid off and, in addition, some permanent workers were discharged.

6. This calculation supposes that women are such a small fraction of the workforce that the firm's hiring rules do not change. Otherwise, while the result remains true that women are assigned to temporary contracts, the firm hires fewer temporary workers than by the rule of comparing expected marginal product less wage to the value h, to allow for the lost investment on exogenously separated women.

7. This assumes that the only discrimination is in assigning women to contracts and that – within a contract – they are treated equally to men. Otherwise women would suffer disproportionate layoffs in either permanent or temporary contracts. Also, if discrimination occurs throughout the economy, the firm would be able to pay women – within a contract – lower wages than men, given their lower opportunity costs.

8. The possibility of avoiding the impact of equal pay provisions between temporary and permanent workers can explain the use of agency workers. This is a rationale for the proposed extension of the European directives to agency temporary workers.

9. Further information on the BHPS can be obtained at http://www.iser.essex.ac.uk/bhps/doc/index.htm.

10. Using the first seven waves of the BHPS, Booth, Francesconi and Frank (2002) provide an overall picture of temporary jobs in Britain and examine the future career development of workers who hold temporary jobs.

11. The BHPS collects information on ethnic group membership distinguishing between seven groups: White, Black–Caribbean, Black–Other, Indian, Pakistani, Bangladeshi, Other ethnic group. On average every year only 5 per cent of the sample is made up of individuals from all 'non-white' groups. Although the labour market heterogeneity within the non-white group is probably as large as the heterogeneity between the non-white and the white groups, the sample size is too small to analyse each non-white group separately.

12. Probationary lecturers, for example, are viewed as permanent since they do not form a 'buffer stock' of easily dismissed employees for the purposes of redundancy.

13. To ease the interpretation of the results, the table reports marginal effects. These are calculated as the derivative of the conditional expectation of the observed dependent variable, and evaluated at the sample means, following the procedure in Greene (1997).

14. The OLS estimates from the BHPS shown in Table 3.2 are very close to random-effects (RE) estimates, which account for the longitudinal nature of the BHPS data. We also estimated fixed-effects (FE) models, which provide us with point estimates that are similar to (albeit quantitatively smaller than) those reported in Table 3.2. For simplicity and comparability

with the estimates from the RES and AUT samples, these additional results are not shown, but can be obtained from the authors upon request. Notice also that the BHPS sample sizes reported in panel B of Table 3.2 are different from those reported in Table 3.1 (and Table 3.3 below). This is because the regressions estimates in Table 3.2 are obtained from models that control for a large number of variables for which there may be missing values, which do not affect the computations reported in Tables 3.1 and 3.3.

15. Booth, Francesconi and Frank (2002) provide independent evidence that there is lower training in these jobs.
16. Similar figures emerge when the sample is restricted to the most recent period 1999–2000.
17. This information is revealed by the equality tests by gender reported in the top part of the table for contract types. The figures show, for example, that there is a difference of (0.941–0.916 = 0.025) between the proportions of men and women on permanent contracts and that this difference is statistically significant (*t*-statistic of 4.603).
18. The relative risk ratios are obtained from multinomial logit regressions, in which N = 7937, with a resulting pseudo $R^2 = 0.140$.
19. Dolado, Garcia-Serrano and Jimeno (2002: F290) provide some evidence of gender differences in coverage by temporary contracts in Spain over the past decade.

REFERENCES

Blackaby, D. and J. Frank (2000), 'Ethnic and other minority representation in UK academic economics', *The Economic Journal*, **110**, F293–311.

Booth, A.L. and J. Burton, with K. Mumford (2000), 'The position of women in UK academic economics', *The Economic Journal*, **110**, F312–33.

Booth, A.L., J.J. Dolado and J. Frank (2002), 'Symposium on temporary work introduction', *The Economic Journal*, **112**, F181–8.

Booth, A.L., M. Francesconi and J. Frank (2002), 'Temporary jobs: stepping stones or dead ends', *The Economic Journal*, **112**, F189–213.

Booth, A.L., M. Francesconi and J. Frank (2003), 'A sticky floors model of promotion, pay, and gender', *European Economic Review*, **47** (2), 295–322.

Booth, A.L., J. Frank and D. Blackaby (2002), *Outside Offers and the Gender Pay Gap: Empirical Evidence from the UK Academic Labour Market*, CEPR Discussion Paper No. 3549.

Dolado J.J., C. Garcia-Serrano and J.F. Jimeno (2002), 'Drawing lessons from the boom of temporary jobs in Spain', *The Economic Journal*, **112**, F270–95.

Frank, J. (2002), *Gay Glass Ceilings*, mimeo.

Ginther, D. and K.J. Hayes (1999), 'Salary and promotion differentials by gender for faculty in the humanities', *American Economic Review Papers and Proceedings*, **89** (2), 52–6.

Greene, W.H. (1997), *Econometric Analysis* (3rd edn), Upper Saddle River, US: Prentice Hall.

Lazear, E.P. and S. Rosen (1990), 'Male–female wage differentials in job ladders', *Journal of Labor Economics*, 8 (1, Part 2), S106–23.

Mitchell, W.F. (1988), 'The buffer stock employment model and the NAIRU: the path to full employment', *Journal of Economic Issues*, **32** (2), June, 1–9.

4. Moving from the external to an internal labour market: job tenure, cycle and wage determination

Leandro Arozamena and Mário Centeno

1 INTRODUCTION

Ever since Doeringer and Piore's (1971) seminal study, considerable attention has been devoted to the analysis of wage determination within firms. The main observation in the resulting literature is that wage setting in such 'internal' labour markets differs substantially from the predictions that stem from regarding the labour market as competitive. As a consequence, research has focused on the reasons why these internal labour markets exist and on how they function. In broad terms, they are characterized by long-term relationships, and these in turn are usually explained by the existence of some form of firm-specific human capital that bonds the worker and the employer together. These explanations can also include issues relating to information and learning, as Gibbons and Katz (1991) and Gibbons and Waldman (1999) have recently shown.

Naturally, however, a worker that could be but has not been hired by a given firm has not entered that firm's internal labour market yet: she is taking part in a competitive, 'external' labour market, one that is much more similar to the analysis in standard, competitive models. Once the worker has been hired, then, a process must occur whereby she moves from the external to an internal labour market. Little effort has been made in attempting to describe and explain this transition. This chapter tries to fill that gap. Specifically, we analyse the shift from the external to an internal labour market as it is reflected in changes in the wage determination process along the transition.

To do so, we rely on the extensive literature in labour economics that studies the issue of returns to tenure.[1] The concept of firm- (or match-)specific human capital plays a key role in this literature. It is interpreted as everything valuable in the match between a worker and her employer that has no value for either party outside the match. Match-specific human capital could then be central to how wages are set: given that it is accumulated in the course of the employment relationship, wages may grow with job tenure. The debate on returns to tenure has also been enriched with the introduction of information and learning aspects (for example Jovanovic, 1979; Felli and Harris, 1996).

Taking this literature as a starting point, we incorporate the issue of specific human capital accumulation and returns to tenure into the analysis of how workers move to an internal labour market. We examine how specific human capital and job tenure on one side, and external labour market conditions on the other, interact in the process of wage determination. We claim that, as the employment relationship progresses and specific human capital is accumulated, the impact of external labour market conditions on wage and turnover decisions changes. Furthermore, we construct a simple model and provide empirical evidence that, in both cases, suggest that external labour market conditions have an effect on wages that *declines* with job tenure. This supports the idea that specific human capital accumulation is connected to the progressive 'internalization' of wages.

In Section 3 we introduce a simple model in the spirit of Jovanovic (1979). Employment occurs by random matching between firms and workers. The quality of any given match is unknown *ex ante* and is learned as the employment relationship progresses[2]. Higher job tenure, then, implies that more information has been gathered about match quality. Such information, common to both parties to the match, can be interpreted as match-specific capital. To this standard framework we add the influence of the business cycle, to capture the effect of external labour market conditions. The expected quality of new matches and the value of any given match vary with those conditions. Hence, we are able to examine the interaction between specific capital accumulation and cyclical effects. The model has three empirical implications. First, there are returns to tenure. Second, there is a cohort effect on wages; that is, current wages are influenced by the labour market stance at the beginning of the employment relationship. Last, and most important, there is an inverse relationship between wage cyclicality and job tenure. As more specific capital is accumulated in a match, the worker, by receiving a fraction of the return to that capital, becomes increasingly protected against variations in external labour market conditions: he gradually enters an internal labour market.

In Sections 4–6 we put these empirical predictions to the test. To account for variations in the external labour market stance, we use the unemployment rate as a proxy. We confirm that wages are increasing in job tenure.[3] In addition there is a cohort effect, although it dies out as tenure progresses. But most significantly, we find that the elasticity of current wages to the local unemployment rate is decreasing in job tenure. This result is robust to different model specifications and sample changes. Additionally we consider the possibility that the main result applies to different wage levels with varying intensity. Resorting to a quantile regression approach, we show that the elasticity of wages at the top quantile is more sensitive to tenure than that of wages at the bottom quantile. Finally, we study the possible existence of non-linearities in the transition to an internal labour market. We show that the internalization of the wage-setting process is much faster during the first year of tenure than later on in the employment relationship. We describe the empirical approaches and the data used to test the model's predictions, respectively, in Sections 4 and 5. In Section 6, we present the empirical results. We conclude in Section 7.

In addition to constituting a first examination of the interaction between the labour market stance and job tenure, these results contribute to the recent debate on changes in human resources management and changes in the nature of employment relationships. It is sometimes argued that an increased sensitivity of wages to unemployment rates reflects the fact that the wage-setting process has become less characterized by internal labour market practices.[4] Our results point to an alternative (though compatible) interpretation. Given the evidence from the human resources literature that restructuring processes and downsizing experiences particularly hurt older workers (see Capelli, 1995), it might be the case that this 'recomposition' of the pool of workers dominates the 'main' effect of the business cycle on wages. If this is true, the empirical evidence of a larger sensitivity of wages to the business cycle might be due to lower average seniority and not to structural changes in the way wages are set.

2   A BRIEF REVIEW OF RELATED LITERATURE

Four papers are strongly related to ours: Beaudry and DiNardo (1991), Felli and Harris (1996), Gibbons and Waldman (1999) and Farber (1999). Beaudry and DiNardo (1991) combine a contract model with cyclical effects. They examine the relation between wages and the business cycle both theoretically and empirically, and conclude that the current unemployment rate does not affect wages after controlling for the best labour market conditions since a worker was hired for her current job. However, their model does not allow for a tenure effect on wages and has no prediction regarding how returns to tenure and the cycle interact in wage determination. Furthermore, our result below, according to which the cyclical behaviour of the wage rate decreases with tenure, constitutes an alternative explanation for their findings. If firms shield more tenured workers from the vagaries of the labour market, whether one is to find a large impact of the business cycle on wages will be a function of the tenure composition of the pool of employed workers at any given moment.

Felli and Harris (1996) introduce a dynamic model of specific capital that incorporates issues of information, matching and turnover. This is the only dynamic model that we know of that has implications for the slope of the tenure–earnings profile. Both Gibbons and Waldman (1999) and Farber (1999) present very stylized models of wage dynamics in internal labour markets and with specific human capital, respectively. In addition, as mentioned above, Jovanovic (1979) presents an example of a more dynamic set-up that combines specific capital and search, which serves as a starting-point for our own model below. None of these papers tackles the issue of how variations in the labour market stance associated with business cycle conditions affect the wage profile as the employment relationship progresses. It is precisely this change in the influence of external labour market conditions as tenure is accumulated that constitutes the object of our analysis.

Our work is also connected to the vast literature on the issue of how real wages vary over the business cycle. In his seminal work, Bils (1985) finds evidence that wages for job changers are strongly procyclical, but wages for job stayers respond only weakly to the cycle. This conclusion has been confirmed by more recent papers (see for example Solon et al., 1994), which find incumbent workers' wages to be procyclical, although less so than they are for job changers. These studies also find evidence that wage cyclicality is strongest among low-wage workers.

3   A SIMPLE MODEL

In this section we present a model that analyses the impact of the business cycle on the process of wage determination as it evolves while tenure and specific human capital accumulate. Such a model can be constructed at different levels of formal complexity. In this chapter, we have chosen a particularly simple framework that nevertheless suffices, on one hand, to illustrate the interaction between tenure and the business cycle in the wage-setting process – which is the main focus of our analysis – and, additionally, to motivate the empirical analysis presented in the following section.

The key components of the model are: (i) the existence of employer-specific human capital – valuable in the match between the firm and the worker but with no value outside the match;[5] (ii) the appropriation by the worker of a fraction of the value of this specific capital; and (iii) the interaction between that value and the labour market stance.

We adopt a basic structure that is a simplified version of the one in Jovanovic (1979) and add a cyclical component to it. Specifically, labour is the only factor of production and firms' technologies exhibit constant returns to scale. Workers and firms are matched randomly. Denote by μ the quality of any given match. A match can be of one of two qualities: G (good) or B (bad). Each worker lives two periods ($t = 0, 1$) and there is no discounting. In each period t, the production k_t that results from any match occurs according to the following stochastic technology:

$$k_t = \begin{cases} 1 \text{ with probability } p \\ 0 \text{ with probability } (1-p) \end{cases}$$

if $\mu = G$, and

$$k_t = \begin{cases} 1 \text{ with probability } (1-p) \\ 0 \text{ with probability } p \end{cases}$$

if $\mu = B$, where $p > 1/2$.

The quality of any match is unknown *ex ante*. It is identically and independently distributed (i.i.d.) across matches, according to a distribution to be specified below. Information on match quality is symmetric between the firm and the worker at all stages, and is updated when production occurs. Hence, we take an informational interpretation of match-specific human capital, as in Jovanovic (1979): as the employment relationship progresses, both parties learn about the quality of the match, and the information so gathered constitutes capital that is valuable only within the match.[6]

Turning to the business cycle, we assume for simplicity that it has two possible realizations: high and low. Denoting the state of the cycle in period t by Ψ_t, we then have $\Psi_t \in \{L, H\}$, $t = 0, 1$. Ψ_t is i.i.d. across periods, with prob($\Psi_t = H$) = ρ for all t.

The business cycle enters into our model in two different ways. First, it affects the value of the production generated in any match. Concretely, we assume that the value of production k_t is given by $\alpha(\Psi_t).k_t$, where

$$\alpha(\Psi_t) = \begin{cases} 1 \text{ if } \Psi_t = H, \\ a \text{ if } \Psi_t = L, \end{cases}$$

$0 < a < 1$. This could reflect fluctuations in demand or changes in technology that make workers more or less productive.[7] Notice that, for simplicity, we assume this cyclical effect is equal for all possible matches.

In addition, the business cycle plays a role in the determination of the prior probability distribution over the two possible qualities of a match. Namely, if an employment relationship begins in period t and $\Psi_t = H$ ($\Psi_t = L$), then the prior probability that $\mu = G$ is h (l), with $h > l$. That is, a match will turn out to be highly productive with greater probability if it starts during a boom than if it starts during a recession. We make this assumption for the sake of simplicity. We could model the job-matching process in a more detailed fashion, having the *ex ante* value of a given match depend on the number of workers searching for jobs and on the number of vacancies. In such a model, the relative abundance of job searchers and vacancies during recessions would generate two opposing effects on the average quality of new matches. First, it would make it easier for firms and workers to attain good matches, since they would be choosing from larger pools. But, on the other hand, it would also generate more search frictions, making good matches less likely to happen. Then, we are implicitly assuming that the second effect prevails. This simplifies our model significantly and allows it to stay very close to Jovanovic (1979), differing only in that the distribution of match qualities varies with the cycle. Furthermore, the empirical evidence in Bowlus (1995) strongly suggests that the average quality of new matches is actually procyclical.

The timing of the model is as follows. In each period, the state of the business cycle is revealed. If the worker was employed in a firm during the previous period, she decides whether to stay in the same job or quit. If she quits or she was not employed before – that is, this is the first period of her life – she is matched randomly to a firm. Then, production occurs and the information on the quality of the match is updated.

We assume that wages are determined by Nash bargaining between the firm and the worker. Specifically, in any given match, the wage in period t, w_t, is given by

$$w_t = (1 - \beta) \left[\begin{array}{c} \text{worker's} \\ \text{outside option} \end{array} \right] + \beta \left[\begin{array}{c} \text{expected value of production} \\ \text{from the match in period } t \end{array} \right],$$

(4.1)

where β is the worker's bargaining power, assumed constant and the same for all workers, $0 < \beta < 1$. Of course, a worker will quit if the expected value of production in the current match is lower than her outside option, that is, employment in a new match.[8]

Note that in a new match we have $w_0 = \alpha(\Psi_0) \cdot \text{prob}(k_0 = 1 \mid \Psi_0)$. A worker staying in her job, however, receives a larger sum, since a fraction of the return to the specific capital is added. This is a crucial part of the model. In a competitive bidding environment, the worker's wage would equal her productivity in the best alternative match, and the productivity increase arising from match-specific human capital accumulation would be fully appropriated by the firm. Wherever this happens, in order to generate returns to tenure it is necessary that the worker's productivity in the best alternative match increases with the accumulation of specific human capital in the current match (as happens for example in Felli and Harris, 1996). Our Nash bargaining assumption can be interpreted as a short cut generating the same result.

Our main concern lies in the evolution of wages as tenure progresses. Just as wages in period 0 are essentially determined by the prior beliefs in the quality of the match, wages in period 1 for workers staying in their jobs will depend on the posterior assessment of that quality. For future reference, then, let us specify the values that such assessment can take. With two prior distributions and two possible production levels, four posterior probabilities that a match is good obtain by straightforward application of Bayes's rule:

$$l^0 = \text{prob } (\mu = G \mid \Psi_0 = L, k_0 = 0) = \frac{(1-p)l}{(1-p)\,l + p\,(1-l)}$$

$$l^1 = \text{prob } (\mu = G \mid \Psi_0 = L, k_0 = 1) = \frac{pl}{pl + (1-p)\,(1-l)}$$

$$\text{(4.2)}$$

$$h^0 = \text{prob } (\mu = G \mid \Psi_0 = H, k_0 = 0) = \frac{(1-p)h}{(1-p)\,h + p\,(1-h)}$$

$$h^1 = \text{prob } (\mu = G \mid \Psi_0 = H, k_0 = 1) = \frac{ph}{ph + (1-p)\,(1-h)}$$

Clearly, we have $l^1 > l > l^0$, $h^1 > h > h^0$.

As mentioned above, at $t = 0$ no human capital has yet been accumulated by the worker in any match, so (4.1) trivially implies that her wage equals her outside option. Since the prior assessment of the quality of the match depends on the state of the business cycle, so do wages. Therefore, the initial wage is a function

$$w_0 : \{L, H\} \to \Re_+,$$

where

$$w_0(L) = a[pl + (1 - p)\,(1 - l)], \qquad w_0(H) = ph + (1 - p)\,(1 - h).$$

At $t = 1$, match-specific human capital has been accumulated in the form of better information about the quality of the match. The worker has to decide whether to remain with the same employer or quit, and in the former case she receives a fraction of the accumulated human capital through Nash bargaining. Accordingly, we have the following period-1 wage function:

$$w_1 : \{0, 1\} \times \{L, H\} \times \{L, H\} \to \Re_+ \cup \{\text{quit}\},$$

where the entries in the Cartesian product are the sets of possible values of k_0, Ψ_0 and Ψ_1, respectively. Note that the worker's outside option is provided by a new match in which wages would be as specified by $w_0(\cdot)$. Therefore, if the worker decides to stay, her corresponding wage level, by 4.1, will be

$$\alpha(\Psi_1) \{(1 - \beta) w_0 (\Psi_1) + \beta[p.\text{prob} (\mu = G \mid \Psi_0, k_0)$$
$$+ (1 - p) (1 - \text{prob} (\mu = G \mid \Psi_0, k_0))]\}$$

This is the value that the worker has to compare with her outside option in her choice between staying and quitting. Thus the worker implicitly compares her expected productivity in the current match with the one in a new match, and selects the highest alternative.

Let us now determine what specific values $w_1(\cdot)$ will take in each possible case, using $w_0(\cdot)$ and the updated probabilities in (4.2):

(i)   Clearly, if $\Psi_0 = L$ and $k_0 = 0$, the worker does not stay in the firm under any value of Ψ_1. The updated probability that the match be good, l^0 lies below the corresponding probability in the worst possible outside option l. Then, $w_1(0, L, \Psi_1) = \text{quit}$ for all Ψ_1.

(ii)   If $\Psi_0 = H$ and k_0 and 1, the worker's expected productivity in the match always exceeds her expected productivity in any possible alternative job, since the updated probability of a good match is now $h^1 > h$. From 4.1, we have

$$w_1(1, H, L) = a\{(1 - \beta w_0(L) + \beta[ph^1 + (1 - p) (1 - h^1)]\},$$

$$w_1(1, H, H) = (1 - \beta)w_0(H) + \beta[ph^1 + (1 - p) (1 - h^1)].$$

The two remaining cases – that is $\Psi_0 = L$, $k_0 = 1$ and $\Psi_0 = H$ and $k_0 = 0$ – can generate different results according to parameter values. To reduce the number of possibilities, we introduce the following assumption:

Assumption 1: $(1 - p) (1 - l) h < pl (1 -h)$
Assumption 1 ensures that $l^1 > h > lh^0$, thereby determining the quitting behaviour in the next two cases.

(iii)   If $\Psi_0 = L$ and $k_0 = 1$, the updated probability of a good match, l^1, exceeds l. Then, the worker stays in the job if $\Psi_1 = L$, and we have

$$w_1(1, L, L) = a\{(1 - \beta)\, w_0(L) + \beta[pl^1 + (1 - p)\, (1 - l^1)]\}.$$

If $\Psi_1 = H$, by Assumption 1, the worker does not quit, since her expected productivity in the match is still higher than in any alternative employment. Hence,

$$w_1(1, L, H) = (1 - \beta)\, w_0(H) + \beta[pl^1 + (1 - p)\, (1 - l^1)].$$

(iv)　Finally, if $\Psi_0 = H$ and $k_0 = 0$ the updated probability of a good match h^0 lies below h. This means that the worker will quit if $\Psi_1 = H$. In addition, if $\Psi_1 = L$, Assumption 1 implies that the worker's expected productivity in the match is lower than in an alternative job, so $w_1(1, L, \Psi_1) = $ quit for all Ψ_1.

We are now ready to state the main results of this section.

Proposition 1:
(a)　There are positive returns to tenure:

$$w_1(k_0, \Psi_0, \Psi_1) > w_0(\Psi_0)$$

for all k_0, Ψ_0, Ψ_1 such that $w_1(k_0, \Psi_0, \Psi_1) \neq$ quit.

(b)　The effect of the business cycle on wages falls with tenure:

$$\frac{w_1(k_0, \Psi_0, H) - w_1(k_0, \Psi_0, L)}{w_1(k_0, \Psi_0, H)} < \frac{w_0(H) - w_0(L)}{w_0(H)}$$

for all k_0, Ψ_0, Ψ_1 such that $w_1(k_0, \Psi_1, \Psi_1) \neq$ quit.

(c)　There is a cohort effect:

$$w_1(k_0, H, \Psi_1) > w_1(k_0, L, \Psi_1)$$

for all k_0, Ψ_0, Ψ_1 such that $w_1(k_0, \Psi_0, \Psi_1) \neq$ quit.

Proof: Given our exposition above, to show that the three assertions in Proposition 1 are true we just have to check that the appropriate inequalities hold in all cases.

(a)

$$w_1(1, H, H) - w_0(H) = \beta(2p - 1)\, (h_1 - h) > 0$$

since $p > 1/2$. The three remaining possibilities ($[k_0, \Psi_0, \Psi_1]$ taking the values $[1, H, L]$, $[1, L, H]$ and $[1, L, L]$) are analogous.

(b) Take the case where $\Psi_0 = H$, $k_0 = 1$. Our claim holds if and only if $[w_0(L)/w_0(H)] < [w_1(1, H, L)/w_1(w_1(1, H, H)]$. But

$$\frac{w_0(L)}{w_0(H)} = \frac{a[pl + (1 - p)(1 - l)]}{ph + (1 - p)(1 - h)} < a, \text{ and}$$

$$\frac{w_1(1, H, L)}{w_1(1, H, H)} = \frac{a\{(1 - \beta) w_0(L) + \beta[ph^1 + (1 - p)(1 - h^1)]\}}{(1 - \beta) w_0(H) + \beta[ph^1 + (1 - p)(1 - h^1)]} = a,$$

so our assertion is true in this case. The only remaining relevant case, $\Psi_0 = L$, $k_0 = 1$, is analogous.

(c)

$$w_1(1, H, H) - w_1(1, L, H) = w_1(1, H, L) - w_1(1, L, L)$$
$$= \beta(2p - 1)(h^1 - l1) > 0.$$

The intuition for each of these results, given the simplicity of the model, is straightforward. Since continuation in the current match follows from a high level of production in period 0 – which entails a favorable update of the information on match quality – wages should increase with tenure. Wages in period 0 are cyclical for two reasons. Not only is it the case that the value of production varies with the cycle; the expected productivity of the (new) match does as well. While the first effect is present in period 1, the second affects only the worker's outside option: since the current match started in the previous period, there are no more cyclical fluctuations in its expected productivity. Hence, period-1 wages are less sensitive to the cycle than their period-0 counterparts. Finally, the cohort effect arises directly from the procyclicality of match quality.

A comment is due on the robustness of these predictions to extensions of the model to more than two periods. Although the formal complexity of the solution would definitely increase, all our results should still hold in a more complete model. In expected terms, good matches would tend to survive, while bad matches would be abandoned. Since only better matches would survive the cyclical fluctuations of the outside option, there would still be positive returns to tenure. As regards the cyclical behaviour of wages, the same reasoning employed in Proposition 1 can be used to show that higher wages will be less cyclical than lower ones. If a worker who has remained in the match longer is expected to have a higher wage, lower cyclicality would follow as well. Finally, the cohort effect would still be present, although it would diminish with increases in tenure.

Among the three results on wage dynamics presented in Proposition 1, we are most interested in the second. The effect of the business cycle on wages becomes less significant throughout the duration of the match. As suggested above, this can be interpreted as a progressive internalization of the employment relationship as tenure is accumulated. The worker becomes progressively shielded from the spot labour market. We should then observe a lower elasticity of wages to variables related to the labour market stance as tenure is accumulated. Such a prediction, as well as the remaining results stemming from our model, is evaluated empirically in the sections that follow.

4 TESTING METHODOLOGY

In this section we introduce the different regression models used to assess the empirical evidence for the predictions presented above. With such a set of empirical strategies we try to address a series of issues that might not be captured by our basic regression models. These issues include the sensitivity of the model's results at different wage levels and the presence of non-linearities in the process of learning about match quality captured by job tenure.

4.1 Basic Empirical Model

The model outlined in Section 3 has several empirically testable implications for the process of wage determination. In particular, it entails that the current wage is related to the worker's tenure in her job, to the opportunities available at the moment she was hired and to the current conditions of the labour market. Equation (4.3), our basic wage equation, encompasses all these three implications of the theory:

$$\ln w(i, t + j, t) = X_{i,t+j}\theta_1 + \theta_2\Psi(t, j) + \theta_3\text{ten}_{i,t+j}$$
$$+ \theta_4\text{ten}_{i,t+j} * \Psi(t, j) + \varepsilon_{i,t+j} \quad (4.3)$$

That is, the wage paid in period $t + j$ for an individual i who began working in period t is a function of a vector of covariates $X_{i,t+j}$ – which includes experience, schooling, race, union and marital status, industry and state dummies – her tenure on the job and the labour market stance. The cycle effect is proxied by the local unemployment rate, $\Psi(t, j)$. Both the initial and the current values of the local unemployment rate will be used below. Since we are mainly interested in the interaction between tenure, which we use as an indirect measure of specific human capital accumulation, and the labour market stance captured through the unemployment rate, the most important coefficients for our purposes are θ_2, θ_3 and θ_4.

Our model predicts that θ_3 and θ_4 will be positive and θ_2 negative. The positive sign of θ_3 derives from the existence of returns to tenure associated with the accumulation of firm-specific human capital in the form of learning about match quality. When the initial unemployment rate is included in the regression, the cohort effect implies a negative value for θ_2. The same is true when we use the current unemployment rate, since external labour market conditions do have an influence on wages. Finally, the sign of the interaction term is implied by Proposition 1(b): the sensitivity of wages to the business cycle should be decreasing with tenure.

4.2   Accounting for Job Heterogeneity

Some relevant information, however, may not be captured in such a basic regression. According to the model proposed above, the wage level is a function, among other factors, of firm- and worker-specific human capital and match quality. Firms (or jobs) that invest more in worker-specific human capital and that prefer (or require) stable long-term relationships are expected to pay higher wages and to have a steeper wage profile. This kind of heterogeneity in firms/jobs could induce variation over the wage distribution in the tenure/cycle effect on the wage profile. Therefore, the role of the internal and external labour markets in wage setting would not be constant over the wage distribution. Higher-paid jobs are expected to involve a higher degree of match specificity and this should be reflected in differences in the impact of tenure and the business cycle on wages. To find out whether this is the case or not, we resort to quantile regression. This technique enables us to characterize the entire conditional distribution of the dependent variable given a set of covariates. Therefore, it becomes possible to study issues related to the response of wages to changes in the market conditions over the length of an employment spell, at different points of the wage distribution.[9]

4.3   Non-linearities in Tenure Effects

In the theoretical literature on returns to tenure and learning it has been suggested that the learning process might not be continuous (see for example Jovanovic, 1979). Learning takes place at a much faster rate at the beginning of the match than later on. Not much empirical work on this issue is available. In a recent paper, however, Farber (1999) presents evidence on match duration. According to his findings, there are three key facts on job tenure: long-term employment relationships are common, most new jobs end early[10] and the probability of job change declines with tenure. These results, particularly the second and third facts, point to a non-linearity in the process of learning about match quality. Consequently, we would expect the process of wage internalization to be much faster during the early period of the relationship.

In order to find out whether this is true in our samples and if it might influence the results of the previous models we estimate equation (4.3) allowing for structural breaks in the tenure effect on wages. We do so by introducing a spline on the tenure variable. More specifically, we model the relationship between wages, tenure and the business cycle as a bilinear spline. With this formulation we allow the wage rate to be a piecewise function of tenure, thus permitting different effects for different levels of tenure.

Let S be the number of knots and $\overline{\text{ten}}_s$ their respective value. Our tenure variable is defined as follows:

$$\text{ten}_1 = \text{ten}, \quad \text{ten}_s = \begin{cases} (\text{ten} - \overline{\text{ten}}_{s-1}) & \text{if ten} > \overline{\text{ten}}_{s-1} \\ 0 & \text{otherwise} \end{cases} \quad (s = 2, \ldots, S)$$

$$x_s = \Psi * \text{ten}_s, \text{ for } s = 1, \ldots, S$$

Given the coefficient vectors $\alpha = [\alpha_1, \ldots, \alpha_S]$, and $\gamma = [\gamma_1, \ldots, \gamma_S]$ and the intercept θ, w is defined as:

$$w = \theta + \delta * \Psi + \alpha * \text{ten} + \gamma * x$$

The interpretation of the coefficients is straightforward. More important here are the coefficients that represent changes in the 'interaction effect' of the unemployment rate and tenure along grid lines $\text{ten} = \overline{\text{ten}}_{s-1}$. Note that the net effects for each s can be found by adding these changes to their initial effects. The net main effect of tenure is $\alpha_1 + \ldots + \alpha_s$ and the net interaction effect is $\gamma_1 + \ldots + \gamma_s$.

In the section on econometric results we describe the particular application of this model to our data, specifically including the question of identifying values for the knots.

5   DATA

In this section, we briefly review the main data sources used in this chapter. For a more detailed description of those sources, we refer the reader to Arozamena and Centeno (2001). We use three different databases to investigate the existence of a tenure effect on wages: a Panel Study of Income Dynamics (PSID) extract, a National Longitudinal Survey of Youth (NLSY) extract and several issues of the Current Population Survey (CPS) between 1979 and 1998. The main advantage of the NLSY and the PSID over the CPS is that, being panels, they allow us to follow individuals over time.

Our NLSY extract corresponds to the 1979–96 period. The NLSY is better for our purposes than the other databases not only because of its larger sample – as compared to the PSID – but particularly because it has better information on job tenure and a larger number of short employment spells. Its major drawback is the fact that it surveys relatively young people, thereby not being as representative of the overall labour force. This makes job turnover much more frequent. However, it enables us to use a greater number of spells, and it is more adequate to study issues related to the timing of match learning and non-linearities in tenure effects.

The PSID data cover the 1976-83 period (except 1979, since that year the tenure question was not included). This is a more representative panel than the NLSY and slightly longer. However, its main problem is that the wording of the tenure question has changed substantially over time.[11] This is particularly troubling given the key role that tenure plays not only in the identification of the employment spells, but also as an explanatory variable in the empirical implementation.

The CPS provides a very large sample. Our extract is a repeated cross-section data set. We use all the CPS supplements between 1979 and 1998 containing information on job tenure (a total of 12 surveys). The drawbacks of the CPS, nonetheless, are very significant. In addition to the irregular wording of the tenure question (see Farber, 1999), we lose the longitudinal component of the sample, and the cyclical variation obtained is much smaller.

These three extracts are merged by state and year with the state monthly unemployment rate, our measure of the state of the business cycle. The unemployment rate information is taken from the Bureau of Labour Statistics for the 1976-99 period.

Table 4.1 presents means and standard deviations of the main variables of interest for the three data sets used in this chapter. We restrict the analysis to male workers. We are interested in the investigation of relatively long-term attachment to the labour force as a way to guarantee the development of the type of implicit agreements investigated here. Since males have more stable labour force participation and matches are less likely to end due to reasons not related to the match itself, one might suspect that they are more likely to be covered by the implicit wage-setting contracts.

The NLSY extract appears to have a lower proportion of unionized workers than the CPS and PSID samples. This is a result of the younger NLSY sample. In fact, the average age in the NLSY sample is 23 years while it is 34

Table 4.1   Descriptive statistics: NLSY, PSID and CPS individual data (mean and standard deviations)

Variables description	NLSY	PSID	CPS
Log real wage[a]	1.378	2.206	5.942
	(0.416)	(0.610)	(0.990)
Log state current unemployment rate	1.892	1.872	1.871
	(0.320)	(0.291)	(0.325)
Log state unemployment rate at start of job	1.876	1.909	1.829
	(0.337)	(0.221)	(0.311)
Age	23.216	34.005	37.344
	(4.031)	(9.995)	(12.077)
Tenure[b]	2.153	4.106	7.921
	(2.375)	(7.320)	(8.562)
White	0.688	0.680	0.889
	(0.463)	(0.467)	(0.315)
Married	0.323	0.795	0.679
	(0.468)	(0.404)	(0.467)
Experience[c]	277.030	16.828	17.748
	(191.593)	(10.918)	(12.308)
Union status	0.151	0.224	0.235
	(0.359)	(0.417)	(0.424)
Highest grade completed	11.790	12.546	13.582
	(2.357)	(2.719)	(2.800)
Northeast region	0.178	0.162	0.220
	(0.383)	(0.369)	(0.414)
North Central region	0.236	0.230	0.252
	(0.425)	(0.421)	(0.434)
South region	0.388	0.442	0.276
	(0.487)	(0.497)	(0.447)
West region	0.198	0.166	0.226
	(0.398)	(0.372)	(0.419)

Notes:
The CPS data are composed of a random subsample of male workers from several CPS supplements covering the 1979–98 period.
The NLSY data are composed of male workers in NLSY over the period 1979–96.
The PSID data are composed of male workers in PSID over the period 1979–93.
When required, variables are deflated using the CPI (1982–84 = 100).
[a] Wages are hourly for the NLSY and PSID extracts and weekly for the CPS.
[b] Tenure is measured in years for the NLSY, PSID and CPS extracts.
[c] Experience is measured in weeks for the NLSY extract and in years for both the PSID and CPS extracts.
State monthly unemployment rates are taken from the Local Area Unemployment Statistics from the Bureau of Labour Statistics for the period 1978–96. The CPI is taken from the BLS.

years in the PSID sample and 37 in the CPS. This is also reflected in the average number of years of schooling for each sample. It is smaller for the NLSY than it is for the other two samples. The proportion of whites is much smaller in the NLSY and PSID samples and the South region is over-represented in these two extracts, when compared to the CPS subsample.

The average length of tenure is, as expected, smaller in the NLSY sample and higher in the CPS sample. This is, again, due to the fact that the NLSY extract consists of a sample of young workers with higher turnover and lower employer attachment. Hourly wages are notably lower in the NLSY extract when compared to the PSID wages. This difference reflects, among other factors, the experience and educational composition of both samples. CPS wages are weekly and hence not fully comparable.

6.   ECONOMETRIC RESULTS

6.1   Basic Results

In this section, we present evidence that higher levels of job tenure reduce the sensitivity of wages to both the current unemployment rate and the unemployment rate prevailing at the start of the job. We discuss first the results obtained with the NLSY sample. This is our preferred data set due to the higher quality of tenure recordings. Next, we present the results obtained using the PSID and the CPS extracts. The PSID extract yields, qualitatively, very similar results but with much higher standard errors. The limitations of the CPS (not allowing us to include work history information, losing the longitudinal characteristic of a panel data set and not covering a complete business cycle) make our findings harder to interpret and, in general, much weaker.

6.1.1   NLSY results
Our main findings are shown in Table 4.2. We use a fixed-effects panel-data model to estimate equation (4.3). We present the effect of tenure on the elasticity of current wages to the current local unemployment rate and to the local unemployment rate at the start of the job. The NLSY results correspond to the first four lines of Table 4.2. Columns (2) and (3) present the results when we measure the business cycle using the current unemployment rate, whereas in columns (4) and (5) we use the unemployment rate at the start of the job. As expected, there are positive returns to tenure, and the main current wage–current local unemployment rate elasticity is negative and significantly different from zero. More importantly, and according to our prediction, that elasticity decreases (in absolute value) with tenure.

Table 4.2   Effect of tenure on the elasticity of current wage to the local unemployment rate: basic regression model (dependent variable: log (w_{ijt}))

	N	Tenure (1)	Log current unemployment rate (2)	Tenure * log current unemployment rate (× 100) (3)	Log unemployment rate at start of job (4)	Tenure * log unemployment rate at start of job (× 100) (5)	Marginal effect of the unemployment rate (6)
1	NLSY		−0.0539 (0.0066)				
2	NLSY	0.0943 (0.0070)	−0.0586 (0.0090)	0.4576 (0.2080)			−0.0487 (0.0089)
3	NLSY				−0.0534 (0.0076)		
4	NLSY	0.0149 (0.0043)			−0.0653 (0.0081)	0.7810 (0.1888)	−0.0485 (0.0081)
5	PSID		−0.0719 (0.0211)				
6	PSID	0.0059 (0.0055)	−0.0881 (0.0248)	0.3518 (0.2698)			−0.0662 (0.0247)
7	PSID				−0.0842 (0.0223)		
8	PSID	0.0250 (0.0032)			−0.0844 (0.0225)	0.4020 (0.1768)	−0.0812 (0.0225)
9	CPS		−0.0150 (0.0061)				

Table 4.2 continued

	N	Tenure	Log current unemployment rate	Tenure * log current unemployment rate (× 100)	Log unemployment rate at start of job	Tenure * log unemployment rate at start of job (× 100)	Marginal effect of the unemployment rate
		(1)	(2)	(3)	(4)	(5)	(6)
10 CPS	67 121	0.0274 (0.0019)	-0.0218 (0.0081)	0.0822 (0.0666)			-0.0153 (0.0091)
11 CPS	56 034				-0.0027 (0.0071)		
12 CPS	56,034	0.0447 (0.0034)			-0.0031 (0.0098)	0.0365 (0.1194)	-0.0002 (0.0011)

Notes:
Data in lines 1 to 4 are composed of a panel of workers from the NLSY over the period 1979–96. Data in lines 5 to 8 are composed of a panel of workers from the PSID over the period 1979–93. Data in lines 9 to 12 are composed of a random subsample of workers from several CPS supplements over the period 1979–98. In columns (2) and (3) the business cycle is measured by the log current unemployment rate and in columns (4) and (5) it is measured by the log unemployment rate at the start of the job.

Covariates included in each regression are 4 region dummies, year dummies, 11 industry dummies and 10 occupation dummies. Additional covariates included in each regression are experience, experience squared, tenure squared, education (years of schooling), marital status dummy, union dummy, white dummy and government job dummy.

The marginal effects on column (6) are computed as the derivative of log wage with respect to the log unemployment rate. The expression is: $\theta_2 + \theta_4\,\overline{\text{ten}}$. Tenure is evaluated at the sample mean. The standard errors are computed as the standard error of the corresponding linear combination of random variables. Standard errors are in parentheses. They are corrected to allow for group effects within state–year cells. N is the sample size.

More significantly, column (6) of Table 4.2 shows the marginal effect of the unemployment rate on wages. Using the results arising from the NLSY sample (lines 1–4 in Table 4.2), we show that, considering the interaction between tenure and the unemployment rate, the effect of a 1 per cent change in the current unemployment rate on wages is about 10 per cent lower than the point estimate obtained when we don't control for the existence of the interaction effect.[12] For the NLSY sample a one-standard-deviation change in tenure reduces the elasticity of wages to the current unemployment rate by more than 1 per cent (note that this represents a reduction of almost 25 per cent over the elasticity computed at mean tenure): at the sample mean for tenure, the elasticity would be reduced from –0.048 to –0.037. These results are stronger if we use the unemployment rate prevailing at the start of the job. The effect of initial conditions dies out over time even more rapidly as tenure is accumulated.

The results in Table 4.2 show that higher values of tenure reduce the elasticity of wages to the current unemployment rate and the unemployment rate at the start of the job. The empirical evidence is favourable to our hypotheses and can be interpreted as an indicator that, not only do initial conditions die out over time as tenure accumulates, but also that the longer the match the more shielded the worker is from the vagaries of the external labour market, as measured by the current local unemployment rate. This is consistent with the explanation presented in the model. The development of an internal labour market is a function of the length of job tenure, in the sense that the worker appropriates a fraction of the return to firm-specific human capital accumulated with tenure.[13]

In a related paper, Beaudry and DiNardo (1991) estimate an equation similar to the one in (4.3) but do not include the interaction term. Their results are that the costless mobility model (in which the relevant measure of the unemployment rate is the minimum unemployment rate since the start of the job) is the one that prevails when confronted with the other hypothesis. We see our results as an alternative explanation to theirs. By simply including a tenure interaction we obtain a result not consistent with a spot labour market in wage determination, and evidence favourable to the existence of some contractual model of the labour market. Furthermore, our finding points to the importance of tenure, a proxy for match-specific human capital, as the source of 'enforcement' of these contracts. As mentioned before, our basic result would not change if we were to include the minimum unemployment rate since the job start in our regressions.

6.1.2 PSID and CPS results

The findings obtained using the PSID and CPS are presented in lines 5 to 12 of Table 4.2. Conclusions are very similar to the ones that follow from using the NLSY sample. Note that the PSID yields larger elasticities but also much larger standard errors. The impact of an additional month of tenure in the current wage–current local unemployment rate elasticity is very similar in the NLSY and PSID extracts. However, evaluated at the sample mean for tenure, in column 6 of Table 4.2 the percentage reduction in the elasticity is smaller for the PSID than it was for the NLSY.

The results from the CPS extract are much weaker. In most cases we do not obtain statistically significant coefficients. Splitting the sample according to the wording used in the job tenure question leads to similarly weak results due to the insufficient cyclical variation of each subsample considered.

We now provide additional evidence of the effect of tenure on the wage-setting process. In order to test the robustness of our basic results, we will consider the effect of job heterogeneity over the wage distribution using quantile regression methods (other dimensions of job heterogenity are considered in Arozamena and Centeno, 2001).

6.2   Job heterogeneity

Table 4.3 exhibits the results corresponding to the quantile regression approach. As we mentioned in Section 4, higher-paid jobs are expected to involve a higher degree of match specificity and this should be reflected in differences on the impact of tenure and the business cycle on wages. If this prior is correct, the impact of the local unemployment rate at the start of the job (the cohort effect) and the current local unemployment rate (the degree of 'shielding' that a firm offers to a worker at a given level of tenure) should be larger for the bottom quantiles of the wage distribution. On the contrary, the impact of tenure on this elasticity should be higher for the top quantiles (that is, the interaction effect should be larger for higher wages).

As expected, for every quantile the main impact of the unemployment rate is negative. However, as before, we need to take into account the total effect, adding the interaction term and computing the elasticity at the average value of tenure.[14] Three models are presented in Table 4.3. In Models 1 and 2, we use the current unemployment rate and the unemployment rate at the start of the job, respectively, while in Model 3 we include both variables.

The results from Model 1 show that the sign of the coefficient on the interaction term goes from negative to positive when we move from the lower to the higher quantiles. This is an indication that the spot market hypothesis for wages is relevant for low-wage/low-skill jobs but not for high-wage jobs.[15] In absolute value, the current wage–current local unemployment rate elasticity decreases from 0.0737 for the 10th quantile to 0.0576 to the 90th quantile (this represents a decrease of about 22 per cent). Note that a one-standard-deviation change in tenure reduces the unemployment rate elasticity by about 0.0182 (this represents 31.5 per cent of the marginal effect computed at the mean value of

Table 4.3   Effect of tenure on the elasticity of current wage to the local unemployment rate: quantile regression model – NLSY data (dependent variable: log (w_{ijt}))

	Quantile				
	0.10	0.25	0.50	0.75	0.90
Model 1					
Log current unemployment rate	−0.0696	−0.0793	−0.0924	−0.0755	−0.0741
	(0.012)	(0.0087)	(0.0095)	(0.0111)	(0.0124)
Tenure	0.0726	0.0794	0.0648	0.0681	0.0316
	(0.0092)	(0.0064)	(0.0067)	(0.0079)	(0.0087)
Log current u. rate * tenure (× 100)	−0.1920	−0.2185	0.7926	0.0687	0.7649
	(0.4285)	(0.2957)	(0.3137)	(0.3682)	(0.3992)
N = 40 836					
Marginal effect of log current u. rate	−0.0737	−0.0840	−0.0754	−0.0740	−0.0576
	(0.0124)	(0.0087)	(0.0094)	(0.0111)	(0.0124)
Model 2					
Log unemployment rate at start of job	−0.0769	−0.0721	−0.0800	−0.0849	−0.0779
	(0.0119)	(0.0087)	(0.0089)	(0.0111)	(0.0116)
Tenure	0.0534	0.0609	0.0669	0.0507	0.0287
	(0.0079)	(0.0058)	(0.0059)	(0.0073)	(0.0075)
Log u. rate at start of job * tenure (× 100)	0.6240	0.6479	0.6016	0.8824	0.8824
	(0.3494)	(0.2579)	(0.2616)	(0.3271)	(0.3219)
N = 40 394					
Marginal effect of log u. rate start job	−0.0634	−0.0581	−0.0670	−0.0659	−0.0589
	(0.0118)	(0.0087)	(0.0089)	(0.0111)	(0.0116)

Table 4.3   continued

	Quantile				
	0.10	0.25	0.50	0.75	0.90
Model 3					
Log current unemployment rate	-0.0236	-0.0702	-0.0820	-0.0670	-0.0307
	(0.0243)	(0.0162)	(0.0168)	(0.0203)	(0.0138)
Log unemployment rate at start of job	-0.0520	-0.0092	-0.0078	-0.0156	-0.0458
	(0.0238)	(0.0157)	(0.0163)	(0.0212)	(0.0226)
Tenure	0.0718	0.0821	0.0723	0.0688	0.0349
	(0.0097)	(0.0067)	(0.0070)	(0.0086)	(0.0097)
Log current u. rate * tenure (× 100)	-0.7113	-0.4222	0.7958	0.7462	0.1398
	(0.5367)	(0.3553)	(0.3726)	(0.4783)	(0.0519)
Log u. rate at start of job * tenure (× 100)	0.5190	0.0285	-0.4196	-0.6984	0.4306
	(0.4690)	(0.3115)	(0.3292)	(0.4212)	(0.4441)
N = 40 394					
Marginal effect of log current u. rate	-0.0389	-0.0792	-0.0649	-0.0519	-0.0006
	(0.0242)	(0.0161)	(0.0168)	(0.0211)	(0.0237)
Marginal effect of log u. rate start job	-0.0408	-0.0025	-0.0169	0.0005	-0.0365
	(0.0237)	(0.0157)	(0.0161)	(0.0203)	(0.0225)

Notes:
Data are composed of a panel of workers from the NLSY over the period 1979–96. In Model 1 the business cycle is measured by the log current unemployment rate. In Model 2 it is measured by the log unemployment at the start of the job. In Model 3 both measures of the business cycle are included.
Covariates included in each regression are 4 region dummies, year dummies, 11 industry dummies and 10 occupation dummies. Additional covariates included in each regression are experience, experience squared, tenure squared, education (years of schooling), marital status dummy, union dummy, white dummy and government job dummy.
Standard errors are in parentheses and are a bootstrapped estimate with 1000 replications. N is the sample size.
The marginal effects are computed as the derivative of log wage with respect to the log unemployment rate. The expression is: $\theta_2 + \theta_4 \overline{\text{ten}}$.
Tenure is evaluated at the sample mean. The standard errors are computed as the standard error of the corresponding linear combination of random variables.

tenure). In Table 4.4 we report the results of the F-tests of the interaction coefficient equality at different quantiles. In doing this we use the variance–covariance matrix of the estimators obtained via bootstrapping, since the coefficients reported in Table 4.3 were estimated using simultaneous-quantile regressions. The results for Model 1 confirm that in most cases we can reject the hypotheses of equality of the coefficients. In particular the estimated coefficients for the 10th and 90th percentiles are statistically different from each other, with a p-value of 0.06. These results show that the interaction coefficient is different when we compare the point estimates above and below the median.

For Model 2 no such relation was obtained. The interaction coefficient is positive for every quantile although larger for higher quantiles. However, the marginal effect does not exhibit a monotonic behaviour, since it is slightly smaller for the 90th quantile but higher for the 50th and 75th quantiles. This may be an indication that the cohort effect dies out over time but is more

Table 4.4　F-tests of coefficients estimates equality for different quantiles (testing the equality of the interaction coefficient estimates from Table 4.3)

	Model			
Quantile comparison	1	2	3	
	Log current u. rate * tenure	Log u. rate start of job * tenure	Log current u. rate * tenure	Log u. rate start of job * tenure
10th – 90th Quantiles	3.48 (0.0622)	0.27 (0.6030)	1.47 (0.2251)	0.02 (0.8916)
10th – 50th Quantiles	5.31 (0.0212)	0.00 (0.9450)	7.43 (0.0064)	4.36 (0.0369)
50th – 90th Quantiles	0.00 (0.9497)	0.72 (0.3971)	1.17 (0.2786)	2.39 (0.1222)
25th – 75th Quantiles	0.63 (0.4283)	0.49 (0.4841)	7.64 (0.0060)	3.29 (0.0712)
25th – 50th Quantiles	12.90 (0.0003)	0.03 (0.8737)	8.96 (0.0028)	1.88 (0.1708)
50th – 75th Quantiles	4.99 (0.0256)	1.06 (0.3036)	0.00 (0.9807)	14.70 (0.0306)

Notes:
1. The table reports the F-statistics from the test of equality between the estimated coefficients for each pair of quantiles regressions.
2. P-values are in parentheses.

important for wage determination for workers with relatively higher wages than for those at the bottom quantiles. For Model 2 we accept the equality hypothesis in all the quantile comparisons reported in Table 4.4.

In Model 3, the results for the bottom quantile contrast with those for the top quantile. The interaction of tenure with the current unemployment rate is negative for the bottom quantiles and positive for the top quantiles and the opposite occurs with the interaction term with the starting unemployment rate. Such a contrast is an indication that with increasing tenure the starting rate of unemployment is more important for high-wage jobs than for low-wage jobs. In the bottom rows of Table 4.3 we present the marginal effect of the unemployment rate for each quantile in Model 3. Again, the absolute marginal effect of the current unemployment rate is decreasing with the wage quantile considered. The marginal effect of the current unemployment rate decreases from –0.0792 for the 25th quantile to –0.0006 for the 90th quantile, and it is statistically insignificant for the higher quantiles. For the unemployment rate at the start of the job the change from the bottom to the top quantiles is much smaller and shows no monotonic pattern. This lack of pattern is reflected in the mixed results obtained for Model 3 in Table 4.4. In this case, contrary to the previous models, no general conclusions can be reached on the quantiles comparisons. On the one hand we reject the equality hypothesis for quantile differences in the lower part of the wage distribution (for example the 10th–50th percentiles comparison), but on the other hand we accept the equality hypothesis test for the 10th–90th percentiles difference.

6.3   Evidence on Non-linearities in Tenure Effects

The last set of results we present relates to the existence of non-linearities in the tenure/unemployment rate interaction. They are obtained by estimating the bilinear spline model introduced in Section 4.3.

There is no theoretical guidance about the determination of the knots for the tenure variable. As we have already noted, some previous empirical evidence on labour mobility suggests a structural break early on in the employment relationship, a period in which a large percentage of all full-time matches is expected to end (see Farber, 1999). However, no general evidence has been presented that might help us in the process of determining the value of the knots. The procedure we follow starts from a general formulation, with a large number of knots, and progressively reduces that number by dropping those knots that are not statistically significant.[16] We are thereby left with a very simple model, with a single knot for tenure – at 52 weeks of employment duration – using the NLSY sample.[17]

The findings presented in Table 4.5 show that there is a statistically significant structural break along tenure equal to 52 weeks. The point estimate

Table 4.5 *Non-linearities in tenure effects on the elasticity of current wage to the current local unemployment rate: bilinear splines estimates – NLSY sample (dependent variable: log (w_{ijt}))*

Log current unemployment rate	–0.0826
	(0.0169)
Tenure(1)	0.0416
	(0.0368)
Tenure(2)	0.2444
	(0.0065)
Schooling	0.0062
	(0.0021)
Log u. rate * tenure(1)	0.0365
	(0.0188)
Log u. rate * tenure(2)	0.0076
	(0.0022)
N	40 836
Marginal effect log current unemployment rate	–0.0342
	(0.0202)

F-tests of the bilinear spline model estimates	
Total effect	60.56
Total unemployment rate effect	16.69
Main unemployment rate effect	23.82
Total tenure effect	69.86
Main tenure effect	54.78
Interaction effect	10.52
Structural change along tenure = 52 weeks	53.98

Notes:
Data are composed of a panel of workers from the NLSY over the period 1979–96. The business cycle is measured by the log current unemployment rate.
Covariates included in each regression are 4 region dummies, year dummies, 11 industry dummies and 10 occupation dummies. Additional covariates included in each regression are experience, experience squared, tenure squared, marital status dummy, union dummy, white dummy and government job dummy.
The marginal effects are computed as the derivative of log wage with respect to the log unemployment rate as $\delta + \alpha_1 \overline{ten}_1 + \alpha_1 \overline{ten}_2$. Tenure is evaluated at the sample means. The standard errors are computed as the standard error of the corresponding linear combination of random variables.
Standard errors are in parentheses. They are corrected to allow for group effects within state–year cells. N is the sample size.

obtained in Table 4.5 indicates that an additional week of tenure in the first year of work has a much larger impact on the current wage–current local unemployment rate elasticity than later on.

This result is extremely interesting when we interpret a match as an experience good. In this case, match tenure defines the period of learning about match quality that took place. Our result, together with the hypothesis over firm-specific capital acquisition, suggests that learning about match quality occurs much faster in the match, bad matches being terminated early as well. The effect of tenure after this first period is much smaller. Nevertheless, it is still statistically different from zero and can be interpreted exclusively as the result of the process of firm-specific human capital accumulation.

Finally, from the results shown in Table 4.5 we can also conclude that a standard-deviation increase on tenure reduces the elasticity of current wages to the current unemployment rate by 0.0247 (the elasticity goes from –0.0342 to –0.0095, which represents a reduction of more than 70 per cent). This is a larger reduction than the one obtained in our previous models.

7   CONCLUDING REMARKS

The relation between internal and external labour markets has been extensively discussed in recent years. So has the issue of the existence of returns to tenure. In this chapter, we have drawn from both these analyses to examine the process by which wages are set in relation to the time a worker has spent in her current job. That is, we have posed the question of how job tenure and labour market conditions interact in the process of wage determination.

First, we presented a simple matching model where tenure in the current job is interpreted as a proxy for the match-specific human capital accumulated in the employment relationship. As tenure progresses, the worker seizes a fraction of the rising value of that specific capital. Such appropriation gradually shields her from cyclical variations in the external labour market conditions. The wage-setting process becomes progressively 'internalized'.

The empirical evidence we presented lends strong support to that prediction. The elasticity of current wages to unemployment rates decreases with tenure. Furthermore, this result still holds when we allow for job heterogeneity. We tested our findings' robustness by carrying a quantile regression analysis. The gradual shielding of wages as tenure is accumulated is not uniform over the wage distribution, being higher for wages at the top quantile. Finally, we considered the possibility that the tenure effect on wages may be non-linear. Our findings lead us to conclude that the internalization of the wage-setting process is faster at the beginning of an employment spell than later on.

The results presented in this chapter suggest that the study of issues related to the cyclicality of wages should take into account the tenure composition of the pool of workers. If one is to find evidence of a greater exposure of workers to the vagaries of the external labour market, that might not be an indication of a change in wage policy in the direction of spot market wage setting. It might be a sign that a non-wage human resources policy is being implemented (see Capelli, 1995). For example, it may be the result of a 'recomposition' of the pool towards a greater presence of less tenured workers, which is consistent with the common wisdom that industry restructuring and downsizing processes hit older and white-collar workers harder – precisely those with higher employer attachment and more likely to be in these types of implicit agreement contracts.

Clearly, however, further research is needed into how our conclusions about the process of wage determination and, consequently, the effects of policies on that process depend on job tenure. A richer dynamic model that captures the timing and different characteristics of match-specific human capital investments would be instructive. Additionally, the availability of better micro data, namely at the firm level, would also help in discriminating how different groups of workers will be affected, and how the process of learning about workers' ability interacts with the process of firm-specific human capital accumulation.

NOTES

1. This literature dates back to the work of Becker (1964) and Ben-Porath (1967), among others.
2. This amounts to regarding match quality as an experience good. Other papers, such as Flinn (1986) and Topel and Ward (1992) have used the idea of jobs as experience goods to study mobility.
3. This effect is well known. See for instance Topel (1991) and Altonji and Williams (1997) for a discussion of returns to tenure.
4. See for instance Bertrand (1999).
5. We need to distinguish between general and employer-specific human capital because the first will be related to returns to experience whereas the second will be related to returns to tenure.
6. To keep the model simple, we do not allow for the accumulation of general (that is, productive in all matches) human capital. The inclusion of such an accumulation would add returns to experience to our results on returns to tenure, leaving all of our findings unaltered.
7. Since the origin of this cyclical effect does not affect our results, we leave it unspecified.
8. We assume that the number of firms in the economy is large enough so that the probability that a worker is matched to a firm where she previously worked is negligible.
9. The main difficulty associated with quantile regression in this case is that wage quantiles can be endogenous to workers' wage experiences, which might result in a sample selection problem.
10. According to Farber's CPS tabulations: one-third of all new full-time jobs end in the first six months, half of all new full-time jobs end in the first year and two-thirds of all new full-time jobs end within two years.

11. Before 1984 the question could have been interpreted as referring to duration of continuous employment rather than time together with the present employer. After 1984 the question explicitly asks about time with the present employer.
12. The value of the elasticity falls from –0.0539 to –0.0487. The model without the interaction term corresponds to line 1 in Table 4.2.
13. In all the specifications of Table 4.2, we have restricted the returns to all the demographic variables to be constant over time. These restrictions might not be realistic, at least for some of these variables. We therefore checked the robustness of these specification assumptions, allowing the returns to some of the variables (namely experience, education, unionization, race and marital status) to vary over time. The basic results were not altered.
14. Remember that we take a low elasticity of current wages to current local labour market unemployment rates and a high elasticity of current wages to the unemployment rate prevailing at the time of job start as an indication of internal labour market practices, that shield the worker from variations in the external labour markets.
15. This result must be interpreted with caution because it may be a consequence of the fact that the wage level is not independent of the match quality (and duration); low-wage jobs might be shorter and thus look 'less protected'. This might cause a sample selection problem and be driving our results.
16. Given that we only test for structural breaks along the tenure variable, the grid dimension does not grow very fast and this does not amount to estimating a large number of regressions.
17. We do not present results for the PSID given the problems of lack of precison mentioned before. In this case these problems were even more acute.

REFERENCES

Altonji, J. and N. Williams (1997), *Do Wages Rise with Job Seniority? A Reassessment*, NBER Working Paper No. 6010.
Arozamena, L. and M. Centeno (2001), *Tenure Business Cycle and the Wage Setting Process*, Banco de Portugal Working Paper Series No. 8/01.
Beaudry, P. and J. DiNardo (1991), 'The effect of implicit contracts on the movement of wages over the business cycle: evidence from micro data', *Journal of Political Economy*, **99**, 665–88.
Becker, G. (1964), *Human Capital*, New York: NBER.
Ben-Porath, Y. (1967), 'The production of human capital and the life cycle of earnings', *Journal of Political Economy*, **75**, 352–65.
Bertrand, M. (1999), *From the Invisible Handshake to the Invisible Hand? How Import Competition Changes the Employment Relationship*, NBER Working Paper No. 6900.
Bils, M. (1985), 'Real wages over the business cycle: evidence from panel data', *Journal of Political Economy*, **93**, 666–89.
Bowlus, A. (1995), 'Matching workers and jobs: cyclical fluctuations in match quality', *Journal of Labor Economics*, **13**, 335–50.
Capelli, P. (1995), 'Rethinking employment', *British Journal of Industrial Relations*, **33**, 563–602.
Doeringer, P. and M. Piore (1971), *Internal Labor Markets and Manpower Analysis*, Lexington, MA: D.C. Heath and Company.
Farber, H. (1999), 'Mobility and stability: the dynamics of job change in labor markets', in O.C. Ashenfelter and D. Card (eds), *Handbook of Labor Economics*, Vol. 3, Amsterdam: North-Holland.

Felli, L. and C. Harris (1996), 'Learning, wage dynamics, and firm-specific human capital', *Journal of Political Economy*, **104** , 838–68.

Flinn, C. (1986), 'Wages and job mobility of young workers', *Journal of Political Economy*, **94** , S89–110.

Gibbons, R. and L. Katz (1991), 'Layoffs and lemons', *Journal of Labor Economics*, **9**, 351–80.

Gibbons, R. and M. Waldman (1999), 'The theory of wage and promotion dynamics inside firms', *Quarterly Journal of Economics*, **114**, 1321–58.

Jovanovic, B. (1979), 'Job matching and the theory of turnover', *Journal of Political Economy*, **87**, 972–90.

Solon, G., R. Barsky and J. Parker (1994), 'Measuring the cyclicality of real wages: how important is composition bias?', *Quarterly Journal of Economics*, **109**, 1–26.

Topel, R. (1991), 'Specific capital, mobility, and wages: wages rise with job seniority', *Journal of Political Economy*, **99**, 145–76.

Topel, R. and M. Ward (1992), 'Job mobility and the career of young men', *Quarterly Journal of Economics*, **107**, 439–79.

5. Wage developments in the early years of EMU

Karl Pichelmann[1]

INTRODUCTION

The formation of EMU was expected to exert a profound impact on the market players, in particular affecting price-setting and wage bargaining behaviour. Economic and Monetary Union has in important ways changed the macroeconomic environment, which is now characterized by a single stability-oriented monetary policy for the euro area and sound national fiscal policies.

The debate about the likely impact of EMU on wage formation has centred around three different though interconnected aspects: (i) the necessary degree of nominal wage flexibility to compensate for the loss of the exchange rate instrument; (ii) the direct impact on the wage-setting curve and thus on equilibrium unemployment; and (iii) the impact on labour market institutions, in particular wage bargaining mechanisms.

It has been widely held that, in general, EMU should provide improved framework conditions for employment-compatible wage bargaining behaviour as the link between wage and employment trends becomes more evident and stringent. With the bailout option of nominal exchange rate devaluation no longer existing, any substantial error in wage-setting would ultimately translate into deteriorating labour market conditions and painful adjustment thereafter.

In EMU it is therefore even more important than in the past for wage developments to be in line with both the macroeconomic framework set at the Community level and the individual country-specific requirements. Thus, employment-friendly wage bargaining behaviour is typically characterized by respect for the following guidelines:[2]

1. Overall nominal wage developments must be consistent with the goal of price stability. Excessive nominal wage increases triggering inflationary risks for the euro zone as a whole – as will hold true in particular in the case of larger countries – will inevitably provoke a tightening of monetary conditions with adverse effects on growth and employment in the entire monetary union.

2. Inflationary wage pressure when confined to one – smaller – country or region alone may not significantly affect overall euro area inflation, but through its effect on relative unit labour cost it will depress competitiveness and employment in this country or region.

3. Real wage developments should be kept in line with labour productivity growth and, where necessary, the need to strengthen the profitability of capacity-enhancing and employment-creating investment should be taken into account.

4. The single currency increases transparency and facilitates wage comparisons which may trigger 'wage imitation effects'. However, wage bargaining mechanisms through which wage demands could tend to converge upwards need to be avoided. As productivity levels and increases differ from country to country, attempts to achieve uniform wage levels or increases across EMU members would have seriously disruptive effects on employment.

5. While not directly related to the functioning of EMU, wage agreements should also better take into account productivity differentials according to qualifications, skills and geographical areas. This would not only help to avoid job destruction and enhance job creation in general; it would also improve the employment prospects for groups such as the young, low-skilled or long-term unemployed and contribute to the efficient reallocation of labour across occupations, sectors and regions.

The responsibility for wage-setting procedures and outcomes compatible with the achievement and maintenance of high employment continues to fall primarily in the domain of the social partners. As indicated above, inappropriate wage developments – or, more generally speaking, inadequate labour market structures – in specific countries or regions, particularly when they are big enough to require an offsetting monetary policy response, may have harmful consequences for other members of EMU as well, thus reinforcing the case for strengthened economic policy coordination.

Against this general background, the purpose of this chapter is to provide a brief assessment of wage developments in the first three years of EMU, also including several years of the run-up to EMU. First it offers a short review of a few stylized facts regarding (i) nominal wage and nominal unit labour cost developments and (ii) the evolution of real unit labour cost, focusing in particular on cross-country patterns as an indicator of the synchronization of wage developments. Second it briefly discusses the main findings with a view to identifying potential problems that might be lurking behind the fairly impressive degree of overall wage discipline prevailing in most of the euro area in recent years.

AGGREGATE WAGE DEVELOPMENTS: SOME STYLIZED FACTS

Nominal Wage Cost Developments

The last decade has seen impressive progress regarding nominal stabilization in the euro area in terms of both prices and wages. Indeed in the 1990s a remarkable disinflation process developed and the inflation rate had fallen below the 2 per cent mark by 1997. While the lacklustre overall economic performance over that period has certainly contributed to a reduction in inflationary pressures, there can be little doubt that the high degree of price stability achieved has primarily been the result of the systemic changes associated with the run-up to EMU. With price stability and a high degree of sustainable convergence being key requirements for adopting the euro, cross-country differences in inflation rates also narrowed drastically in this process.

For the euro area as a whole, nominal wage growth per employee has declined almost in parallel with the achievement of price stability, with nominal compensation per worker estimated to increase on average by around 3 per cent annually over the period 2001 to 2003 (Figure 5.1). From a bird's-eye

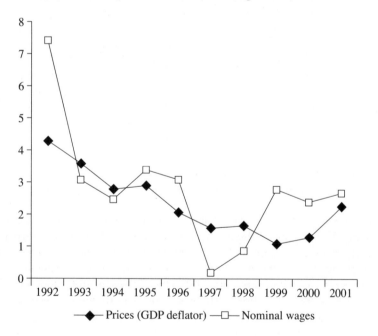

Figure 5.1   Inflation and nominal wage growth per employee in EUR-12, 1992–2001

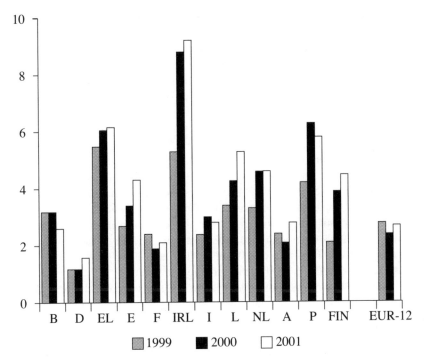

Key: B: Belgium; D: Germany; EL: Greece; E: Spain; F: France; IRL: Ireland; I: Italy; L: Luxembourg; NL: Netherlands; A: Austria; P. Portugal; FIN: Finland.

Figure 5.2   Nominal wage growth per employee in EUR-12, 1999–2001

view, the actors in the wage bargaining process appear in general to have taken on board the price stability objective set by the ECB.

As a by-product of nominal stabilization, the absolute dispersion of nominal wage growth across countries has also diminished significantly over the past decade, resulting in fairly similar nominal wage developments in the recent past, in particular in the euro core countries (Figure 5.2). However, in 2001 the absolute dispersion of nominal wage growth per worker among the 'big four' euro countries (Germany, France, Italy and Spain) still amounted to 2.7 percentage points (ranging from 1.6 per cent in Germany to 4.3 per cent in Spain). Money wages increased somewhat faster in Finland and the Netherlands, probably reflecting different cyclical positions. The highest rates of nominal wage growth were observed in Ireland, Portugal and Greece. Thus there still remains a significant dispersion of rates of growth in money wages in the EUR-12, rendering any notion of fully harmonized wage developments in the euro area as clearly inadequate.[3]

It should be noted, though, that cross-country differences in productivity levels and growth rates limit the extent to which wage synchronization is warranted. In fact, allowing wages to reflect these differences is not inefficient or inequitable but rather a means to allow real wage levels to converge over time. Thus stronger nominal wage increases in some countries enjoying faster growth of per capita output and of labour productivity need not be a particular cause for concern.

In order to take different developments in labour productivity growth across countries into account, Figures 5.3 and 5.4 look at the evolution of nominal unit labour costs. The evidence as presented below is indeed indicative of an impressive amount of stabilization in nominal unit labour cost developments. Moreover the cross-country dispersion in nominal unit labour cost increases has apparently also been quite significantly reduced. However, 2001 saw nominal unit labour cost growth in excess of 2 per cent and therefore above the ECB's quantitative definition of price stability. There is similarly clear evidence of relatively rapid nominal unit labour cost growth in a number of smaller countries, mainly in the euro area periphery.

The slowdown in economic activity in 2001 has been accompanied by a

Figure 5.3   Nominal unit labour cost growth in EUR-12, 1992–2001

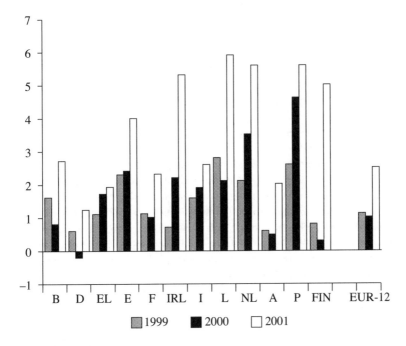

Figure 5.4   Nominal unit labour cost slippage in EUR-12, 1999–2001

pick-up in nominal unit labour cost growth. For the euro area as a whole, nominal unit labour costs have risen by about 2.5 per cent in 2002. While this is to some extent a reflection of weaker than expected labour productivity growth, several countries – mainly in the euro area periphery – have undoubtedly shown some signs of overheating. Nevertheless, for the area as a whole, current expectations are for a deceleration of nominal unit labour cost growth, forecast by the EU Commission to return below the benchmark value of 2 per cent in 2003.

In summary, and with the notable exception of the last two years, nominal unit labour cost inflation in the euro area as a whole has quickly fallen within the bandwidth consistent with the price stability goal as defined by the ECB. Moreover, despite a marked reduction in unemployment over the past few years, thus far there have been few signs of a significant re-acceleration of nominal unit labour cost growth in the area as a whole. Admittedly several countries which have experienced a few years of sustained growth and where the labour market has become relatively tight, namely Ireland, the Netherlands and Portugal, appear to be relatively more exposed to eventual wage pressures.

Furthermore, the labour cost impact of the reduced working week in France may be felt more strongly once compensating productivity increases start abating. However, overall there can be little doubt that the early years of EMU, including several years of the run-up to monetary union, have seen an impressive amount of nominal wage discipline, which can hardly be explained without recourse to changes in underlying behavioural relations.[4]

Real Wage Cost Developments

Corroborative evidence for overall wage discipline is to be found in the evolution of real product wages adjusted for productivity. Obviously in its simplest form this boils down to the analysis of real unit labour cost developments, mirroring changes in the share of labour in total income. Indeed, for the euro area as a whole, the labour income share has remained broadly constant in the first three years of EMU after having fallen continuously in the preceding five years, though the downward trend in the labour share started much earlier than this, in the early 1980s (Figure 5.5).

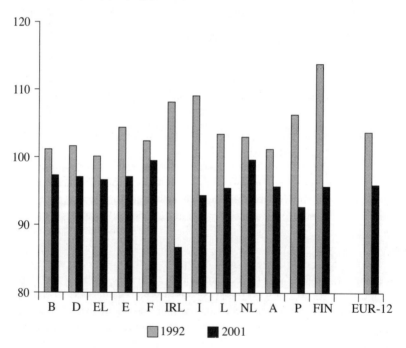

Key: see Figure 5.2

Figure 5.5   Real unit labour cost index, EUR-12, 1992 and 2001

A REAL WAGE GAP INDICATOR FOR THE EURO AREA

This box presents a simple indicator for shifts in the aggregate wage-setting curve in the euro area, basically by comparing real wage developments to productivity growth. However following the lines of Blanchard (1997, 1998), apparent labour productivity is replaced by a measure of labour efficiency based on Harrod-neutral technical progress, thus computing a measure of real wages in efficiency units. Furthermore, to construct a somewhat refined real wage gap indicator, real product wages are augmented by a factor representing the wage-dampening effect of a positive unemployment gap.

Put more formally, the wage gap indicator is derived from a simple wage-setting equation relating the real product wage in efficiency units (w/e) to the unemployment rate UR and a shift parameter Z that captures other relevant labour market conditions affecting wage pressure in a log-linear manner: $\log (w/e) = -b\ UR + Z$, with b denoting the elasticity of real efficiency wages with respect to unemployment. The real product wage w is the gross nominal wage (including employers' contributions to social security) divided by the GDP deflator (at factor costs?). The series for labour efficiency e is derived under the assumption of Harrod-neutral technical progress as the Solow residual divided by the labour share, reflecting the condition for labour productivity growth along the balanced growth path. A real wage gap indicator can then be constructed using $Z = \log (w/e) + b\ UR$, with b set to 1 (a value of one for the wage elasticity of unemployment may be regarded as a compromise between different estimates; plausibly, the value is smaller in the short run, but higher in the long run) and finally normalizing the series to equal zero at the start of the data series in 1970.

Figure 5.6 below gives the results for the evolution of the refined wage gap indicator for the EUR-12, assuming a value of one for the unemployment elasticity of real wages. Overall the series shows a large increase in the wage gap indicator variable over the 1970s with a peak of more than 10 per cent in the early 1980s. Thereafter wage pressure gradually abated, with the exception of the 1991–94 period, when the wage gap started to widen again, despite unemployment still hovering around 8 per cent.

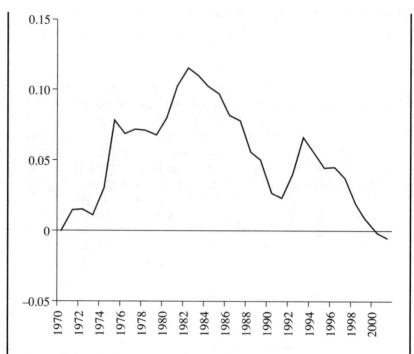

Figure 5.6   Real wage gap indicator, EUR-12, 1970 = 0

The second half of the 1990s was characterized by a continued process of wage moderation resulting in a monotonic decline
of the wage gap indicator. At present the real wage in efficiency
units for the area as a whole appears to have even fallen below
its level at the beginning of the 1970s. Taking the increase in
unemployment into account, the real wage gap indicator has
approximately returned to its value 30 years ago.

A somewhat closer look at real unit labour cost developments in the past
three years reveals the following patterns (Figure 5.7):

1. Real wage discipline has prevailed in almost all countries of the euro area.
    Only in France, Luxembourg and Portugal were real unit labour costs
    higher in 2001 than three years before.
2. In the countries of the former DM bloc plus Italy real unit labour cost
    growth was basically flat over the past three years. Spain also saw a pause
    in the trend decrease of the wage share last year.

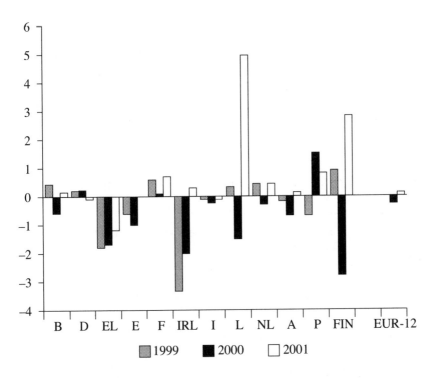

Key: see Figure 5.2.

Figure 5.7   Real unit labour cost growth, EUR-12, 1999–2001

3. In Ireland and Finland, which had both seen significant declines in real unit labour costs in the pre-EMU years, the fall in the labour income share came to a halt and real unit labour cost started to increase.
4. A pronounced fall in real unit labour cost over the past three years was registered in the case of Greece (which entered EMU two years later than the other countries), compensating for the real wage push experienced in the pre-EMU years.

Evidently real wage moderation has borne fruit and contributed to the dynamism in job creation in recent years. The unemployment rate of the area has decreased significantly from its peak of 11.5 per cent to below 8.5 per cent, yet wage developments have remained subdued. Thus the most recent assessment by DG ECFIN (European Commission, 2002a) indicates a decline of the NAIRU for the euro zone by about 1.5 percentage points, suggesting therefore that about half of the improvement in actual unemployment can be considered structural in nature. By and large, other international bodies such as the OECD (2002) and the IMF (2001) have arrived at broadly similar conclusions. Obviously an understanding of the underlying mechanisms resulting in the observed wage discipline is required for an assessment, whether or not this process of wage moderation can be sustained. Moreover, the relatively positive picture at the aggregate level may mask several potential problems that might be lurking behind the wage discipline observed in most euro area countries in recent years.

FACTORS BEHIND THE OBSERVED WAGE DISCIPLINE IN RECENT YEARS

In terms of having a better understanding of the nature of the observed wage discipline, as reflected in the fall of the NAIRU, the second half of the 1990s has indeed witnessed relatively widespread product and labour market reforms in most euro area countries, spurring competition in goods and services markets and cracking down on insider–outsider divisions in the labour markets. Employment-stimulating reform efforts have addressed *inter alia* tax and benefit systems, for example in the form of cuts in payroll taxes for targeted groups or in-work financial support for low-wage earners, more active and preventive labour market policies and a modernization of work organization, including the facilitation of part-time work and more flexible work contract arrangements.

Moreover, the introduction of the single currency is bound to increase the degree of competition in product and service markets by enhancing price transparency across EMU member states.[5] Thus EMU provides an additional impetus to already ongoing efforts in the context of the Single Market Programme to improve the functioning of product and service markets. As a result, the potential for rent-sharing behaviour between workers and firms will be strongly reduced; an effect equivalent – in the context of the Calmfors–Driffill hypothesis – to a forced decentralization of wage bargaining.

While it is certainly difficult to establish precisely the contribution of the various reform efforts, there can be little doubt that they have left their traces in a reduction of the NAIRU by helping to keep a lid on wage demands. However, it must also be acknowledged that reform progress has been fairly uneven across countries – with all the major economies of the euro area still plagued by relatively high structural unemployment – and of a rather piecemeal character. This suggests that the various labour market policy initiatives implemented over the past few years may offer only a partial explanation for the apparent area-wide improvement in the short-run unemployment–inflation trade-off. Thus it is difficult to account for the observed widespread wage moderation without invoking the role of informal incomes policies in a number of countries.[6]

In the past few years tripartite agreements on wage policy have (again) been reached in Finland, Greece, Ireland, Italy and Portugal, typically committing the actors in collective bargaining to some form of wage discipline in order to meet EMU stability goals and to improve competitiveness. Governments' involvement may take various forms, for example trading tax cuts and/or specific labour market policy measures against wage restraint as has recently been the case in Finland and Ireland. Finland has also made an interesting attempt to increase nominal wage flexibility by the introduction of so-called 'EMU buffer funds',[7] but their impact will probably remain fairly limited.

In Belgium and the Netherlands bipartite intersectoral agreements are in place. Belgium provides probably the clearest instance of explicitly taking competitiveness considerations into account. In 1996 the government enacted an 'employment and competitiveness' law which included a legal wage norm for 1997–98, whereby pay increases were not to exceed average increases in Belgium's neighbouring countries, France, Germany and the Netherlands. Indeed the social partners concluded new intersectoral agreements in 1998 and 2000, again incorporating the concept of a wage norm related to wage trends in neighbouring countries as the key reference for average Belgian wage increases.[8]

Another example for the development of 'wage norms', coming to some extent as a response to the Belgian 'legal standard', is provided by the so-called 'Doorn initiative' of Belgian, German, Luxembourg and Dutch union confederations in 1998 containing an 'orientation formula' for national bargaining, whereby trade union negotiators should 'aim to achieve collective bargaining settlements that correspond to the sum total of the evolution of prices and the increases in labour productivity'. More or less the same approach has been taken by the European Metalworkers' Federation when adopting a 'European coordination rule', whereby 'the wage policy of unions in all countries must be to offset the rate of inflation and to ensure that workers' incomes retain a balanced participation in productivity gains'.

In EMU there are indeed some clear incentives working towards coordinated bargaining, since substituting nominal wage flexibility for monetary policy autonomy, which may be required to smoothly absorb asymmetric shocks, may be easier under such conditions. However, experience suggests that a number of other conditions have also to be met to uphold such bargaining arrangements. Among these, trading tax cuts for wage restraint has figured prominently, but flanking policy measures to increase labour supply availability and some degree of inbuilt wage differentiation flexibility appear to be crucial as well.

It is worth noting in this context that coordinated bargaining may indeed deliver fairly differentiated outcomes. Moreover, recent years have seen a move towards 'centralized decentralization' in wage bargaining in several countries, for example in the form of so-called opening clauses allowing for some degree of firm-level differentiation. With labour market policies geared to mobilize the labour force potential, overall wage pressures may indeed remain subdued and thus the infant years of EMU may well see sustained wage moderation supported by coordinated wage bargaining at national level.

However, such arrangements face a fundamental problem of time consistency, making it difficult to lock in the bargain. In particular, with free capital mobility the effectiveness of mechanisms bonding the employers' side to policies of high investment is fairly limited. In turn this reduces the incentives for labour to exercise wage restraint in anticipation of future investment. Moreover, governments may find it increasingly difficult to design supportive policies deemed acceptable by the main actors in wage bargaining.

Thus, given an inherent fragility of social pacts over the medium to long term and against a background of strong trends towards more decentralization of bargaining to firm and local levels, wage bargaining coordination efforts may ultimately fail. Unfortunately it cannot be ruled out that such a failure may result, at least temporarily, in wage bargaining outcomes that tend to be less employment-friendly. Thus EMU could probably see more wage turbulence at its stage of puberty.

Moreover, the evidence from some of the smaller countries participating in EMU such as Portugal suggests that wage-setting out of line with productivity developments may not be quickly self-correcting. Rather, the ensuing loss of competitiveness may build up over quite some time, before the inevitable, yet then even more painful, adjustment processes will kick in.

Despite these caveats there can be little doubt that wage bargaining institutions and wage-setting practices have responded in general quite favourably to the new economic environment, both in the run-up to EMU and during its first three years. Over the medium term all the major elements of the Marshall–Hicks rule of labour demand are likely to be operative, increasing the real wage elasticity of demand for labour. Thus the driving forces of price transparency, increasing capital mobility, trade integration and competition should provide a strong and probably dominating countervailing power to foster employment-compatible wage bargaining behaviour as the link between wage and employment trends will ultimately become much more evident and stringent.

NOTES

1. Research Adviser, EU Commission DG for Economic and Financial Affairs, and Associate Professor, Institute d'Études Européennes, ULB Brussels. The views expressed in this chapter

are strictly personal and do not necessarily represent those of the European Commission or its services.
2. See for instance European Commission (2002b).
3. Indeed, when the coefficient of variation in nominal wage growth rates is taken as a yardstick, the relative dispersion of nominal wage increases appears to have even somewhat increased over time. However, the distinctive behaviour of a core group of EUR-12 countries exhibiting more closely synchronized nominal wage behaviour is also preserved when looking at measures of relative dispersion.
4. Put more formally, out-of-sample predictions of wage equations estimated up to the early 1990s generally tend to over-predict wage developments in subsequent years (OECD, 2002).
5. Note, however, the more sceptical view of several observers that integration may not necessarily imply intensified competition, because integration also facilitates the strategies of transnational firms, potentially enabling them to establish product market domination across Europe.
6. For a detailed discussion see for example EIRO (2000).
7. In periods of economic upturn social security contributions are levied at a slightly higher rate than necessary. During cyclical downturns the accumulated funds can then be used to pay for additional social security costs.
8. The most recent framework agreement, concluded in December 2000, caps increases in nominal wages per employee to a total of 6.4 per cent for the period 2001–2002.

REFERENCES

Blanchard, O. (1997), 'The medium run', *Brookings Papers on Economic Activity*, **2**, 89–158.

Blanchard, O. (1998), *Revisiting European Unemployment: Unemployment, Capital Accumulation and Factor Prices*, NBER Working Paper No. 6566.

EIRO (2000), *Wage Policy and EMU*, Dublin: European Industrial Relations Observatory.

European Commission (2002a), *The EU Economy: 2002 Review*, European Economy No. 6/2002, Brussels.

European Commission (2002b), *The Euro Area in the World Economy – Developments in the First Three Years*, Communication from the Commission, 332 final, Brussels.

IMF (2001), *World Economic Outlook, October 2001*, World Economic and Financial Surveys, Washington, DC.

OECD (2002), *OECD Economic Outlook No. 72*, December, Paris.

6. Wage formation in the Italian private sector after the 1992–93 Income Policy Agreements

Piero Casadio[*]

INTRODUCTION AND MAIN CONCLUSIONS

This chapter analyses the effects of a decade of incomes policy on wage formation in Italy. The wage bargaining structure (henceforth BS) stemming from the 1992–93 Income Policy Agreements is widely seen as having been crucial in bringing about wage moderation by linking wages to the government's target inflation. This has also been viewed as instrumental for the major fiscal adjustment in the 1990s and thereby supportive of Italian participation in the European single currency. This cooperative bargaining structure, that has been called the *Concertazione* between social partners has, *inter alia*, supported the adoption of performance-related wage premia at the firm level, temporary contracts and flexible working time arrangements. Nevertheless, the compressed wage differentials between skills and regions have remained unchanged.

Since 1992–93 the main sectoral national contracts (SNCs) have precluded any price–wage spiral by aiming at increasingly lower inflation targets and eschewing the previous policy of automatic indexation for price increases. The coverage of firm-level contracts (FLCs) has increased only slightly. In the year 2000 more than half of the workers in firms with above ten employees were still excluded from such contracts. Inside the covered segment there has been a widespread adoption of performance-related wage premia, which are generally used more regularly than other forms of premia, but nevertheless remain relatively small in relation to the productivity trend. Only some elements of wage flexibility and differentiation have been introduced at the company level.

The chapter is organized as follows. The next section provides an overview of the long-run developments in wages and wage dispersion in Italy. In the third section, the recent evolution of wage bargaining institutions is considered. The fourth section discusses the role of the inflation target used in the wage agreements in inducing and maintaining wage moderation. The coverage and adoption of firm-level contracts and the use of performance-related wage premia and their effects on wage differentials are considered in the fifth section. Finally, the increasing relevance of individual wage-setting at the firm level and some open questions are assessed.

THE LONG-RUN EVOLUTION OF WAGES, PRODUCTIVITY AND WAGE DIFFERENTIALS IN ITALY

Econometric evaluations of the recent Italian income policies have typically concentrated on the period following the 30 per cent devaluation of the Italian lira. During 1993 the inflation rate remained around 4 per cent, despite a direct impact on domestic inflation from the devaluation of at least three percentage points.[1] Surprisingly, many formal investigations failed to identify any regime change relating to the Income Policy Agreements as a source of moderation in wages, inflationary expectations and firms' mark-ups.[2] In particular, it was difficult to immediately disentangle the role of the income policies, because of the contemporaneous severe domestic recession and the introduction of a large restrictive fiscal package. Without any wage indexation Italian firms became more cautious in raising their profit margins after the devaluation and the need to secure price stability became more widely accepted by all social partners.[3] Only since 1996 has it become possible to identify econometrically the results of the new patterns of wage bargaining. In particular, by means of counterfactual simulations Fabiani et al. (1997) showed that, without the income policy, Italy might have experienced a 2–3 per cent higher inflation in 1996. To have maintained the 1993–98 disinflationary path solely by means of monetary policy would have required a major slowdown in activity which would have, in turn, seriously undermined the fiscal adjustment. In a longer-run perspective it is reasonable to argue that joining the single currency would have been far more difficult without the 1992–93 Income Policy Agreements.

In the private sector, per capita real wages have remained broadly constant over the last decade, closing the gap with the productivity trend which emerged due to the higher wage growth of the 1970s and the 1980s (Figure 6.1). The same pattern emerged in all the main economic sectors, pointing to a high degree of coordination. Since 1995 a moderate recovery in real wages has been accompanied by an increase in employment. The labour share of value added has decreased since 1992 in all the main sectors.[4] The dispersion of individual real incomes, net of taxation, declined continuously until 1991 (Figure 6.2). Then, between 1991 and 1993 the dispersion index jumped up by about 25 per cent, due also to the more than 1.5 million newly unemployed, caused by the Italian recession. These were generally median wage earners, mature unskilled workers with a high tenure. In 1993 some of them probably enlarged the lower quantiles of the distribution, receiving some unemployment benefits. The relatively higher wage dispersion in the following years may largely reflect changes in the composition of employment. The bulk of the additional two million jobs created since 1995 are accounted for by young part-time or temporary workers, which enlarged the gap between the total dispersion index and the full-time

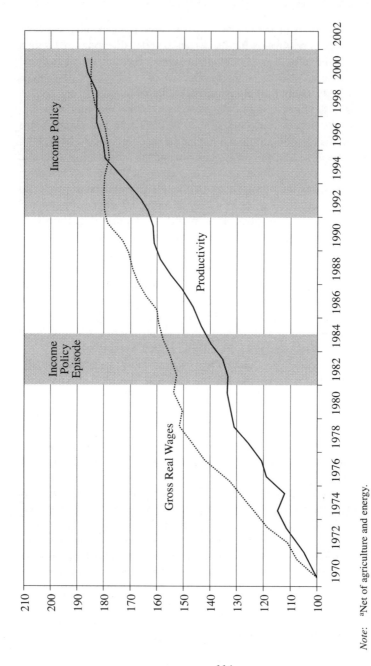

Note: [a]Net of agriculture and energy.

Source: Istat National Accounts.

Figure 6.1   Per capita gross real wages and productivity in the Italian private sector[a] (index 1970 = 100)

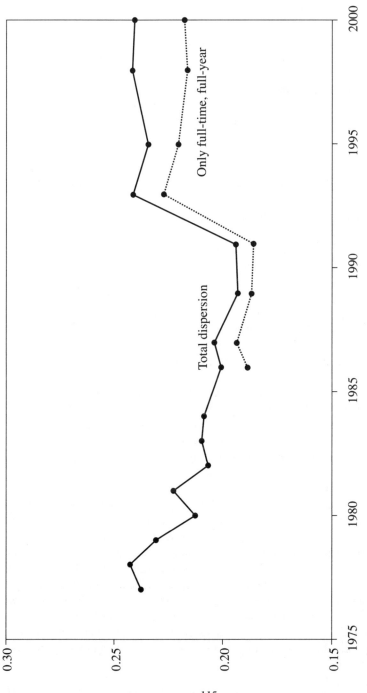

Source: Bank of Italy Survey on Households Income and Wealth (SHIW).

Figure 6.2 Dispersion of the Italian individual real wages, net of taxation (Gini index, percentage values)

and full-year one (Figure 6.2). Moreover, total dispersion can be decomposed into a 'between sector' part – which slightly declined in the 1990s – and in a 'within sector' part, which slightly increased. Total dispersion remained fairly constant if one imposes a fixed employment composition by contractual category of the 1990.

In the following section we seek to assess the main effects on wage dispersion and differentials of the different wage components: national contracts minima, premia set in a firm-level contract and premia unilaterally decided by the firm.

THE INSTITUTIONAL FRAMEWORK EVOLUTION

The Heritage from the 1970s and 1980s

During the 1970s high inflation and faster labour cost growth undermined the international competitiveness of the Italian economy, which was periodically but temporarily restored by exchange rate devaluations. In the second half of the 1980s the Banca d'Italia's adoption of a tighter monetary policy inside the Exchange Rate Mechanism of the European Monetary System was explicitly designed to curb inflation and wage dynamics. The resulting increase in goods market discipline due to international competition supported, *inter alia*, wage moderation in manufacturing while private services remained a source of inflationary pressure.[5]

The wage bargaining structure was based primarily on national contracts, with company-level agreements playing a supplementary role. Without any specialization, all issues were covered at each bargaining level. This introduced an inflationary bias, as wage behaviour was the cumulative outcome of cost-of-living adjustments – the so-called *Scala Mobile* – and pay increases set at the company level. The indexation induced substantial real wage resistance, with respect to terms of trade and oil shocks as well as to changes in indirect taxation.[6] Over time, indexation strongly reduced wage differentials, both regional and skill differentials, causing severe distortions.[7] Firm-level individual and unilateral wage increases were used in order to reduce such distortions. Little room remained for negotiated collective wage incentives and profit-sharing schemes. The government did not play a consistent role over this period, neither in defining a general macroeconomic framework, nor did it regulate public sector earnings coherently. Overall, the Italian wage bargaining structure was characterized by an intermediate degree of centralization and a small degree of coordination among sector national contracts renewals prevailed.[8] Many of these problems have been addressed in the last decade.

The Wage Bargaining Structure Designed in 1992–93

At the beginning of the 1990s after a prolonged expansion the Italian economy slowed down. At the end of 1991 the former indexation mechanism was frozen under a growing perception of an impending crisis due to losses in competitiveness and the poor state of the public finances. Indexation was abolished with the July 1992 partial agreement in combination with a substantial short-term wage freeze.[9] In September 1992, together with the crises of the European Monetary System, the Italian lira was devaluated by about 30 per cent over a short period of time. The sustainability of public debt was in doubt and an emergency fiscal package was imposed.

At this point the social partners recognized the macroeconomic need for wage moderation and set about sterilizing the major terms-of-trade shock. Some other microeconomic longer run targets were: (1) increasing wage flexibility with respect to the economic performance of the firms; (2) reducing wage compression; and (3) sustaining employment by means of more flexible working contracts.

The July 1993 agreements between social partners set up a hierarchy of specialized bargaining levels, with the national contracts devoted to maintaining the purchasing power of wages while firm-level contracts were devoted to the distribution of productivity gains. National contracts were set for four years for their non-wage components and two years for wages. The new instrument of the government's target inflation was introduced to lead inflation expectations down and facilitate coordination among social partners. The new wage increases granted in SNCs were forward looking, reflecting the government's target inflation set for the two years ahead. As a safety net, an ex post compensation should be provided for the difference between the actual and the target rates of inflation in the two preceding years. Such a difference should be adjusted to eliminate the effects of changes in the terms of trade due, for example, to a devaluation. The lack of a clear formulation about the compensation for past non-targeted inflation remained a source of conflict. In addition, nothing was specified in the agreement about tax variations.[10]

In practice, the SNCs specified the money amount of the increases in contractual base pay for each level of employment. Increases are generally divided into two equal instalments.[11] In industry, base pay incorporates the former cost-of-living adjustment and corresponds to around 80 per cent of total pay. In the market services sector the proportion was even higher. Incentives for the speedy renewal of national contracts were provided for in the 1993 agreements.[12] The wage part of the Italian bargaining structure always regulated the standard or contractual monthly bill, with only a loose determination of the hourly wage and no real link with hourly productivity.[13]

The hierarchically subordinated[14] firm-level contracts, which should have a four-year duration, provided for their expiry to be staggered with respect to the related SNC. The firm-level contracts should grant flexible wage increases, linked to the economic performance of the firm, and thus should be productivity-stimulating and non-inflationary by nature. In particular, such flexible wage premia are not to be subsequently transformed into a fixed component of earnings, as was the case in the past.

Opening Clauses and Wages below the Contractual Minimum

In Italy contractual wages are normally used as the benchmark in case of legal disputes, providing a natural minimum wage that is differentiated by sector and category of worker. The two lowest categories serve as the entry level for young people and apprentices,[15] especially in small enterprises and less developed areas. The cost of labour can fall below the contractual minimum: (1) because of the territorial pacts and the area contracts;[16] (2) due to relief of social contribution or the concession of tax credits for employees;[17] and (3) by the work provided by self-employed workers, on the basis of contingent contracts which are similar to those of salaried workers, apart from the reduced fiscal contributions and the absence of firing costs.[18]

Furthermore, wages below the contractual minimum levels are frequently paid in the underground economy which, according to some recent estimates, might account for about 15 per cent of Italian GDP. Underground employment, expressed in full-time equivalent units, was about three and a half million in 2001, about a million and a half of which is estimated to be irregular full-time employees, not covered by any national contract.[19]

NATIONAL-LEVEL CONTRACTUAL WAGES AND THE EFFECTIVENESS OF TARGET INFLATION

On the basis of the available econometric and institutional evidence, the government's inflation target proved to be very effective in reducing inflation expectations and in fostering coordination of the different sectors' contractual wages.

On the econometric side, using the quarterly model of the Bank of Italy, only shortly after the 1995–96 strong recovery in production was it possible to identify the main features of the new wage determination regime. Between 1970 and 1991 a standard Phillips curve was estimated for the pre-income policy regime.[20] Thus a systematic pattern in forecasting errors emerged, with an overestimation of the wage dynamics between 1992 and 1995, corrected by a small underestimation in 1996. The catching up of wages with respect to the target inflation raised to a year and a half. The main changes in the wage

Table 6.1   *Inflation and wage cumulative growth (indexes, 1992 = 100;*
            percentages)

	1994	1996	1998	2002
Actual inflation	108.3	118.6	122.7	134.7
Target inflation (a year ahead)	107.1	113.6	118.6	126.0
Private sector per capita contractual wages:	106.1	114.1	121.6	131.1
Contribution to the total wage growth[a]	105.6	112.9	119.7	128.4
Private sector: % share of contractual wages on total wages	88.8	87.7	87.8	84.8

Note: [a]Computed assuming that all the other wage components but the national contracts mimima remain constant.

Source: Our calculations based on Istat data.

formation were: a small reduction in the NAIRU and a decrease in the speed of adjustment of wages to the previous-quarter inflation. Hence, a new wage determination regime was now identified, because since 1993 the nominal wage dynamics was driven by the target inflation rather than actual inflation.

Target inflation persistently underestimated actual inflation. Between 1992 and 2002 the cumulative forecasting error, a year ahead, was –8.7 percentage points (126.0 versus 134.7, Table 6.1) and it was –10.2 two years ahead.[21] Due to the ex post compensation mechanism, the cumulative increase in the private sector per capita contractual wages was five points above the target inflation (Table 6.1). The remaining 3.6 points' distance from the actual inflation could be fully attributed to terms-of-trade shocks. Therefore, the Income Policy Agreements were formally respected. However, this experience illustrates that even constant contractual real wages make a negative contribution to the total wage bill. In fact, in the private sector such a contribution was cumulatively 6.3 percentage points below inflation (128.4 versus 134.7, Table 6.1). Overall, the reduced protection operated by the SNCs left to the firm-level negotiations the task of coping with the productivity trend and the above-mentioned inflation differential.

On the institutional side we can explain the small and temporary deviations of contractual earnings from the target inflation (Figure 6.3) by means of the ex post real losses compensation.[22] Four periods can be identified. First, in 1992–94 the suspension of the former wage bargaining structure[23] sharply reduced the rate of growth of private per capita wages from above 9 per cent to below 2 per cent. Second, in 1995–96 the first new regime national contracts were applied. The acceleration of the contractual earnings indicator above the target inflation embodied the full credibility of such a target. Only a

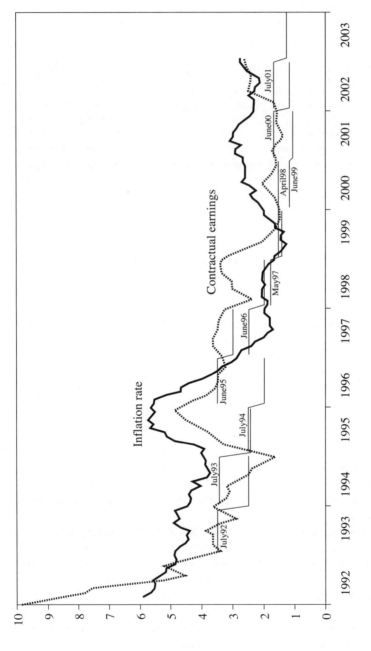

Note: [a]The target inflation date is referred to the release by the government for the following two years.

Source: Istat. Consumer Price Index; government target inflation (DPEF, various years).

Figure 6.3   Actual inflation, target inflation[a] and contractual earnings in the Italian private sector (percentage changes)

partial ex post compensation for the 1992–94 real losses (two percentage points) was added to the cumulative target inflation for 1995–96 (4.5 per cent).[24] The third period, 1997–98, started out with a considerable potential for conflicts, because during the 1995–96 period the actual inflation rate had exceeded the target inflation one by about four percentage points. Some trade unions attempted, unsuccessfully, to introduce a new form of automatic wage indexation. The following helped in solving these tensions: (a) the diffusion in 1995–96 of firm-level contracts with flexible wage premia (see next paragraph), and (b) the target inflation for 1996–97 set at a level about a percentage point higher than the actual inflation. Finally, since 1999 the wage bargaining structure was increasingly questioned by social partners. However, two opposite requests to reduce/increase the relevance of wages set at the national level neutralized each other, and the debate gradually shifted to reforming employment protection legislation.

The two-year length of wage settlements under national contracts is unusual. In the past, it was thought that annual renewals might generate too much conflict in the Italian system. In addition, agreeing two years of increases in advance introduces considerable nominal inertia. This no doubt worked in favour of wage moderation up to 1995, but it then set workers to recoup several years of decline in real wage at one fell swoop with the contract renewals of 1997. Again, when the oil price substantially increased in the year 2000, the biannual length turned out to be quite useful. The nominal wage inertia prevented the temporary upward pressure from imported prices from being embodied in the medium-run firms' costs.

FIRM-LEVEL CONTRACTS AND PERFORMANCE-RELATED WAGE BONUSES

To summarize, in Italy at the end of the 1980s: (i) a very small fraction of workers were covered by firm-level contracts, concentrated in large industrial firms; (ii) often in non-covered firms, small payments, additional to the SNCs, were unilaterally decided by firms; (iii) the expired firm-level contracts often remained unrenewed for years; (iv) all types of firm-level wage premia were in fixed amounts of money, definitely embodied in the wage bill; and (vi) high inflation rapidly reduced the real value of such wage premia.

The full exploitation of the 1992–93 agreements should imply: a pervasive diffusion of firm-level contracts, their regular renewals after four years and a continuous increase in flexible performance-related wage premia. However, the coverage of firm-level contracts has only partly increased. Moreover, even inside the covered segment, the cumulative amount of performance-related premia remained markedly below the productivity trend. Overall only limited elements of wage flexibility and differentiation were introduced at the company level.

A long-run analysis of all the different data and sources on firm-level contracts in Italy is presented by Rossi and Sestito (2000). They show how different sources give a similar picture, once corrected for differences in definitions. In 1995–96 about 40 per cent of workers in firms with more than ten employees was covered by a FLC,[25] corresponding to 3.2 million employees, with about a half of them being concentrated in industry. The coverage was strongly positively correlated with firm size and markedly lower in the south. Since 1997 there is evidence of only a slight increase in the FLCs' coverage, almost solely due to the banking sector and the large store chains. The Bank of Italy Survey on Investment in Manufacturing (SIM henceforth) shows a high and fairly constant coverage of FLCs since 1994[26] (Table 6.2). The reduced coverage in the south and in smaller manufacturing firms (20–49 employees) was confirmed in 2001. Overall, currently about half of the workers in private firms above ten employees, and almost all of those working in smaller firms, are estimated to be still excluded by FLCs' coverage.

There has been a widespread adoption of performance-related pay within the covered segment. In 1994–95, together with the first renewals of the new regime national contracts, a large fraction of firms covered by an FLC immediately introduced some performance-related wage premia.[27] The Istat Survey for 1995–96 shows that about a quarter of employees in industry and a fifth in services received such premia. In the south the diffusion was only 7 per cent. In contrast to many other countries, in Italy the adoption of flexible firm-level premia was not helped by fiscal incentives.[28]

According to the SIM, a particularly strong adoption of performance-related wage bonuses was registered in the last decade, among medium and large manufacturing firms[29] (Table 6.2). However, in 2001, such wage bonuses were used in only 13 per cent of firms with between 20 and 49 employees. The traditional 'fixed amount' wage bonuses are still given in the south (more than 40 per cent of firms) and by firms with fewer than 200 employees (30 per cent).[30] The share of manufacturing workers covered by performance-related wage bonuses has increased faster: up to nearly 75 per cent in 1999 (Table 6.2). Again in 2001 this share was below 15 per cent in firms with 20 to 49 employees. At the end of 2001, considering only manufacturing firms with more than 20 employees, the total number of workers receiving flexible wage bonuses would be around two million.

The relationship between FLCs and actual wage increases is not an automatic one. Many firm-level contracts provide such increases irregularly, or just conditionally on specific targets. However, even firms without a formal firm-level contract can pay wage increases, individually and unilaterally. Using the Bank of Italy SIM data, we analyse the sector of the Italian economy which has

Table 6.2 Firm-level contracts coverage by type of wage bonuses: manufacturing sector (percentages of firms and employees)

| | Firms with more than 50 employees | | | | | | Between 20 and 49 employees | |
| | End of 1994 | | End of 1996 | | End of 1999 | | End of 2001 | |
Types of firm-level contract	Firms	Employees	Firms	Employees	Firms	Employees	Firms	Employees
(a) Without company contract	**14.1**	**7.6**	**10.2**	**5.7**	**11.6**	**5.2**	**66.4**	**66.4**
(b) With a company contract	**85.9**	**92.4**	**89.8**	**94.3**	**88.4**	**94.8**	**33.6**	**33.6**
of which: by type of wage premia								
(b.1) No additional firm-level premia	**0.0**	**0.0**	**0.0**	**0.0**	**0.0**	**0.0**	**10.1**	**10.1**
(b.2) Traditional bonuses	**64.9**	**35.0**	**42.7**	**26.9**	**25.3**	**19.7**	**9.9**	**9.9**
of predetermined amount	60.5	32.7	39.9	25.4	22.3	17.5	8.8	8.8
for organizational change	4.4	2.3	2.9	1.5	3.0	2.2	1.1	1.1
(b.3) Bonus related to performances	**21.0**	**57.4**	**47.1**	**67.4**	**63.1**	**75.1**	**13.6**	**13.6**
of the whole company	16.8	47.9	39.0	50.0	N.A.	N.A.	N.A.	N.A.
of single production units	4.3	9.5	8.1	17.4	N.A.	N.A.	N.A.	N.A.
or								
partly related to performances	N.A.	N.A.	N.A.	N.A.	31.6	35.3	5.5	5.5
totally related to performances	N.A.	N.A.	N.A.	N.A.	31.5	39.8	8.1	8.1
Total (a) + (b)	100.0	100.0	100.0	100.0	100.0	100.0	100.0	100.0

Source: Bank of Italy, Survey on Investment in Manufacturing (SIM).

123

shown the most widespread adoption of firm-level contracts – manufacturing firms with more than 50 employees – and find that additional wage bonuses, even if frequent, are still not paid continuously.[31] The result is the insufficient distribution to workers of the productivity gains.

In the SIM, the increase in total wages due to additional bonuses set at the firm level – both unilaterally paid or contracted upon – was about 0.3 per cent in 1995, reached peaks of 1.3 per cent in 1996 and 1.1 per cent in 1998 and then remained around 0.8 per cent until 2001. During the two peaks the increases were particularly marked for firms with more than 500 employees, for those paying flexible wage premia and for firms in the north (Figure 6.4).

In the last decade, firm-level contracts have tended to (1) reduce wage dispersion inside the firm;[32] (2) enlarge the wage differentials among similar workers in firms with different productivity/profitability; and (3) slightly increase regional wage differentials between firms located in the north or in the south of Italy. In particular, the SIM data show that in the south the average incidence of total firm-level wage increases was 0.3 percentage points smaller per year, compared to the other Italian regions. Cumulatively, between 1995 and 2001 the induced wage drift in the south was some 2.5 per cent smaller. That reflects compositional effects and productivity differentials.[33] Even assuming a proliferation of fully flexible company-level bonuses, it will take several years to create significant differentials across regions characterized by different productivity levels. We should interpret this as allowing the possibility to enlarge and institutionalize firm-level wage premia in the north – given the insufficient distribution of productivity gains pointed out before – and not as a means to reduce wages in the south.

In the income policy framework the existence of a performance-related pay firm-level contract could signal more collaborative labour relations which favour the adoption of a more flexible organization of the firm.[34] With the SIM data the adoption of FLCs with performance-related pay was recently shown to be a complement to a more intensive utilization of fixed-term contracts and to standard working time variability with respect to production fluctuations.[35]

THE INCREASING RELEVANCE OF FIRMS' INDIVIDUAL WAGE-SETTING

Individual wage-setting in Italian firms is generally underestimated, particularly by the international literature, because of the lack of reliable data. Only for the important metalworking and engineering sector[36] are long-run data available that show the changing composition of wages.

In this sector the share of wages determined by the national contracts was about 79 per cent in 1991 and then steadily declined to 75 per cent in 2000.

(a) By firm size

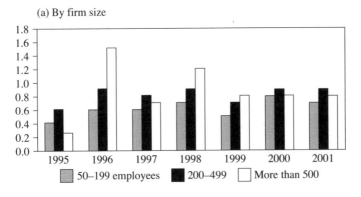

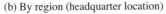

(b) By region (headquarter location)

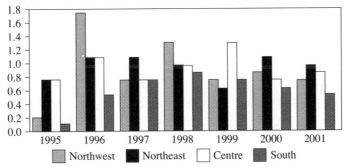

(c) By type of firm-level contarct

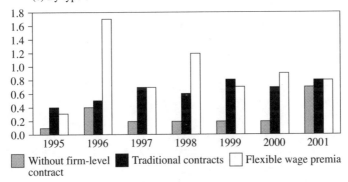

Source: Bank of Italy SIM, Survey on Investment in Manufacturing, telephonic follow-up.

Figure 6.4 Incidence of firm-level wage increases on the previous year total wage bill: all firms, paying or not such premia (percentage incidence; manufacturing firms with more than 50 employees)

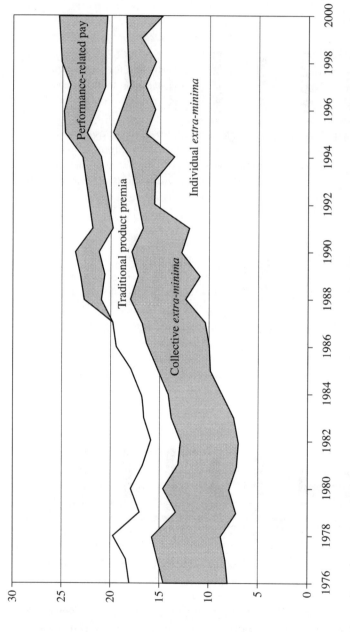

Notes: [a]The overtime premia are excluded from the total. The *extra-minima* wage premia are computed as the difference – catagory by category – between actual monthly paid wage bills and the national contract ones. The individual *extra-minima* are based on the *Assolombarda* Survey.

Source: Federmeccanica and Assolombarda Surveys.

Figure 6.5 Share of the metalworking and engineering total wage bill[a] determined at the firm level by component (percentage values)

The complementary 25 per cent determined at the firm level is mainly composed of the *extra-minima*[37] (see Figure 6.5). From the incentives and wage differentials point of view the individual and collective *extra-minima* are fairly different. The individual one tends selectively to increase internal wage differentials and skill premia. The collective *extra-minima* generally reproduce the compressed SNCs' wage differentials by category. With some simplifying assumptions[38] it is possible to distinguish between the two categories, showing the sharp increase in the individual *extra-minima* share, to above 15 per cent of total metalworking wage bills in the last six years. The incidence of the performance-related pay increased by three points since 1992, consistent with the Income Policy Agreements prescriptions, but almost completely at the expense of the collective *extra-minima*. Therefore a more efficient and variable team-productivity incentive – generally maintaining or reducing internal wage differentials – substituted the previous more rigid instrument. No real changes in the incentive policy of metalworking and engineering firms can be identified.

SOME OPEN QUESTIONS

In relation to wage-setting and income distribution in the long run, the Italian 1992–93 agreements dealt only indirectly with the regulation of the distribution of income between wages and profits. At the end of any biannual-length SNC, an *ex post* compensation should be provided only with respect to the differential between the actual and the target inflation, that is, the real contractual wages, net of the terms-of-trade effects. Therefore a short-run reduction of the labour share should be expected after major devaluations or oil price shocks, to reduce their inflationary impact. No direct appraisal or correction is related to the actual distribution of productivity gains.[39] In particular, nothing can enforce the adoption of firm-level contracts in the majority of firms. In the long run an equilibrium relation should emerge between real wages and productivity, and the labour share should be stationary.

The simple model presented by Casadio (2003) shows how the 1992–93 agreements are likely to be biased towards the reduction of the labour share in the long run and may not support a reduction in the share of wages fixed at the national level. The main result points to a slow tendency towards actual real wage reduction, induced by the link with inflation for contractual wages only,[40] and the insufficient aggregate distribution of productivity gains induced by the exclusion of a big fraction of employees by firm-level wage premia. Interestingly, the long-run tendency to reduce the labour share should emerge, even assuming that firms without an FLC unilaterally pay some additional wage premia to maintain constant the share of wages determined at the firm level.

An often-quoted weakness of the Italian wage structure is the rigidity that stems from its having inherited pay scales that are relatively flat and in reproducing them mechanically by granting all employees roughly the same nominal increases regardless of rank. In the traditional view, sectors and dimensions, but not the territory or the specific firm characteristics, are the main determinants of the wage differentials, reflecting the embodied human capital.

In recent years many changes in Italian wage-setting have occured, but the literature has presented only limited evidence of them.[41] In particular, on the aggregate side many authors have shown the substantial irrelevance of the local unemployment rates in determining wage dynamics during the 1980s and the early 1990s.[42] Using more disaggregate data, a few recent studies have found interesting results about the effects of regional unemployment on the lower quantiles of the wage distribution.[43]

FUTURE DEVELOPMENTS

The 1992–93 wage bargaining structure has not been fully supported by social partners, especially since 1999, but it has survived mainly because of the repeated crises that have been faced. In more recent years, trade unions have preferred to maintain the current wage bargaining system, while asking for new instruments to distribute the productivity growth at the central level. The employers' associations have alternated between calling for a significant reduction in the importance of national contracts and demanding a larger role for company-level contracts within the existing system.

After the May 2001 change of government, the effectiveness of the *Concertazione* among social partners was challenged directly. In July the metalworking SNC was renewed without the subscription of the bigger union in the industrial sector. In July 2002 a new pact was signed by the government, again without the subscription of the bigger union in the industrial sector. The main issue was the introduction of some temporary increase in the possibility of firing workers without just cause. This would increase the government's autonomy, reduce the role for unions and definitely end the *Concertazione* and incomes policy experience. This new phase has already been accompanied by a resurgence of social conflict.

The next contractual round, opening at the beginning of 2003, will face a large *ex post* excess in inflation compensation at a time of a cyclical downturn and the ending of the *Concertazione*. In recent months the three bigger unions presented for the first time separate wage demands for the relevant metalworking and engineering national contract renewal. The degree of wage coordination is dropping sharply, because at the same time the credibility of the government target inflation is strongly questioned.[44]

In the short run some wage acceleration will probably emerge, but overall wage moderation seems not to be at risk. In our opinion, what is more vulnerable, is the set of flexible arrangements contracted upon at the firm level since 1995–96 under the general cooperation induced by the *Concertazione*.

NOTES

* Bank of Italy, Research Department. The views expressed here are personal and do not necessarily reflect those of the Bank of Italy. For helpful comments I thank A. Brandolini, P. Cipollone, L. D'Aurizio, M. Magnani, F. Mongelli, J. Morgan, P. Pini, R. Torrini, the participants to the ECB workshop on 'Wage Formation in Europe' in Frankfurt, December 2001, and the participants in the Italian Labour Economists' Annual Conference in Salerno, September 2002. Special thanks to F. Giorgi and R. Nizzi for research assistance.

1. A few weeks before the devaluation, under the hypothesis of a 10 per cent depreciation of the Italian lira, the Bank of Italy econometric model simulated a 4 per cent consumer price increase in a year and a 7 per cent increase in three years (Siviero and Terlizzese, 1997). Because of the recent elimination of the wage indexation, the Phillips curve was no longer a valid forecasting tool. Using some *ad hoc* link with the value-added deflator or the input–output tables framework, there was a consensus about a considerably reduced impact elasticity, around 0.1, with a medium-run elasticity largely uncertain, around 0.5 (Fabiani et al., 1997).
2. See Nicoletti Altimari (1997) and Siviero and Terlizzese (1997).
3. See Gavosto, Sabbatini and Sestito (1994) for the firms' price policy, Dell'Aringa (1994) for the strongest anti-inflationary environment and Onofri (1997) for the major effects of the fiscal package.
4. In private services the 1990s' reduction followed that of the previous decade and was amplified by technological change and privatizations. In industry the labour share was still high in 1991–92 and started declining only after the Income Policy Agreements.
5. Compared to Germany and France, the output price dynamics in the service sector remained remarkably high and productivity stagnant (see Visco, 1994).
6. Automatic wage increases due to indexation were quarterly before 1986 and then half-yearly until the 1992 abolition. The degree of coverage of the *Scala Mobile* – ratio of the percentage changes of the indexed components of wages to the rate of change of the cost-of-living index – was very high. In manufacturing the coverage was about 60 per cent at the beginning of the 1970s. It was elevated to above 90 per cent in the centralized 1975 agreement, when any differentiation by skill or contractual category in the indexed increases was eliminated. The degree of coverage gradually declined towards 80 per cent in the following decade. As a paradox, in that period the degree of coverage for the lower categories of blue-collar workers was slightly above 100 per cent. In 1986, after some centralized income policy episodes, the indexation mechanism was reformed. The automatic wage increases became semi-annual and the degree of coverage fell to 50–60 per cent. See Visco (1995), Bank of Italy (1986) and Manacorda (2002) for more details.
7. The trade union organizations too have always favoured little differentiation of wage increases, both across sectors and qualifications. The regional wage differentials are analysed in Manacorda (2002) and Brandolini, Cipollone and Sestito (2001).
8. According to Calmfors and Driffill (1988) such a combination had adverse effects. A more centralized structure could neutralize the negative externalities of a rapid wage increase. On the other hand a more decentralized structure could benefit from the discipline induced by competition in the goods market.
9. Waiting for a full reform, any firm-level wage increase was suspended until the end of 1993, compensated by a one-off undifferentiated payment equal to 0.7 per cent of the average wages in January 1993.
10. Indirect taxes, like VAT, are often excluded by the core inflation indicators. We should

assume it was excluded even from the definition of target inflation. How to consider changes in the tax wedge and the social contributions was not specified. The question is relevant, because all the social partners often asked for a reduction of the tax wedge and because the degree of real wage resistance affects the outcomes of wage bargaining.

11. In general, the first instalment is paid immediately at the renewal, and the second one 12 months later. The contractual earnings indicator is typically stair-shaped. Most settlements provide for a one-off payment compensating for the months of delay not fully covered by the contract. The median delay in the private sector during the 1990s was about four months.

12. In the period between the expiry of a contract and its renewal, employees receive an automatic wage increase equal to one-third of the official target inflation rate after three months and half that rate after other three months.

13. The SNCs set the standard weekly working hours, about 38–39 hours, corresponding to the standard monthly wage bill. Without any major change in those weekly hours, the actual number of hours worked per year changed markedly in the last three decades (see Casadio and D'Aurizio, 2001).

14. The national contracts can set ceilings for company-level pay increases and provide for their suspension in given periods.

15. The new apprenticeships introduced in 1996 allow newly hired young workers to be paid an initial wage equal to 80 per cent of the contractual minimum wage for the lowest category, rising gradually to 100 per cent over the three- to four-year duration of the contract.

16. In the last five years so-called territorial pacts and area contracts have been introduced (see Bank of Italy, 2002). Both these instruments permit the non-application of minimum contractual wages in backward areas subject to authorizations negotiated between trade unions, employers and local authorities. Some incentives are provided for the northern firms to open new plants in the south.

17. The tax credit introduced at the end of the year 2000 is the most important active labour market policy applied in Italy because of the large size of the relief and its nation-wide applicability. The measure, supporting the creation of permanent jobs, seems to be quite effective but provides a low level of selectivity; see Bank of Italy (2002) and Cipollone and Guelfi (2003) for more details.

18. According to the Labour Force Survey, the share of self-employed workers is above 25 per cent in Italy (about six million) compared to less than 10 per cent in the other main European countries. Even excluding the employers and a large part of family workers, to account for the Italian small firms' structure probably about two and a half million Italian workers would have been classified as employees in other countries or under different regulations (see Torrini, 2003).

19. Such an amount is obtained excluding the approximately 600 000 irregular self-employed, and excluding occasional jobs and multiple irregular activity added to a regular job.

20. See Fabiani et al. (1997). The average private sector wage growth was regressed on the consumption inflation rate and on both actual and expected inflation, with a homogeneity restriction. In the estimation the following were included: the unemployment rate, capacity utilization, hours of strike, the replacement ratio and the unemployment rate differential between the north and the south. In such a formulation there is no response of wage growth to the productivity gains, which should have been a logical long-run assumption, because any tendency towards the long-run equilibrium was not yet visible (see Figure 6.1). In the estimates it was mainly the unemployment rate in the north that influenced the wage dynamics.

21. As a comparison, in the same period the Consensus Survey forecasts cumulatively overestimated the actual Italian inflation respectively by 1.2 and 3.2 percentage points, one year ahead and two years ahead.

22. For more details see Istat (2002), CNEL (1997, 2000).

23. At the end of 1991 the former indexation mechanism was frozen and in July 1992 abolished. Waiting for a full reform of the BS, any firm-level wage increase was suspended until the end of 1993 and compensated by a one-off undifferentiated payment amounting to 0.7 per cent of the average total wages in January 1993.

24. In November 1994 and in January 1995 the two most important SNCs were renewed: the wholesale and retail trade one (eight months' delay) and the metalworking SNC (six months'

delay). Both the contracts added to the cumulative target inflation an extra payment (less than 2 per cent) as a partial compensation for the previous year's real losses and for the delay. Many other SNCs were then renewed quickly and without strikes.

25. The Istat Survey (1999) – conducted interviewing 8000 firms with more than ten employees – measured the cumulative flow of FLCs renewals in 1995–96, which was quite a good approximation of the stock of new regime contracts because of the first generalized implementation of the Income Policy Agreements.

26. See Bank of Italy (1996) for more information about the annual survey conducted on a representative sample of about 1000 firms with more than 50 employees. In the SIM the estimated FLCs' coverage is higher than in Istat, because even earlier FLCs, paying the pre- 1992–93 fixed-amount payments, are included.

27. In 1994, many firms simply added some decimal points to the 0.7 per cent wage increase decided centrally in the July 1993 agreement, as a start of more cooperative relations at the firm level. Often some sequential FLCs were signed in the following two years, renegotiating and monitoring the new performance-related bonuses.

28. The incentives announced by the government at the end of 1997 were formally introduced in 1999, but only took effect in 2000. Firms with flexible wage premia gain bonuses on social contributions equal to the amount of such premia, up to 3 per cent of workers' wages. In 2000 total fiscal incentives amounted to about 400 million euro. The corresponding number of employees can be estimated at 650 000 to 800 000 employees.

29. The share of firms above 50 employees with performance-related wage bonuses was negligible before 1992; and increased up to 21 per cent at the end of 1994 and to 47 and 63 per cent in 1996 and 1999 respectively.

30. The flexible payments are equally divided between partly and totally variable with respect to performance. A total variability is predominant in firms with more than 500 employees (nearly 50 per cent of those firms); see Casadio (2003) for more details.

31. Since 1996 the share of employees actually gaining additional firm-level premia in the reference year fluctuated around 65–70 per cent in the larger industrial firms and in the north; and remained between 25 and 40 per cent in firms below 200 employees and in the south. Even in firms with performance-related premia, the probability of gaining an additional wage premium was markedly lower than one, fluctuating between 60 and 75 per cent. Such a probability was between 35 and 50 for workers covered by old-fashioned FLCs, paying only fixed-amount premia; it was on average about 20 per cent for workers not covered at all by FLCs, with a clear cyclical pattern.

32. Generally the wage premia contracted upon at the firm level pay the same amount to all the workers, or at most differentiate by category, on the basis of the compressed SNCs' scale. The idea is to incentivize all the workers as a team, assigning to the other unilateral payments the role of selectively incentivizing some high-skilled workers.

33. Controlling for sectors, dimensions and the peculiar kind of FLC, some panel data estimations conducted on over 700 SIM firms between 1995 and 1999 pointed to bigger performance-related wage bonuses in the northeast of Italy. Compared to that region, firms in the northwest paid annual average per capita wage bonuses 0.2 percentage points lower. Such differentials in wage bonuses were 0.3 percentage points for firms located in the centre of Italy and 0.4 for the southern firms, see Casadio (1999).

34. See Cainelli et al. (2002), Leoni (2001), Pini (2002) and their references.

35. See Casadio and D'Aurizio (2001).

36. This sector accounted for 2 100 000 employees in 2000, corresponding to 16 per cent of Italian production and a half of both the exports and the production of investment goods. The sector is considered a leader in wage determination, together with the wholesale and retail trade. The *Federmeccanica* – representative association of the employers of the sector – has since 1976 provided yearly data about the wage composition by category of worker and by wage components, which is set in the national contract or at the firm level.

37. In Italian *Superminimi*, which includes both individual and collective premia, additional to the national contracts minima. Such *extra-minima* are paid on a monthly basis and by a fixed amount, definitely embodied in the wage level.

38. The total *extra-minima* coming from the *Federmeccanica* data were decomposed in indi-

vidual and collective *extra-minima* on the base of the *Assolombarda* Survey, formally the subsample of firms and plants located in Milan province, which is one of the biggest and most productive Italian industrial districts. The incidence of individual *extra-minima* in the *Assolombarda* data should be upward biased, but the bias could be constant over time.

39. In contrast, a sort of distributional neutral wage growth rule is adopted in Germany. Some compensation should be considered if the past year wage growth differed substantially from the sum of the planned rate of inflation and the medium-run productivity growth.

40. If the contractual wages are the α per cent of total wages, and increases at the inflation rate π, the actual real wages decrease at the rate $(1 - \alpha)\, \pi$. For example, in manufacturing, contractual wages are about 85 per cent of the total; therefore in this sector total real wages decreased by 0.5 per cent per year if the inflation rate was 3.4 per cent.

41. It depends partly on the delay in the release of administrative data, currently up to 1997, and partly on the low quality of the information on the wage drift one can get as a difference between national accounts and contractual wages.

42. See Dell'Aringa, Ghinetti and Lucifora (2000) for a review.

43. See Brunello, Lupi and Ordine (1999, 2000) and their references.

44. The July 2002 Italian Government Financial Programming Document set the target inflation for 2003 and 2004 respectively at 1.4 and 1.3 per cent. All three bigger unions announced that they would consider as a reference point for the next renewals a 2 per cent inflation expectation for both 2003 and 2004, which is in line with the Consensus forecasts.

REFERENCES

Bank of Italy (1996), *Metodi e Risultati dell'Indagine Sugli Investimenti delle Imprese Industriali*, Supplemento al Bollettino Statistico, Note metodologiche e informazioni Statistiche, **59** (6).

Bank of Italy (various years), *Annual Report of the Governor*, 31 May, Rome.

Brandolini, A., P. Cipollone and P. Sestito (2001), 'Earnings dispersion, low pay and household poverty in Italy, 1977–1998', in D. Cohen, T. Piketty and G. Saint-Paul (eds), *The New Economics of Rising Inequalities*, Oxford: Oxford University Press.

Brunello, G., C. Lupi and P. Ordine (1999), *Widening Differences in Italian Regional Unemployment*, Fondazione ENI Working Paper No. 54.

Brunello, G., C. Lupi and P. Ordine (2000), 'Regional disparities and the Italian NAIRU', *Oxford Economic Papers*, **52**, 146–77.

Cainelli, G, R. Fabbri and Pini, P. (2002), 'Performance-related pay or pay for participation? The case of Emilia-Romagna', *Human Systems Management*, **21** (1), 43–62.

Calmfors, L. and J. Driffill (1988), 'Bargaining structure, corporatism and macroeconomic performance', *Economic Policy*, **3** (6), 7–12.

Casadio, P. (1999), 'Diffusione dei premi di risultato e differenziali retributivi territoriali nell'industria', *Lavoro e Relazioni Industriali*, **1** (gennaio–giugno), 57–81.

Casadio, P. (2003), *Wage Formation and Wage Differentials in the Italian Private Sector after the 1992–93 Income Policy Agreements*, Temi di discussione, Bank of Italy Working Papers, forthcoming.

Casadio, P. and L. D'Aurizio (2001), 'Working hours flexibility, employment flexibility and wage flexibility in the Italian industry: Complements or substitutes?', presented at the EALE Conference 2001, September, Jivaskila University, Finland, and *Economia e Lavoro*, **3** (settembre–dicembre, anno XXXV), 71–91.

Cipollone, P. and A. Guelfi (2003), *Tax Credit Policy and Firms' Behaviour: The Case of Subsidies to Open-End Labour Contracts in Italy*, Temi di discussione, Bank of Italy Working Papers no. 471.

CNEL (1997, 2000), *Rapporto Sulle Retribuzioni e il Costo del Lavoro*, Documenti CNEL, n. 30, maggio.

Dell'Aringa, C. (1994), *Caratteri Strutturali dell'Inflazione Italiana*, Bologna: Il Mulino.

Dell'Aringa, C., Ghinetti, P. and Lucifora C. (2000), 'Pay Inequality and Economic Performance in Italy: A Review of the Applied Literature', presented at the PiEP LSE Conference, 3–4 November 2000, London.

Fabiani, S., A. Locarno, G. Oneto and P. Sestito (1997), *NAIRU: Income Policy and Inflation*, OECD Economics Department Working Paper No. 187, and *Risultati e Problemi di un Quinquennio di Politica dei Redditi: Una Prima Valutazione Quantitativa*, Temi di discussione, Bank of Italy Working Paper No. 9, March 1998.

Gavosto, A., R. Sabbatini and P. Sestito (1994), 'Inflazione e ciclo economico: alcuni elementi di analisi per interpretare i recenti avvenimenti in Italia', *Moneta e Credito*, **188** (47), 495–514.

Istat (1999), *Indagine Sulla Flessibilità nel Mercato del Lavoro nel 1995–96*, Rome.

Istat (2002), *Annual Report*, 15 May, Rome.

Leoni, R. (ed.) (2001), *Disegni Organizzativi, Stili di Management e Performance d'Impresa*, Milano: Franco Angeli.

Manacorda, M. (2002), *Can the 'Scala Mobile' Explain the Fall and Rise of Earnings Inequality in Italy? A Semi-parametric Analysis, 1977–93*, Centre for Economic Performance, LSE Working Paper.

Nicoletti Altimari, S. (1997), 'Uno studio sulle aspettative di inflazione in Italia: 1970–1995', Banca d'Italia, *Ricerche Quantitative per la Politica Economica 1995*, **1**, 1–46.

Onofri, P. (1997), 'La capacità previsiva dei modelli econometrici nella recente fase ciclica', Banca d'Italia, *Ricerche Quantitative per la Politica Economica 1995*, **2**, 819–40.

Pini, P. (ed.) (2002), *Innovazioni Organizzative, Risorse Umane e Relazioni Industriali*, Milano: Franco Angeli.

Rossi, F. and P. Sestito (2000), 'Contrattazione aziendale, struttura negoziale e determinazione decentrata del salario', *Rivista di Politica Economica*, ottobre–novembre, 129–84.

Siviero, S. and D. Terlizzese (1997), 'Crisi di cambio e innovazione nei comportamenti: alla ricerca di discontinuità strutturali nel modello econometrico della Banca d'Italia', Banca d'Italia, *Ricerche Quantitative per la Politica Economica 1995*, **2**, 841–904.

Torrini, R. (2003), *Cross-Country Differences in Self-Employment Rates: The Role of Institutions*, Temi di discussione, Bank of Italy Working Papers, forthcoming.

Visco, I. (1994), 'Caratteri strutturali dell'inflazione italiana: 1986–1991', in C. Dell'Aringa, *Caratteri Strutturali dell'Inflazione Italiana*, Bologna: Il Mulino.

Visco, I. (1995), 'Inflation, inflation targeting and monetary policy: Notes for discussion on the Italian experience', in L. Leiderman and L. Svensson (eds), *Inflation Targets*, London: CEPR, pp. 142–68.

7. A widening scope for non-wage components in collective bargaining in the EU?[*]

Véronique Genre, Ramón Gómez Salvador, Nadine Leiner-Killinger and Gilles Mourre

1 INTRODUCTION

Collective bargaining is increasingly taking place against the background of a growing importance of 'qualitative labour-related aspects', a development which may have contributed to wages increasing less in the second half of the 1990s than in the past. These 'qualitative labour-related aspects' can be defined to include non-wage components of collective bargaining such as non-wage compensation (for example employers' social security contributions and fringe benefits) and working conditions. Indeed, the European Trade Union Confederation (ETUC) has put forward a guideline for the coordination of collective bargaining, which demands the 'total value of the agreement' to encompass nominal wage increases and an improvement in 'qualitative aspects of work', implying a trade-off between wage developments and non-wage issues.[1] At the same time European governments have been calling for an increased focus on such qualitative labour-related aspects. The Lisbon European Council in 2000 concluded that the European Union (EU) has 'to become the most competitive and knowledge-based economy in the world capable of sustainable economic growth with more and better jobs and social cohesion'.[2] In 2001 the Stockholm European Council stated that

> regaining full employment not only involves focusing on more jobs but also on better jobs . . . including equal opportunities for the disabled, gender equality, good and flexible work organization permitting better reconciliation of working with personal life, life-long learning, health and safety at work, employee involvement and diversity in working life.[3]

Non-wage compensation such as training and improved working conditions may have a positive effect on labour productivity. If this were to be the case, employers would have an incentive to enlarge spending on these non-wage components until the resulting increase in real wages equals the increase in labour productivity. With workers placing increased emphasis on non-wage compensation and working conditions, this might support a trade-off between wage and non-wage components in remuneration, where nominal wage increases lag behind increases in productivity.

Against this background, we analyse whether collective bargaining in EU countries has increasingly broadened its scope to encompass non-wage components such as non-wage compensation and working conditions. In doing so, we take a first step towards an assessment of whether non-wage components in collective bargaining have been conducive to moderate wage developments and price stability in recent years. We consider changes in four bargaining areas – continuing vocational training, health and safety at work, reconciling work and private life and, finally, working time.

The chapter is structured as follows. Section 2 briefly reviews existing literature on the relevance of non-wage components in collective bargaining. Section 3 provides and assesses information on the importance of selected non-wage components in EU countries. Section 4 concludes.

2   NON-WAGE COMPONENTS IN COLLECTIVE BARGAINING: SURVEY OF THE LITERATURE

Trade unions' objectives cover a wide range of issues, including as a basic objective the maximization of their members' economic welfare which, next to employment, broadly encompasses all aspects associated with employee rewards such as wages and non-wage-labour-related aspects, including non-wage compensation and working conditions.[4] Some aspects of non-wage compensation, for example employers' social security contributions and costs associated with maternity and sick leave, are largely determined by legislation. At the same time non-wage compensation also includes firms' voluntary provision of services ('fringe benefits') such as expenditures for education or training, bonuses, occupational pension schemes, childcare facilities, cheap mortgages and company cars, as well as health services or insurance. Similarly, working conditions, including for example permitted breaks, health and safety at work or disciplinary procedures, are determined both by legislation and by firms' provision.[5] Generally, the higher the level of non-wage components in remuneration due to existing legislation, the smaller should be the trade unions' incentives to bargain on these aspects. Booth (1995) for example argues that the fact that US collective agreements cover a wider set of issues than in Britain reflects the relative lack of US social welfare legislation. Furthermore, unions' demand for fringe benefits depends on the age composition of the organized workers (see, for instance, Freeman and Medoff,

1984). Consequently the shares of wage and non-wage components in unions' collective bargaining objectives will be affected by the preferences of union members for wage and non-wage remuneration, which tend to differ with respect to age structures and depend on the existing legislation concerning non-wage components.

The literature on union behaviour has paid relatively more attention to bargaining on wages than on non-wage compensation and working conditions. Like wage costs, both non-wage compensation and working conditions involve resource costs for employers. The analysis of non-wage-related aspects in collective bargaining should therefore proceed along broadly similar lines as the analysis of wage compensation (see, for example, Calmfors et al., 2001). In the same way that trade unions' success in increasing wages depends in the longer run on the generation of a surplus in production, their success in achieving improvements in non-wage components also requires such a surplus. In the case of non-wage-labour-related aspects the size of this surplus may also depend on the impact of non-wage components on labour productivity. As with wage outcomes, unions' ability to increase non-wage compensation and to improve working conditions necessitates sufficient trade union bargaining power. The impact of unions on non-wage components should tend to rise with the level of their monopoly power.

The early empirical studies on the effects of trade unions on non-wage compensation – Freeman (1981) and Freeman and Medoff (1984) – focus on comparing the non-wage outcomes of workers in union and non-union firms. For the US labour market in the late 1960s and mid-1970s they find a higher proportion of labour costs spent on fringe benefits for union workers than for non-union workers. In a study of the US labour market in the 1980s, Freeman and Kleiner (1990) find only a modest impact of newly established unions on wages, but a substantial impact on various working conditions such as grievance systems and seniority protection. Booth (1995) reports evidence regarding the change in the percentage of British establishments with a recognized trade union or staff association that bargain on non-wage issues such as physical working conditions, major changes in production methods, holiday entitlement and length of working week. From 1984 to 1990, for manual workers, bargaining on these aspects seems to have declined slightly, whereas negotiation over these non-wage issues seems to have increased slightly for non-manual workers.[6,7]

To our knowledge, empirical evidence on whether the importance of non-wage compensation and working conditions relative to wages in collective bargaining has increased and contributed to moderate wage developments in European countries remains scarce. This is because any analysis of this kind is hampered by non-wage components in collective bargaining taking very different forms, and particularly because working conditions are difficult to measure. As a first step towards a more thorough analysis, this chapter surveys developments in selected non-wage components across EU countries in the second half of the 1990s which have gained renewed interest in the discussion on the so-called qualitative aspects of work organization. The starting point of our analysis, which is qualitative throughout, is the question of whether non-wage components have gained momentum against the background of demands for moderate wage developments.

3 A WIDENING SCOPE OF COLLECTIVE BARGAINING IN EU COUNTRIES?

The non-wage components considered in this chapter include continuing vocational training, health and safety at work, reconciling work and private life, as well as reduction and reorganization of working time. This list of non-wage components is not meant to be exhaustive, but to focus on some of the aspects that appear to have become more relevant in the last few years. Moreover, the aim is not to show that these non-wage components are relatively new aspects subject to collective bargaining. On the contrary, most of them have been on the bargaining table for some decades.

The understanding of developments in non-wage components requires the use of a large set of information on bargaining practices at the national, sectoral and firm levels. This information is mainly obtained from the European Industrial Relations Observatory (EIRO) and, to a lesser extent, from the European Trade Union Institute (ETUI). When possible, indirect evidence of available macro-indicators from Eurostat or OECD is presented to check the consistency of the findings.

3.1 Continuing Vocational Training

Until the late 1980s, continuing vocational training, that is opportunities offered to workers during their working life to enable them to acquire, update and adapt their knowledge, skills and competencies, was a relatively minor issue in collective bargaining in most EU countries. It was not until the late 1980s that it gained importance in the strategies of social partners and in collective bargaining, being especially marked since the mid-1990s.[8] Possible reasons for a rise in the importance of continuing vocational training include the increased appreciation of staff training by management and the increasing importance of lifelong training in public employment policies as a key factor in maintaining the employability of workers and in promoting and sustaining company competitiveness.

The role of collective bargaining in continuing vocational training depends on the characteristics of the industrial relations system and on the education and training systems of each country. Three groups of EU countries are broadly identifiable, depending on the influence of collective bargaining on continuing vocational training. The first group comprises those EU countries where the continuing training system is based on agreements between employers' organizations and trade unions. Social partners therefore have a high degree of joint responsibility in the regulation and management of training (mainly through sectoral collective bargaining). This group includes, for example, France, Belgium, the Netherlands and Spain. France pioneered this kind of agreement in the early 1970s. Since then, the development and management of the continuing training system has been mainly influenced by mainly sectoral collective bargaining.[9] In the second group of EU countries, continuing training is the responsibility of the public authorities and therefore not greatly considered in collective bargaining. For instance in Greece and Portugal the public authorities play a major role in the financing and organization of training. A third group includes countries in which continuing training depends largely on the initiative of individual employers, such as Germany and the United Kingdom. In Germany, for instance, collective bargaining plays a certain role and continuing training is gaining importance in the strategies of social partners. In the United Kingdom continuing training is almost entirely an employer's prerogative, and in Ireland, although the state plays a major role in the organization and financing of continuous training at the national level, firms decide at local level on what training is required in each case.

The main objective of collective bargaining as regards continuing vocational training has been to establish a regulatory framework to promote training in companies and to institutionalize the role of social partners. Three main roles for bargaining on the regulation of continuing training can be distinguished: funding and management, participation of worker's representatives in company training plans, and the content and recognition of training councils. Collective bargaining has however mainly focused on the first two of these roles. Regarding funding and management, intersectoral collective agreements have resulted in an obligatory levy on employers in some countries.[10] Provisions for the division of costs of continuous training between employers and employees have been made in some agreements. The employer may fund both the training and the time in which it takes place,[11] or the worker may contribute time.[12] Social partners generally share the management,[13] although the state also participates in some cases.[14]

Turning to participation of work councils, continuing vocational training is one of the areas in which works council-type bodies have statutory participation rights in some EU countries.[15] In other EU countries, collective agreements may contain provisions that guarantee the participation of company-level workers' representatives in continuing training or, alternatively, sectoral collective agreements may lay down such a possibility.[16]

Finally, with regard to the content of training and its recognition/certification, collective bargaining does not cover in general the specific content of continuing vocational training in companies. Experiences vary among countries and are linked to the general role of collective bargaining in vocational continuing training described earlier. In those countries in which the continuing training system is more closely linked to sectoral collective bargaining, social partners usually set up bipartite training institutions which establish the training priorities in each sector and are also responsible for teaching and certifying the training. Continuing training is, in this model, generally highly recognized between companies.[17] In countries in which public authorities have a greater role, social partners usually play an advisory role in the evaluation of needs and the content of training. The extent to which continuing training is regarded as important varies significantly among countries.[18]

Although it was already included in collective agreements before the 1990s, the use of continuing vocational training seems to have gained momentum in the second half of the 1990s. In Belgium, for example, 80 per cent of sectors were covered by agreements that include provisions relevant to training in 2000. This was the case for 40 per cent of agreements signed in Portugal in 1999. In the Netherlands such provisions affected 21 per cent of employees covered by collective agreements in 2000 and in Spain 27 per cent in 1999. In most cases such agreements took and continue to take place at the sectoral level or at a higher level in which the government plays an important role. Table 7.1 presents some examples of the agreements signed throughout the 1990s at the country level.

The quantitative measurement of whether there has been a reinforcement of continuing training in collective bargaining over recent years is hindered by the fact that only indirect evidence provided by collective bargaining agreements is available. According to OECD figures,[19] between 1995 and 1999 the number of participants in training, public or quasi-public, for employed adults increased significantly in most of the EU countries for which this information is available compared to 1990–94 (see Figure 7.1). Interestingly, this picture is not so clear for public expenditure on these kinds of programmes, measured as a percentage of GDP, which declined in the same period. This very likely reflects greater use of better-targeted labour market policies and reduced emphasis on expensive programmes, such as long periods of training (see OECD, 2001).

3.2 Health and Safety at Work

The prevention of industrial accidents started to be tackled early on in the discussions on how to improve working conditions. Wide-ranging legislative

Table 7.1   *Major changes in agreements concerning continuing vocational training in some EU countries*

Country	Date	Change in agreement
Belgium	1988	Bipartite intersectoral agreement followed by a law providing for an obligatory contribution by firms.
	1992	The amount spent on continuing vocational training was set at 0.25% of the pay bill, 0.10% for state-promoted training for groups with difficulties and 0.15% for continuing training organized by companies.
	1997	Increase in the employers' contribution in some sectors.
	1999– 2000	Intersectoral agreement: additional efforts with a view to achieving an investment in training equivalent to the mean level reached by its three main neighbouring countries (ranging from 1.2% to 1.9% of total pay bill) within six years. For the period 1999–2000 it means an increase in employer contributions from 1.2% to 1.4% of the pay bill. 80% of the sectors are covered by agreements which include some provisions relevant for training.
	2001– 2002	Intersectoral agreement: companies will increase their spending on continuing vocational training to 1.6% of pay costs.
Spain	1992	Intersectoral national agreement on continuing training (Acuerdo Nacional de Formación Continua – ANFC) signed by the social partners and the administration. It establishes an obligatory financial contribution by firms, joint management and the pre-eminence of sectoral bargaining.
	1996	Amendment of the ANFC: increasing the number of recipients, improving the management and promoting the certification of training. Other goals for the future: increase the quality of training and promote the participation of SMEs and less-qualified workers.
	1999	The number of agreements that regulate training plans has increased annually in recent years, although since 1997 the number of workers affected seems to be falling. Clauses on training plans were found in 20.2% of agreements recorded up to May 1999, covering 27.2% of workers.
	2000	Third national agreement on continuing training, which introduced changes in the administration and funding of continuing training.
France	1970	Central intersectoral agreement followed by a law that has been reformed several times. It provides for the rights of all employees for continuing training, the obligation for all firms to finance it and joint management through bipartite sectoral bodies.

Table 7.1 continued

Country	Date	Change in agreement
France	1999	A government white paper proposed the creation of an individual entitlement to training, safeguarded by collective agreements and the certification and validation of vocational experience and knowledge. The proposals, broadly welcomed by the social partners, form part of a phased reform process, with much emphasis on dialogue and negotiation with the social partners.
	2000	Agreements dealt with issues such as adapting employees to changing skills needs, improving job opportunities for young people, developing training in SMEs and offering lifelong learning. At the company level bargaining activity was limited, with training dealt with in less than 4% of agreements.
Finland	1998–99	A 'job rotation model' to assist people in their acquisition of skills is to be launched in the near future in cooperation with the social partners, in order to give people with atypical employment contracts training opportunities. Training is supposed to correspond better to the needs of the labour market and to improve employees' general capacity to seek and gain employment.
	2001–2002	Measures are agreed to promote employees' 'ability to cope' at work and to promote training, including a clause stating that projects will be set up to promote lifelong learning. Training benefit schemes for persons of working age, equal to about 80% of unemployment benefit, are granted only for full-time vocational training of up to one and a half years' duration. Undertaken at the initiative of employees.
United Kingdom	1997	National agreement in local government emphasizing the importance of training and development and requiring unions and employers to develop local schemes.
	1998	The social partners emphasized their view of the importance of effective vocational training throughout working life in order to meet rapid changes in markets, technology and work organization.
	1999–2000	Trade unions are increasingly attempting to incorporate training into the bargaining agenda through initiatives such as the Bargaining for Skills Project of the Trades Union Congress (TUC). Company-sponsored employee development schemes and open learning facilities appear to be on the increase. These typically encompass employer-funded or subsidized voluntary personal development activities, which need not be job-specific and which take place in employees' own time. Such developments are likely to be given further impetus by government initiatives to promote lifelong learning.

Source: EIRO, ETUI. Annual country reviews.

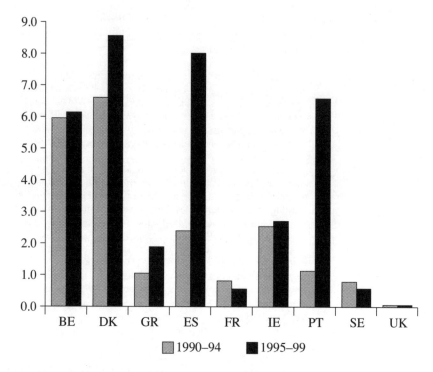

Key: BE: Belgium; DK: Denmark; GR: Greece; ES: Spain; FR: France; IE: Ireland; PT: Portugal; SE: Sweden.

Source: OECD, Labour Market Programmes database.

Figure 7.1   Participant inflows in continuing vocational training (as a percentage of the labour force)

tools[20] were implemented in all European countries, so that by the end of the 1990s the involvement of social partners in matters of health and safety at work remained driven by either the implementation or the enhancement of the legal framework. In practice this led to the signature of bi- or tripartite agreements in nearly all European countries between 1997 and 2001. These agreements generally laid out the practical rules to ensure health, hygiene and safety in the workplace and define the respective responsibilities of employers and employees.[21] On a few occasions employers have been drawn to the negotiating table under the threat to shift the focus on wage increases if health and safety matters were not dealt with (for example in the Netherlands in 1998).[22] Although the current trend regarding the prevention of accidents at the workplace very much depends on the coverage of the existing legislation, an analysis of recent EIRO publications (annual country reviews) shows that social partners are increasingly taking an active role in motivating, providing incentives and increasing awareness at company level in many European countries.

At the end of the 1990s European surveys on working conditions pointed to a generalized intensification of work pressures.[23] Thus one important development of the social dialogue concerning health matters in recent years is the increasing attention given to stress and psychological strain linked with work. In most countries stress is not an issue widely dealt with in collective bargaining, but it shows a strong potential for gaining importance in the social dialogue across the European Union.[24] Collective agreement clauses referring explicitly to stress or psychosocial risk factors with a view to applying a policy of prevention exist in Belgium (where an intersectoral agreement was signed in 1999), Denmark, Germany, Luxembourg, the Netherlands, Finland, Sweden and the UK and most agreements were signed after 1997. Generally these clauses provide for studies to determine the extent of the issue, introduce indicators of stress and lay down procedures to tackle specific problems.

While no data are available on the exact coverage of health and safety issues in European collective agreements, the European surveys on working conditions report that the number of European workers considering themselves as well (or fairly well) informed on risks attached to their job rose from 71 per cent in 1995 to 76 per cent in 2000. In 2000 more than 70 per cent were also offered the possibility to discuss working conditions generally with colleagues and superiors, and for 75 per cent of them, these discussions led to improvements at the personal level. In general there has been a decrease in the number of accidents at work in the second part of the 1990s (see Figure 7.2). Although this is undoubtedly related to a secular increase of less dangerous economic activities (for example services), it may also reflect some success of increased efforts and campaigns to prevent industrial accidents, and thereby a growing awareness about related issues.

3.3 Reconciling Work and Private Life

Reconciling work and private life has started to be dealt with relatively more recently compared with health and safety issues in the latter part of the 1990s in most European countries. The idea is to promote changes in institutional practices and in the organization of working time in order to accommodate changing family structures and lifestyles, to promote changes in parental roles (for both men and women) and to allow for personal development for all. Reaching a better balance between work and private life encompasses a whole range of various initiatives. This consists, for instance, in making the organization of working time more flexible, with special leave or career breaks, in facilitating voluntary part-time work, chosen progressive retirement, annualized

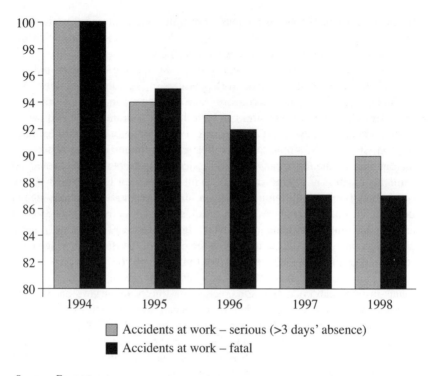

Source: Eurostat.

*Figure 7.2   Health and safety at work in the European Union (accidents per
100 000 employed; 1994 = 100)*

hours schemes or flexi-time (that is, personalized working time), as well as
teleworking. It also includes measures related to elderly and childcare support.
Collective agreements promoting the reconciliation of work and private life
generally complement legislation in achieving more tailored approaches to
working conditions, according to the needs, interests and priorities of men and
women.

Examples of collective agreements with provisions promoting a better
balance between work and private life can be found in all Member States and
in all sectors of the economy. The extent and number of these agreements vary
substantially across countries, however, as reported by the European
Foundation for the Improvement of Living and Working Conditions (1999,
2002). In a first group of countries (Germany, Greece, Spain, Luxembourg and
Austria), reconciling work and private life is hardly dealt with in collective
agreements.[25] When they exist, collective agreements on balancing work and

private life in these countries tend to mainly focus on 'mother-friendly' measures.

In a second group of countries (Belgium, France, Italy, Ireland, Portugal and the United Kingdom) collective bargaining on reconciling work and private life has started to develop and some agreements are spreading even at company and sectoral levels. For example in Italy the issue of teleworking has been covered by a national agreement in 2001, following several major industry-wide agreements (in particular in telecommunications). In France more than 75 per cent of company-level collective agreements contain provisions supplementing a relatively generous basic legal framework (in terms of parental leave, care leave, crèche-type facilities). In Ireland the tripartite agreement (Programme for Prosperity and Fairness, followed by Partnership 2000) contains a range of work–life balance initiatives (for example special leave, career break, flexi-time, and so on). In some countries, such as Ireland, employers have been led to address the work–private life issue in order to attract and retain workers in a tight labour market.

Finally in a smaller number of countries (Denmark, the Netherlands, Finland and Sweden) collective bargaining on reconciling work and private life has been undertaken for some time but nevertheless has developed further over the 1990s. It combines company agreements with sectoral agreements on a wide range of proposals (possible career breaks, flexible working time for all, paternity leave, creation of crèches within the firm, and so on) going far beyond the scope of 'mother-friendly' solutions and aiming towards personal development for all.[26]

It seems that, as with stress-related issues, reconciling work and private life has become a very topical issue in the late 1990s. Although employers may consider employee-friendly policies as being outside their sphere of responsibility or not cost-effective in terms of improving productivity, recent microeconomic studies have stressed that work–life balance practices improve staff motivation and commitment and reduced labour turnover and absenteeism.[27] In addition, voluntary part-time work has increased, in some cases substantially, from 1995 to 2000 in those countries where initiatives have been taken to improve the reconciliation of work and private life (see Figure 7.3). The increase in the proportion of people voluntarily working part-time may be a sign that part-time work has increasingly become a means for workers to achieve a better balance between work and private life.

A striking aspect of these agreements on reconciling work and private life remains their close relation with gender equal opportunities issues and their attempt to address the pronounced phenomenon of gender segregation at work observed in the EU. Equal opportunities in general and discrimination on ethnicity, beliefs or age grounds in particular, are also matters linked to the improvement of job quality that have recently gained ground in collective bargaining.

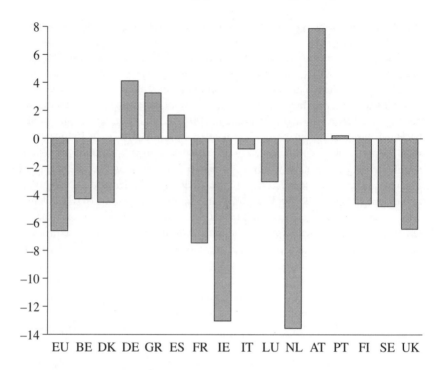

Key: BE: Belgium; DK: Denmark; DE: Germany; GR: Greece; ES: Spain; FR: France; IE: Ireland; IT: Italy; LU: Luxembourg; NL: Netherlands; AT: Austria; PT: Portugal; FI: Finland; SE: Sweden.

Source: Eurostat.

Figure 7.3   Developments in the share of involuntary part-time work in total part-time employment (in percentage points, 1995–2000)

An analysis of recent EIRO publications shows that intersectoral collective agreements related to these issues have been signed in most European countries in recent years.

3.4   Reduction and Reorganization of Working Time

In most EU Member States, working time has received particular attention in the collective bargaining process since the second half of the 1990s. 'Working time' refers to the organization and the number of hours worked in firms within a given time period (day, week, several weeks or year). The various themes addressed in negotiations include working-time reduction and working-time reorganization (for example atypical work, computation on an annual basis, payment for overtime with compensating rest,[28] and so on). The reduction of working time is often linked to initiatives made to reconcile work and private life. Conversely this issue does not cover measures such as early retirement schemes and changes in the effective retirement age, which deal with working-life duration rather than usual working time.

In many sectors in most EU countries[29] collective bargaining in the second half of the 1990s has led to a slight and gradual reduction in collectively agreed working time for employees in exchange for the increased working-time flexibility sought by firms, as reported by EIRO (1997, 1998b, 2000, 2001, 2002) and Fajertag (1999, 2000, 2001). This has not been associated with requirements in terms of employment creation. Working-time reduction has translated mainly into the granting of bank holidays (Finland), individual days off (Denmark, Germany), the reduction of annual working hours (Spain, Italy, Sweden), the crediting of extra hours to 'individual working-time accounts' (Italy) and, though much more seldom, into a decrease in weekly working hours (Germany, Greece, Portugal). Enhanced flexibility has mainly taken the form of a calculation of working time over a reference period[30] varying from a few weeks to a year, or similarly the replacement of overtime payment by rest periods or extra hours credited to time accounts. The use of atypical work (evening work, weekend work, shift work) seems to be less emphasized by collective agreements, because of the reluctance of trade unions. In general flexibility remains mostly a theme raised by employers to increase productivity and has not been implemented primarily in order to improve employees' working conditions. In general, the bargaining process on working time has occurred at a decentralized level, although in addition, some national agreements (Austria, Portugal) or legislation (Italy) have been implemented, providing for a reduction in statutory working time.

However, two groups of countries fit less in this general pattern of working-time reduction. The first group comprises countries such as the Netherlands over the period 1982 to 1996, France and, very recently and to a much lesser extent, Belgium, which have adopted substantial reductions in the statutory working hours as a way of reaching macroeconomic targets, which are primarily creating/safeguarding jobs ('work sharing') or securing wage moderation. In this group of countries the government appeared to have initially encouraged the inclusion of working-time issues in the collective bargaining process.[31] Although law or national agreements imposed working-time reduction, its specific modality in terms of work reorganization was most often determined by a company-level agreement taking into account the particular situation of the firm considered.

On the opposite side there exists a second group (the UK and to a lesser extent Ireland), where most collective agreements have only consisted of applying the minimum European standards in terms of working time defined by the new national legislation adopted to comply with the 1993 EU Directive.[32] Available measures, especially in the UK, indicated that at least initially, most employers sought to minimize the impact of the legislation by securing the flexibility via collective agreements and by encouraging individual opt-outs from the 48-hour limit on average weekly working hours.[33] However, the legal limitation of average weekly working hours recently applied in Ireland and the UK is reflected in the diminution in usual working hours of full-time workers in the late 1990s.

In conclusion, compared to the first half of the 1990s, negotiation on working time is now a common concern across countries and will gain increasing attention in collective bargaining and in the public debate in the medium run. It seems that the number of employees actually covered by working-time agreements, albeit still limited in some countries and uneven across sectors, has increased in the 1990s.

As shown in Figure 7.4, the reduction in negotiated working time is visible in the decline in the usual working hours of full-time employees in several countries (Ireland, Italy, the Netherlands, Portugal, Sweden and the UK) and the European Union as a whole. The magnitude of the decline seems to be positively related to the initial number of usual hours worked per week, which may point to a 'convergence' process of usual working time across the European Union.

This indicator (which includes in particular the impact of overtime) is of course too indirect to actually measure the change in negotiated working hours and, for some countries where the actual coverage of working-time agreements is still limited, too aggregate to take into account sectoral developments. However, it shows that despite the cyclical upswing, the increase in usual working hours in the late 1990s was lower than that seen earlier in the decade (except for Denmark, Greece and Luxembourg, probably owing to cyclical overtime).

CONCLUSIONS AND ISSUES FOR FURTHER RESEARCH

Non-wage issues seem to have gained importance in collective bargaining as the descriptive evidence gathered regarding continuing vocational training, health and safety at work, as well as reduction and reorganization of working time seems to indicate. Indeed, although precise information is lacking, it seems that in many EU countries the number of agreements actually covering these non-wage-labour-related aspects, albeit still limited in some countries, has increased in the latter part of the 1990s.

It is possible to interpret the bargaining on these non-wage components as beneficial for both workers and firms. On the one hand employees obtain a compensation in exchange of moderate wage developments. On the other hand

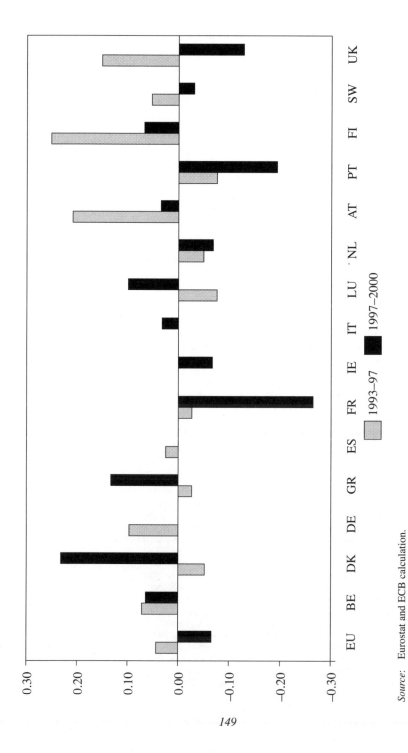

Source: Eurostat and ECB calculation.

Figure 7.4 Average annual change in usual hours works per week by full-time employees (in minutes)

factors such as training and working-time flexibility can increase workers' productivity. Thus the emergence of non-wage components in wage bargaining in a context of high unemployment might have supported continuing wage moderation in the late 1990s.

Further research should be carried out better to measure the trade-off between wage and non-wage components in collective bargaining. Such an analysis would need to shed more light on the driving factors behind overall labour cost developments and provide an assessment of future upward/downward risks to labour costs on the basis of the expected developments in the non-wage component.

NOTES

* We thank Neale Kennedy, Gerard Korteweg, Reiner Martin, Ad van Riet, Wolfgang Schill and Melanie Ward-Warmedinger for valuable comments.
1. 'Qualitative aspects of work' includes non-wage components such as working time, lifelong learning and retirement – see ETUC (2000, 2001).
2. See European Commission (2000).
3. See European Commission (2001a, 2001b). Against this background, the Employment Guidelines 2002 emphasize the need to ensure 'quality in work'.
4. See Booth (1995), ch. 4 for a discussion of the trade union objective function.
5. Although collective bargaining between firms and trade unions on non-wage-labour-related aspects of remuneration will tend to focus on the fringe benefits and working conditions voluntarily provided by firms, trade unions and employers' federations might also be able to influence the legislative process concerning any changes in non-wage components.
6. Based on Millward et al. (1992).
7. An indirect approach to assessing whether a trade-off between wage and non-wage outcomes has actually taken place during the late 1990s is to estimate wage curves which describe the relation between wages and unemployment as the outcome of bargaining between employers and employees (see, for example, IMF, 2001 and Friberg and Uddén Sonnegård, 2001).
8. See EIRO (1998a).
9. Belgium, the Netherlands and Spain have models similar to the French, but started in the late 1980s and early 1990s. In addition, Italy signed an agreement of this kind in 1996. Finally in Sweden, Finland and, to a lesser extent, Denmark, collective agreements at the sectoral level also have an influence on continuing vocational training, although in all three countries it falls in a more general context of adult training that is part of their educational culture.
10. There are examples in Belgium, France, Spain and Italy.
11. There are examples in France, Austria and Luxembourg.
12. There are examples in Austria, Finland, Germany and Luxembourg.
13. As in Belgium, Denmark, France, the Netherlands and Spain.
14. As in Finland, Greece, Ireland and Portugal.
15. For instance in France, Finland and the Netherlands.
16. For instance in Austria, Denmark, Germany and Sweden.
17. Such as in France, the Netherlands and to a lesser extent Belgium.
18. While in Denmark the adult training system leads to formally recognized qualifications, in Ireland and Portugal the level of recognition is more limited. A special case is the UK, in which continuing training depends largely on the initiative of individual employers. There is a system of national certification that defines the skills that the labour market demands and it is widely used to certify continuing training.

19. OECD Labour Market Programmes database.
20. The European legal framework is based on two core directives: the framework directive 80/1107/EEC, which is designed to protect health and safety of workers against risks arising from exposure to chemical, physical or biological agents in the workplace, and the directive 89/391/EEC, which contains basic provisions for health and safety organization and outlines the respective responsibilities of employers and employees. This initial basic framework was supplemented and strengthened with a number of other directives and amendments, such as the directive 92/85/EC on the introduction of measures to encourage improvements in the health and safety at work of pregnant women. The transposition process in domestic legislation generally took place in the second part of the 1990s.
21. In particular the most recent national or intersectoral agreements (in Spain in 1997, in Ireland for the Partnership 2000, in France in 2000 or in Portugal in 2001) create safety committees to monitor the implementation of decisions. By doing so, they provide new spaces for increased social dialogue about these issues.
22. EIRO (1999).
23. In the 1990s the publication of three European working condition surveys pointed to tighter deadlines and to a pace of work increasingly dictated by human demands rather than by industrial constraints (such as production targets or automatic speed of machines). In 2000 about a third of European workers considered that their health and safety was at risk at their workplace, and nearly 60 per cent considered that their work affected their health (in particular in causing backaches, stress, overall fatigue and muscular pain). Violence and harassment at work were also shown to be persistent. (See, for example, the European Foundation for the Improvement of Living and Working Conditions, 1999, 2001).
24. While such issues have become increasingly important on trade unions' agenda (via research projects, information campaigns, advice and training), the approach taken by employers' organizations seems to remain more heterogeneous. This could be due to the difficulty of defining intangible concepts and of measuring the amount of stress specifically linked to work organization and not rooted in the private life or the personal characteristics of the employee. Employers' attitudes range from little concern expressed so far (in countries like Greece, Spain, Luxembourg or Italy) to growing concern leading to some publications on the linkage between stress and productivity, motivation and involuntary absence from work (Ireland, Denmark, the Netherlands and the UK).
25. In Greece, Spain and Italy trade unions tend to advocate legislative changes rather than trying to improve conditions through collective bargaining. In Germany, Luxembourg and Austria legislation plays an important role and existing action from social partners takes rather the form of symbolic declaration of intent as they might not feel the need to improve the current legal framework.
26. During the late 1990s a large part of the negotiations in these countries tried to address the risks of abuse or misuse of flexible forms of work and reorganization of working time.
27. See Dex and Scheibl (1999) for a survey undertaken among 102 large private service sector employers. Similarly in a representative survey of US employers only a minority (18 per cent) perceived the costs of flexible work arrangement policies as outweighing the benefits, while nearly half (46 per cent) perceive the benefits from such policies as outweighing costs (see Galinsky and Bond, 1998). Hogarth et al. (2001) also carried out a study showing a consensus among employers that work–life balance practices fostered good employment relations (72 per cent). Many agreed that work–life balance practices improved staff motivation/commitment (58 per cent) and helped lower labour turnover (52 per cent), reduced absenteeism (53 per cent) and retained female employees (51 per cent).
28. Days off or half-days off, which should be taken within a certain period of time and/or could be saved in an individual working time account.
29. Denmark, Germany, Greece, Spain, Italy, Luxembourg, Austria, Portugal, Finland and Sweden.
30. This enables employers not to pay overtime premia for hours worked above the average in any day, week, month and so on, as long as the average number of hours is respected over the reference period.

31. It generally agreed with trade unions and employers' federations as part of a 'comprehensive package'. In this package employers benefit from more working-time flexibility, cuts in social security contributions and/or commitment to wage moderation in the near future in exchange for working-time reduction and job creation. The calculation of working time on an annual basis together with increased leave time for executives appears to be the main pattern of working time flexibility (EIRO 1998b).
32. The directive is fairly complex. It provides, with possible numerous exemptions, an average 48-hour maximum week, 11 hours' daily rest period, weekly rest period of 35 hours, rest breaks at work, four weeks' annual holiday, Sunday working provisions and limitation on hours worked at night.
33. Long working hours remain common and there have been only limited signs of innovations such as annualized hours.

REFERENCES

Booth, A. (1995), *The Economics of the Trade Union*, Cambridge: Cambridge University Press.

Calmfors, L., A. Booth, M. Burda, D. Checci, R. Naylor and J. Visser (2001), 'The future of collective bargaining in Europe', in T. Boeri, A. Brugiavini and L. Calmfors (eds), *The Role of Unions in the Twenty-First Century*, Oxford: Oxford University Press.

Dex, S. and F. Scheibl (1999), 'Business performance and family-friendly policies', *Journal of General Management*, **24** (4), 22–37.

EIRO (1997), *Collective Bargaining on Employment in Europe*, Dublin: European Industrial Relations Observatory.

EIRO (1998a), *Collective Bargaining and Continuing Vocational Training in Europe*, Dublin: European Industrial Relations Observatory.

EIRO (1998b), *Flexibility of Working Time in Europe*, Dublin: European Industrial Relations Observatory.

EIRO (1999), *1998 Annual Review for the Netherlands*, Dublin: European Industrial Relations Observatory.

EIRO (2000), *Working Time Developments – Annual Update 1999*, Dublin: European Industrial Relations Observatory.

EIRO (2001), *Working Time Developments – Annual Update 2000*, Dublin: European Industrial Relations Observatory.

EIRO (2002), *Working Time Developments – Annual Update 2001*, Dublin: European Industrial Relations Observatory.

European Commission (2000), *Lisbon European Council – Presidency Conclusions*, Brussels.

European Commission (2001a), *Stockholm European Council – Presidency Conclusions*, Brussels.

European Commission (2001b), *Employment and Social Policies, a Framework for Investing in Quality*, Brussels.

European Foundation for the Improvement of Living and Working Conditions (1999), *Pacts for Employment and Competitiveness – Concept and Issues*, Dublin.

European Foundation for the Improvement of Living and Working Conditions (2001), *Ten Years of Working Conditions in the European Union*, Dublin.

European Foundation for the Improvement of Living and Working Conditions (2002), *Reconciliation of Work and Family Life and Collective Bargaining: an Analysis of EIRO Articles*, Dublin.

ETUC (2000), *Annual Report on the Coordination of Collective Bargaining in Europe (2000)*, Brussels: European Trade Union Confederation.

ETUC (2001), *Annual Report on the Coordination of Collective Bargaining in Europe (2001)*, Brussels: European Trade Union Confederation.

Fajertag, G. (ed.) (1999), *Collective Bargaining in Western Europe 1997–1998*, Brussels: European Trade Union Institute (ETUI).

Fajertag, G. (ed.) (2000), *Collective Bargaining in Europe 1998–1999*, Brussels: European Trade Union Institute (ETUI).

Fajertag, G. (ed.) (2001), *Collective Bargaining in Europe 2000*, Brussels: European Trade Union Institute (ETUI).

Freeman, R.B. (1981), 'The effect of unionism on fringe benefits', *Industrial and Labor Relations Review*, **34** (4), 489–509.

Freeman, R.B. and M.M. Kleiner (1990), 'The impact of new unionization on wages and working conditions', *Journal of Labor Economics*, **8** (1, pt 2), S8–25.

Freeman, R.B. and J.L. Medoff (1984), *What do Unions do?*, New York: Basic Books, Inc.

Friberg, K. and E. Uddén Sonnegård (2001), 'Changed wage formation in a changing world?', *Sveriges Riksbank Economic Review*, **1**, 42–69.

Galinsky E. and J.T. Bond (1998), *The 1998 Business Work–Life Study: A Sourcebook*, New York: Families and Work Institute.

Hogarth, T., C. Hasluck, G. Pierre, M. Winterbotham and D. Vivien (2001), *Work–Life Balance 2000: Results from the Baseline Study*, UK Department for Education and Employment Research Report No. 249.

IMF (2001), *Rules-Based Fiscal Policy and Job-Rich Growth in France, Germany, Italy and Spain*, Washington, DC: IMF.

Millward, N., M. Stevens, D. Smart and W.R. Hawes (1992), *Workplace Industrial Relations in Transition*, Aldershot: Dartmouth.

OECD (2001), *Employment Outlook*, Paris: OECD.

8. Aggregation and euro area Phillips curves

Silvia Fabiani and Julian Morgan[1]

INTRODUCTION[2]

Since the start of Stage 3 of EMU, attention has increasingly been paid to euro area aggregate rather than national developments. This is true for a wide range of economic and financial information, reflecting the notion of the euro area as a single economic entity – 'Euroland'. At the same time, while a single monetary policy has been adopted, it is recognized that many important differences in economic structures remain across countries. Nowhere is this more evident than in labour markets. Structural features relating to labour market institutions, the legislative framework and social security systems differ to a large degree across the euro area countries. Such differences raise issues about whether one should analyse labour market developments at the area-wide level or whether it is more appropriate to conduct analysis at the national level and aggregate the outcomes to the euro area level.

There is a growing literature on aggregation issues which is summarized in Dedola et al. (2001). Much of the recent work has focused on the aggregation of money demand relationships (Fagan and Henry, 1998; Dedola et al., 2001) but some analysis has also been undertaken with respect to labour markets (Turner and Seghezza, 1999; OECD, 2000). The question that is often addressed by researchers is whether there is an aggregation bias that emerges when estimating relationships at an aggregate rather than national level. As discussed in Fagan and Henry (1998), an aggregation bias will emerge unless either the estimated parameters in such relationships are identical across countries or the independent variables are perfectly correlated. Neither of these conditions appears likely to hold – particularly in the field of labour market analysis – so it seems highly probable that some form of aggregation bias is present.

It is then necessary to investigate how large such a bias is and whether there are any potentially offsetting factors that make it more useful to conduct an area-wide analysis rather than estimating national relationships. As Fagan and Henry (1998) discuss, the magnitude of the bias depends positively on the extent to which the parameter coefficients are different and inversely on the degree of correlation in the movement of the independent variables at the national level. A potential offsetting factor is what is known as the statistical averaging effect. This emerges because, typically, the variance of the weighted sum of the country equation residuals is lower than the variance of the residuals in any one country. In other words, some residuals will tend to offset each other, leading to lower residuals at the aggregate rather than national level. The extent to which this happens clearly depends on the degree of correlation in the residuals across countries. Another way of looking at this, as argued by OECD (2000), is that the national equations may be mis-specified in that they wrongly exclude important area-wide variables. For example, in the context of money demand, national equations would be affected by foreign variables if there were currency substitution within European portfolios. This may lead to negative cross-country correlations in the residuals from national money demand equations.

The issue of the validity of aggregation therefore becomes an empirical question of the extent to which parameters differ across countries and of the comparison of the correlations in both the independent variables and the residuals. In the context of money demand, Fagan and Henry (1998) estimate a long-run money demand function on 14 EU countries and at the aggregate level. Despite the fact that there are marked differences in the parameter estimates between the national equations, they find a superior performance of the aggregate equation with a lower standard error and stronger evidence for cointegration than the national equations. The statistical averaging effects are found to lower the standard error at the aggregate level, as there is a small tendency towards a negative correlation in the residuals from national equations. However, a point forcefully made by Dedola et al. (2001) is that it is not necessarily appropriate to compare the performance of an aggregate equation against the performance of a typical national equation. Rather, comparison should be made between the performance of the aggregate equation and the performance of the aggregated results from the national equations. This way the statistical averaging effect of residuals falls out of the comparison and no longer serves to favour the aggregate approach. Nevertheless, in the paper by Fagan and Henry (1998), the aggregate money demand equation still outperforms the aggregation of national equations.

This chapter aims to make a practical contribution to this debate in the context of labour market analysis by seeking answers to three questions. The first is, to what extent is the relationship between wage growth, inflation and the tightness of the labour market similar across the large euro area countries? The second is, what are the potential gains and losses from pursuing aggregate as opposed to country-level analysis of such a relationship? The third is, if, since the start of EMU, one had used country-level or aggregate analysis to forecast the rate of growth of trend unit labour costs, which would have performed better?

To seek to answer the first question we estimate Phillips-type relationships for the five largest euro area countries, both individually and as an aggregate. We test the extent to which there is a common relationship across the five countries between wage growth and the cyclical position of the economy, measured by the gap between the current unemployment rate and its long-run value. To address the second question we examine the evidence of correlations in both the independent variables and the residuals from the national equations. In addition we compare the performance of the aggregate equation against the aggregated results from national equations with and without imposing a common parameter on the unemployment gap variable across countries. Finally, to address the third question we undertake a comparison of the out-of-sample forecast properties of the country and area-wide equations since the start of EMU.

The chapter is structured as follows. In the next section we discuss the specification adopted to model the dynamics of wage growth. Next we report estimates of the aggregate and national equations. In the latter cases these are estimated separately and as a system to test whether the restriction of a common parameter on the unemployment gap is accepted. We also provide evidence on the correlation structure in the independent variables and the single equation residuals. The residuals of the various approaches are compared. The chapter then gives details of the out-of-sample forecast properties of the approaches before concluding.

AN OVERVIEW OF THE WAGE GROWTH EQUATION

We examine the potential importance of aggregation biases in labour markets using a simple wage–price Phillips curve (following Gordon, 1997). The equation describes a disequilibrium adjustment process in the labour market: the change in nominal wages adjusted for trend productivity growth provides a measure of trend unit labour costs. This is postulated to depend on price inflation and labour market tightness. Price inflation is measured by the first difference in (the log of) consumption deflator (current and lagged values). In the absence of a specific measure of expected inflation, this lag structure is assumed to capture both price inertia and the formation of inflationary expectations. Labour market tightness is measured by the unemployment gap, that is, the difference between the actual rate of unemployment and the NAIRU, where the latter is computed as a filtered version of observed unemployment. The equation also contains shocks to import prices as an additional factor which might influence wage growth other than the stance of the labour market.

The specification chosen includes among the regressors lagged values of the dependent variable, lagged values of the change in (the log of) consumer prices and import prices (in second differences) and current values of the unemployment gap.

$$\Delta \ln ulc_t = a + bgap_t + \sum_{j=1}^{k} c_j \Delta \ln ulc_{it-j} + \sum_{j=0}^{h} d_j \Delta \ln p_{cit-j}$$

$$+ \sum_{j=0}^{p} g_j \Delta\Delta \ln pm_{it-j} + z_t \qquad (8.1)$$

where *ulc* is the ratio of nominal wages to trend labour productivity, p_c is the consumers' expenditure deflator, *pm* is the import deflator, *gap* is the difference between the unemployment rate (ILO measure) and the time-varying NAIRU and *z* is an error term.

As is standard practice in Phillips curve-based analysis, a long-run nominal homogeneity restriction is imposed. This assumption guarantees the existence of an equilibrium in the labour market and implies that inflation depends only on nominal factors in the long run, that is:

$$\sum_{j=1}^{k} c_j + \sum_{j=0}^{h} d_j = 1.[3]$$

The choice of analysing a reduced-form relationship such as the Phillips curve described above is partly motivated by the idea that an area-wide approach might be more justified for an empirical analysis of the euro area labour market based on this type of relationship rather than, say, on a structural model. It is in fact sometimes argued that the Phillips curve approach and, relatedly, the concept of NAIRU, is more relevant for large closed economies (such as the USA) than for small open ones, where domestic factors play a lesser role in determining inflation when compared to foreign variables such as the exchange rate and competitiveness. Indeed, as indicated in Fabiani and Mestre (2000, 2001), area-wide estimates of the NAIRU show significant inflation forecasting ability and are able to produce sensible measures of the output gap at the euro area level.

THE DATA

Data for the five largest euro area countries are seasonally adjusted quarterly time series collected from various sources, namely the ESA95 database published by Eurostat, the Quarterly National Account (QNA), the Quarterly Labour Force Statistics and the Main Economic Indicators (MEI) databases published by the OECD and the BIS database. The time range covered by the series differs across countries. In order to achieve the highest possible degree of comparability we selected a common sample period, starting in 1982q1 and ending in 2000q4.

Data on GDP, final consumption of households, imports of goods and services (all at constant and current prices), the number of employees and total compensation of employees at current prices are available in the ESA95 database from 1978q1 for France, 1970q1 for Italy, 1980q1 for Spain and 1991q1 for Germany.

For Germany, data prior to 1991 were reconstructed by the authors using time series for West Germany from different sources: namely the QNA database for GDP at current and constant prices, private final consumption expenditure at current and constant prices, imports of goods and services at current and constant prices and the BIS database for compensation of employees and the number of employees for the whole economy. In order to be coherent with the seasonally adjusted ESA95 data available since 1991, as a first step the data prior to 1991 from the QNA database were adjusted for seasonal effects by the authors.[4]

For the Netherlands, ESA95 data on GDP and imports at constant and current prices are available from 1977q1, while time series on private final consumption started only in 1995. For the latter, the BIS private consumption deflator series, seasonally adjusted and starting in 1977q1, was used.

For the unemployment rate, Eurostat standardized unemployment rate series available on the OECD MEI database were used for all countries, with the exception of Italy, for which the series for unemployment in the Centre–North provided by Banca d'Italia was adopted.[5] Finally, data on total employment for all countries were taken from the OECD Quarterly Labour Force Statistics database. Trend unit labour costs time series were constructed as follows. First an estimate of whole economy productivity was derived as the ratio of real GDP to total employment. This series was smoothed with a Hodrick–Prescott filter to obtain a measure of trend productivity. Trend unit labour costs were then calculated as the ratio of wages (compensation per employee) to trend productivity. The consumption deflator was computed as the ratio of nominal to real private consumption expenditure, with the exception of the Netherlands, as mentioned above. The import deflator was obtained as the ratio of nominal to real imports of goods and services, for all countries.

In order to compare the results at the single-country level with those obtained at the area-wide level, the national data for trend unit labour costs, the consumption deflator, the import deflator, the unemployment rate described above were aggregated into area-wide variables.[6] For this purpose, we adopted the so-called index method: national nominal and price variables were transformed into logarithms and then aggregated using fixed weights, namely GDP at PPP exchange rates for 1995. These weights were also used to compute the area-wide unemployment rate. As stressed by Fagan and Henry (1998), this approach has the advantage of facilitating the comparison of results from area-wide and national equations.

EMPIRICAL EVIDENCE

Cross-correlations in the Independent Variables

As discussed in the introduction, the degree of correlation in the national independent variables is an important indicator of the extent to which aggregation biases may be relevant. To recap, the higher the degree of correlation in the movement of the independent variables at the national level, the smaller the expected magnitude of the aggregation bias. As shown in Table 8.1, which gives details of the correlations in the independent variables across countries, we generally find a positive and statistically significant correlation coefficient. In the case of the change in the log of trend unit labour costs the correlation coefficient is around 0.4 to 0.6 for France–Italy, France–Spain and Italy–Spain and highly statistically significant. The correlation coefficients for each country with respect to Germany are also positive, but lower in magnitude and not statistically significant. However, in the case of the Netherlands the correlation coefficients with the other countries are generally negative. The overall average of the correlation coefficients was 0.14. As for the unemployment gap, there is a significant and generally large positive correlation for all pairs of countries. The overall average correlation coefficient was 0.65. For the inflation variable, that is, the first difference of the log of the consumers' expenditure deflator, all correlation coefficients are positive, and most are statistically significant, with an overall average of 0.41. Finally in all cases there is a positive correlation in the change in the log of import price growth across the five countries, with the overall average being 0.32. In all but one case these correlation coefficients are statistically significant.[7]

The Aggregate Equation

We estimated an area-wide Phillips curve described in equation 8.1 using data obtained by aggregating the time series of the five countries. Prior to the estimation, we tested for stationarity of the unit labour cost growth and inflation time series by means of standard Augmented Dickey–Fuller tests. As the last two rows of Table 8.2 show, it is possible to reject the null hypothesis that both

Table 8.1   Correlation matrix for independent variables

	Germany	France	Italy	Netherlands	Spain
(a) Trend unit labour costs growth					
Germany	1.000	0.078	0.122	0.089	0.268
France		1.000	0.622***	–0.356***	0.404***
Italy			1.000	–0.350***	0.564***
Netherlands				1.000	–0.109
Spain					1.000
(b) Unemployment gap					
Germany	1.000	0.636***	0.748***	0.569***	0.764***
France		1.000	0.725***	0.239**	0.788***
Italy			1.000	0.638***	0.856***
Netherlands				1.000	0.560***
Spain					1.000
(c) Inflation					
Germany	1.000	0.346***	0.345***	0.198*	0.216*
France		1.000	0.884***	0.211*	0.775***
Italy			1.000	0.174	0.842***
Netherlands				1.000	0.139
Spain					1.000
(d) Change in import price growth					
Germany	1.000	0.363***	0.407***	0.391***	0.096
France		1.000	0.309***	0.405***	0.274**
Italy			1.000	0.390***	0.270**
Netherlands				1.000	0.265**
Spain					1.000

Note: *Significance at the 90% level; **at the 95% level; ***at the 99% level.

series have a unit root when an order of augmentation of the test of at least two is selected.

Having ascertained that the series were stationary, we searched for the preferred specification of the Phillips curve. Both Akaike and Schwartz selection criteria suggested the introduction of only one lagged value of the dependent variable among the regressors. As for the independent variables, the preferred specification was one that included three lags of price inflation, the current change in import price inflation. For the variable measuring the stance of the labour market, we followed Gordon (1997) in including the current value of the unemployment gap and, as a result of our specification search,

Table 8.2 Stationarity tests

Variable	ADF		ADF(1)		ADF(2)		ADF(3)		ADF(4)	
	c	c,t	c	c,t	c	c,t	c	c,t	c	c,t
France										
DULC	−4.36	−5.55	−3.07	−3.48	−2.86	−3.18	−3.41	−4.10	−3.07	−3.68
DPC	−3.89	−4.76	−4.04	−4.03	−3.97	−3.67	−4.37	−4.73	−4.68	−4.42
Germany										
DULC	−9.13	−9.34	−5.32	−5.52	−3.98	−4.19	−2.98	−3.18	−2.04	−2.22
DPC	−5.23	−5.18	−4.24	−4.21	−2.89	−2.87	−2.16	−2.13	−2.02	−1.98
Italy										
DULC	−4.79	−6.39	−3.78	−5.33	−3.02	−4.03	−2.85	−3.74	−2.73	−3.52
DPC	−2.80	−3.90	−2.64	−3.26	−2.85	−2.92	−2.95	−2.88	−2.83	−2.86
Netherlands										
DULC	−3.01	−3.72	−2.29	−2.91	−2.13	−2.77	−2.62	−3.39	−2.41	−3.23
DPC	−10.28	−10.36	−5.91	−5.91	−5.14	−5.14	−3.22	−3.23	−2.65	−2.64
Spain										
DULC	−5.50	−6.37	−3.58	−3.98	−3.37	−3.79	−3.24	−3.71	−2.69	−2.92
DPC	−3.19	−5.31	−2.33	−3.46	−2.21	−3.22	−2.18	−3.30	−2.12	−2.54
Aggregate										
DULC	−5.63	−7.31	−3.25	−4.28	−2.49	−3.27	−2.29	−2.99	−2.02	−2.50
DPC	−3.28	−3.88	−2.91	−3.31	−2.71	−2.61	−2.69	−2.57	−2.77	−2.50

Notes: For each lag, the two columns report the results of Dickey–Fuller regressions including an intercept (c) and including an intercept and a time trend (c,t), respectively. The 95% critical value for the ADF statistics is −2.9 in the regression (c) and −3.5 in the regression (c,t).

we chose not to enter first differences of the unemployment rate as an additional regressor capturing hysteresis effects. The final specification adopted was:

$$\Delta \mathrm{ln}ulc_t = a + bgap_t + c\Delta \mathrm{ln}ulc_{it-1} + \sum_{j=1}^{3} d_j \Delta \mathrm{ln}p_{cit-j}$$

$$+ e\Delta\Delta \mathrm{ln}pm_{it} + D84q2 + D91q2 + D98q1 + z_t \qquad (8.2)$$

where $D84q2$ and $D91q2$ are time dummy variables accounting for large outliers in German data. The first relates to a major period of industrial unrest while the second relates to reunification. The dummy variable labelled as $D98q1$ accounts instead for a break in the series of compensation of employees for Italy, due to the introduction of a new tax scheme (IRAP). In order to achieve nominal dynamic homogeneity in the long run, we imposed the restriction $c + d_1 + d_2 + d_3 = 1$.

The OLS estimates of the aggregate Phillips curve for the period 1982q1, 2000q4[8] are reported in the last column of Table 8.3. The unemployment gap term is correctly signed and significant with a coefficient of –0.0016.

The statistical properties of the model are quite satisfactory. The long-run homogeneity restriction is not rejected by the data. The goodness of fit is high, considering that the equation is specified in first differences and that the estimation period is quite long. The LM test for serial correlation shows that the chosen specification captures quite well the dynamic properties of the endogenous variable, while the RESET test supports the validity of the linear specification. The estimated equation exhibits no signs of heteroscedasticity. In order to verify whether the relationship linking nominal wage growth to inflation and the unemployment gap has undergone significant modifications during the estimation period, we followed two different strategies. First we estimated the equation up to 1998q1 and used the obtained coefficients to predict the wage growth pattern over the following two years. The Chow test for the adequacy of such predictions does not seem to signal the existence of a structural break in the relationship. Second, given that the timing of structural breaks cannot in general be established a priori, we performed a Hansen test aimed at detecting instability of a general form (which is approximately an LM test of the null of constant parameters against the alternative that they follow a martingale). The test was carried out on the overall equation and on some relevant parameters. As the last column of Table 8.4 shows, none of the parameters shows signs of instability and the statistic for the entire equation is well below the 5 per cent critical value.

Table 8.3 OLS estimation for individual countries and five-country aggregate

Variable	France	Germany	Italy	Netherlands	Spain	Aggregate
Constant	-0.0017 (2.98)	-0.0013 (1.55)	-0.0031 (3.42)	-0.0006 (1.32)	-0.0012 (1.57)	-0.0021 (4.91)
GAP	0.0001 (0.07)	-0.0037 (2.79)	-0.0014 (0.70)	-0.0027 (2.63)	-0.0019 (2.88)	-0.0016 (2.04)
$DULC_{t-1}$	0.2872 (2.16)	-0.1278 (1.50)	0.2085 (1.88)	0.7079 (9.37)	0.2408 (1.91)	0.0696 (0.75)
DPC_{t-1}	0.3326 (1.44)	0.3951 (2.37)	0.4203 (1.61)	0.1008 (1.73)	0.6244 (3.00)	0.5010 (2.79)
DPC_{t-2}	0.0329 (0.15)	0.1876 (0.93)	0.5068 (1.59)	0.0675 (1.20)	-0.1144 (0.57)	0.0723 (0.32)
DPC_{t-3}	0.3473 (2.25)	0.5451 (3.29)	-0.1356 (0.50)	0.1237 (2.11)	0.2493 (1.38)	0.3570 (2.11)
$DDPM_t$	0.0124 (0.44)	0.1324 (2.39)	0.0497 (1.47)	0.0019 (0.10)	-0.0568 (1.09)	0.0682 (2.22)
d84q2		-0.4107 (5.61)				-0.0176 (5.03)
d91q2		0.0337 (4.59)	-0.0283 (4.18)			0.0153 (4.38)
d98q1						-0.0062 (1.82)
$\bar{R}^2$	0.4864	0.6002	0.5646	0.5808	0.3651	0.6923
DW	2.0974	1.6625	1.9021	2.1314	2.1465	1.9138
SE	0.0044	0.0068	0.0066	0.0034	0.0061	0.0032
Homogeneity restriction – $\chi^2(1)$	5.6465 [0.017]	0.5097 [0.475]	2.1928 [0.139]	5.2967 [0.021]	9.6705 [0.002]	2.5692 [0.109]
A – Serial correlation – $\chi^2(4)$	15.8336 [0.003]	4.6366 [0.327]	2.5431 [0.637]	5.6370 [0.228]	7.0066 [0.136]	5.0731 [0.280]
B – Functional form – $\chi^2(1)$	2.8795 [0.090]	1.2975 [0.255]	0.3080 [0.579]	0.0496 [0.824]	3.2031 [0.073]	0.4721 [0.492]
C – Normality – $\chi^2(2)$	1.2284 [0.541]	0.3772 [0.828]	0.1249 [0.939]	1.3269 [0.515]	0.3238 [0.851]	1.8520 [0.396]
D – Heteroscedasticity – $\chi^2(1)$	5.3481 [0.021]	0.1826 [0.669]	1.3452 [0.246]	2.3690 [0.124]	0.4509 [0.502]	1.2277 [0.268]
E – Predictive failure $\chi^2(8)$	11.4063 [0.180]	7.2976 [0.505]	1.6240 [0.990]	4.9867 [0.759]	3.1129 [0.927]	7.6699 [0.466]
F – Chow test $\chi^2(6)$	11.2071 [0.082]			4.0573 [0.669]	2.9360 [0.817]	

Notes:

Parentheses show absolute values of t-statistics, square brackets show the significance level of the reported tests.

A: Lagrange multiplier tests of residual serial correlation.

B: Ramsey's RESET test using the square of fitted values.

C: Based on a test of skewness and kurtosis of residuals.

D: Based on the regression of square residuals on squared fitted values.

E: Test of adequacy of predictions for 1999:1–2000:4 based on the estimates for the period up to 1998:4 (Chow second test).

F: Test for stability of the regression coefficients for 1999:1–2000:4 based on the estimates for the period up to 1998:4 (Chow first test).

Table 8.4   Hansen stability tests for individual countries and five-country aggregate OLS equations

Variable	France	Germany	Italy	Netherlands	Spain	Aggregate
Equation	2.655	3.025	1.034	1.676	1.618	1.783
GAP_t	0.384	0.078	0.088	0.679	0.132	0.055
$DULC_{t-1}$	0.274	0.094	0.086	0.081	0.097	0.066
DPC_{t-1}	0.074	0.254	0.129	0.477	0.062	0.176
DPC_{t-2}	0.039	0.062	0.122	0.486	0.036	0.139
DPC_{t-3}	0.074	0.099	0.117	0.280	0.093	0.130
$DDPM_t$	0.225	0.199	0.316	0.084	0.113	0.092

Notes:
The 5% critical values are 0.470 for individual coefficients and 2.110 for the whole equation.
The test for Germany and for the aggregate was run without including the dummy variables.

The National Equations

Having investigated the stationarity properties of the national series of trend unit labour cost growth and inflation (see Table 8.2), we estimated equation (8.1) for each single country. The results of the OLS regressions are reported in the first five columns of Table 8.3. Excluding the case of France, the unemployment gap always has the expected negative coefficient, ranging from –0.0014 in Italy to –0.0037 in Germany. For France and Italy the coefficient is not significantly different from zero. For the other countries, the statistical significance of the unemployment gap coefficient is quite high, as it has a *t*-statistic in the range of 2.6–2.9.

As each national model is specified exactly as the one chosen for the aggregate equation, its performance varies quite widely across countries. The estimated equation performs quite poorly in the case of France, showing signs of residual autocorrelation and heteroscedasticity, but reasonably well for the remaining countries. Hansen tests (reported in the first five columns of Table 8.4) point to a certain degree of instability of the overall equation for France and Germany, although the result for the latter is driven by the necessity to exclude the dummy variables from the specification for carrying out the test. In the case of the Netherlands the test finds evidence of instability for the unemployment gap coefficient. Conversely, Chow tests for stability of the regression coefficients for 1999: 1 – 2000:4 and predictive failure tests based on estimates for the period up to 1998:4 both reject the hypothesis of a structural break at the start of Stage 3 of EMU.

Table 8.5 gives details of the cross-correlation matrix of the national OLS residuals. In general there is somewhat mixed evidence on the co-movement of these residuals, but in almost all cases the results are not statistically significant. The correlation coefficients for the residuals of the German equations and each of the other countries are negative except in the case of Italy. A negative pattern

Table 8.5   Correlation matrix for the residuals from the national OLS equations

	Germany	France	Italy	Netherlands	Spain
Germany	1.000	–0.141	0.139	–0.115	–0.202*
France		1.000	0.012	0.309***	–0.031
Italy			1.000	0.066	0.101
Netherlands				1.000	–0.126
Spain					1.000

Note: *Significant at the 90% level; **at the 95% level; ***at the 99% level.

emerges also for the correlation coefficients for the residuals of Netherlands–Spain and France–Spain. It appears that there is some sign of a small mutual positive correlation in the other residuals, although the coefficients are nearly all below 0.3. The lack of a strong positive correlation in the residuals means that the aggregate equation should benefit from the statistical averaging effect described in the introduction, leading to a lower standard error than is present in the typical national equation.

System Estimation: Imposing Restrictions across Countries

The national Phillips curves were then estimated together as a panel system with fixed effects and (following Turner and Seghezza, 1999) tested for the imposition of a common unemployment gap term across countries.[9] As this assumption was not rejected by the data, it was imposed and the results reported in Table 8.6. Overall, the pattern of results is similar to the individual OLS regressions. The main notable improvement is an increase in the significance of the unemployment gap term which, at –0.002, is slightly larger than in the aggregate equation.

It is noteworthy that this finding of a common parameter on the unemployment gap for these countries finds some support from other studies. Morgan and Mourougane (2001), who estimate a panel system including a structural wage and labour demand equation for the same five countries and in addition the UK, find that it is possible to impose a common unemployment parameter. Turner and Seghezza (1999), who estimate a Phillips curve with an output gap variable using a SURE system, also find that it is possible to impose a common coefficient for the gap variable for a wide group of OECD countries.

Although the restriction required for the long-run nominal dynamic homogeneity in the wage–price system was imposed in all countries, we did not investigate the extent to which it would be possible to impose a common price dynamics, that is, common coefficients on trend unit labour cost, consumer and import prices. It is clear from the tables that although it may be possible to group individual parameters in some countries, it is highly unlikely to be possible to group them all given the range of outcomes reported in the tables (as for some of them the estimated coefficients are positive and significant while for others they are negative and significant).

In-sample Properties

Despite the generally satisfactory nature of the area-wide equation, as Dedola et al. (2001) point out, it is necessary to compare its residuals with those obtained by aggregating the residuals from the national equations. For this

Table 8.6   Restricted pooled estimation for individual countries

Variable	France		Germany		Italy		Netherlands		Spain	
Constant	-0.0017	(-2.22)	-0.0013	(-1.90)	-0.0032	(-4.09)	-0.0005	(-0.74)	-0.0012	(-1.71)
GAP_t	-0.0020	(-4.39)	-0.0020	(-4.39)	-0.0020	(-4.39)	-0.0020	(-4.39)	-0.0020	(-4.39)
$DULC_{t-1}$	0.3218	(1.90)	-0.0866	(-1.31)	0.1995	(2.19)	0.7357	(6.73)	0.2306	(2.09)
DPC_{t-1}	0.2384	(0.82)	0.4040	(2.93)	0.4205	(1.91)	0.0926	(0.97)	0.6283	(3.29)
DPC_{t-2}	0.0732	(0.27)	0.1613	(0.96)	0.5084	(1.89)	0.0553	(0.61)	-0.1117	(-0.61)
DPC_{t-3}	0.3666	(1.85)	0.5213	(3.81)	-0.1284	(-0.57)	0.1164	(1.21)	0.2528	(1.53)
$DDPM_t$	0.0102	(0.28)	0.1310	(2.86)	0.0490	(1.72)	0.0000	(0.00)	-0.0587	(-1.24)
d84q2			-0.0422	(-7.00)						
d91q2			0.0362	(6.15)						
d98q1					-0.0284	(-4.96)				
$\bar{R}^2$	0.6232									
SE	0.0056									

$\chi 2(4)$ test for the equality of the coefficient of GAP_t for all countries = 5.0855 [p-value=0.279]

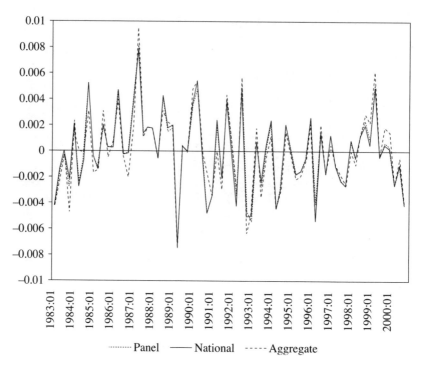

Figure 8.1   Residuals from the aggregate, national and panel equations

purpose we have aggregated the national residuals derived from the estimation exercises (both single OLS and system estimates) described in the first part of this section, using the same weights adopted to construct the area-wide variables. Figure 8.1 compares the aggregated residuals from the single OLS and the restricted system estimation with the residuals from the area-wide equation. Table 8.7 also gives details of the respective standard errors. Both the table and the graph clearly show that the volatility of the area-wide residuals is slightly higher than that of the aggregated national ones. In particular the OLS single-country estimation seems to generate residuals that, once aggregated, provide the lowest standard error. According to the test of Grunfeld and Griliches (1960), this provides grounds for selecting the disaggregate model over the aggregate one. However, it should be noted that the differences in the standard errors are not particularly large – ranging from 0.29 per cent for the aggregated national equations to 0.30 per cent for the system and the aggregate approach. The difference of 0.01 per cent compares with an average quarterly change in aggregate unit labour costs of 0.7 per cent over the estimation period.

Table 8.7   Standard error of residuals

National OLS	0.0029
Restricted pooled system	0.0030
Aggregate OLS	0.0030

Forecast Properties

The last part of this empirical section focuses on the performance of our Phillips curves in forecasting aggregate trend unit labour costs. More precisely, we investigate the out-of-sample forecast properties of the area-wide equation as compared with the aggregation of the out-of-sample forecasts based on the national equations. It should be emphasized that the results presented here should be seen as simple tests of the performance of the equations analysed thus far in this chapter and are not the outcome of a careful fine-tuning of equations providing optimal forecasts of area-wide wage growth.

The approach to out-of-sample forecasting that we adopt here is that of Staiger et al. (1997), based on recursive least squares. This approach provides a consistent way to evaluate real-time forecasting performance, since at each point in time the forecast is truly out of sample. We examined what forecasts would have been made during each quarter from the start of 1999 to the end of 2000 based on quarterly data for the period from 1982q1 up to the quarter when the forecast was made, by estimating our equations on actual data over the same time period.[10] For example, for 1999q1 we estimated the equation up to this quarter, we derived a forecast for the next four quarters, and we saved the 1-, 2-, 3- and 4-step-ahead forecast errors. The process was then repeated for 1999q2, using data up to that date and a new set of 1-, 2-, 3- and 4-step-ahead errors was saved. Having repeated this exercise recursively until the quarter before the last (that is, 2000q3), we computed the mean absolute error (MAE), the root mean square error (RMSE) and the Theil's U-statistics (U) for 1-, 2-, 3- and 4-step-ahead errors (Table 8.8).[11]

Table 8.8 is divided into two panels. The first is based on forecast errors generated by aggregating the five national wage growth forecasts; the second panel refers instead to the forecasting performance of the area-wide equation. In both cases the equations used to compute each forecast have exactly the same specification as those adopted in the OLS exercise described above.

Both the RMSE and the Theil's U-statistic are lower in the top panel for the first two rows, corresponding to the forecasts for 1 and 2 steps ahead. However, the better forecasting performance of the national equations is not maintained for the 3- and 4-step-ahead forecasts. Hence the results presented

Table 8.8   Out-of-sample recursive forecasts of aggregate wage growth

	Mean absolute error	Root mean squared error	Theil-*U*
Steps ahead		National equations	
1	0.0023	0.0031	0.9389
2	0.0027	0.0031	0.9934
3	0.0021	0.0026	1.2059
4	0.002	0.0024	0.7320
Steps ahead		Aggregate equations	
1	0.0027	0.0033	0.9854
2	0.0028	0.0033	1.0478
3	0.0021	0.0024	1.1079
4	0.0020	0.0024	0.7097

Note:
Theil-*U* is computed as the ratio of the root mean square error to the root mean square error of a 'naïve' forecast of no change in the dependent variable.

in the table indicate that if one had used the Phillips curve to forecast aggregate trend unit labour cost growth since the start of 1999, then such a variable would have been better predicted if one had relied on national equations and then aggregated the results rather than adopting an area-wide specification. However, if one had wished to predict the rate of growth of trend unit labour costs more than six months ahead, then there would have been no benefit in using national equations. The gain from using the national equations, in terms of lower RMSEs, was 0.02 for both the 1- and 2-period-ahead forecasts. This compares with an average quarter-on-quarter growth rate in the variable about 0.3 per cent over the forecast horizon.

In specifying the Phillips curve, we have so far computed the NAIRU in each country and at the area-wide level as a smoothed version of observed unemployment. In order to check the robustness of the results, we also considered an alternative framework, based on the assumption that the NAIRU is constant over the whole time horizon. In other words, we modelled trend unit labour cost growth as depending on the actual unemployment rate instead of the unemployment gap.[12] The pattern of results obtained under this alternative hypothesis framework was very similar to that described above, as are the standard errors for both the aggregated and aggregate results. However, under the hypothesis of constant NAIRU the forecasting ability of the area-wide equation was markedly worse than when using a time-varying NAIRU. Although the performance of the national equations also worsened when using a constant NAIRU, the deterioration in the forecast performance of the area-wide equation was much more marked.[13]

CONCLUSIONS

At the start of this chapter we set out to find information to help answer three questions. The first was the extent to which the relationship between wages and productivity growth, inflation and the tightness of the labour market is similar in the large euro area countries. Our analysis suggests that freely estimated Phillips curves do generate different estimates of the impact of the rate of unemployment on wage formation. However, when estimated jointly in a panel system, these differences do not prove to be statistically significant and it is possible to impose a common unemployment gap effect. Nevertheless, many national idiosyncrasies remain, which, within the reduced-form equation considered in this chapter, are captured by the constant and by the dynamic pattern of consumer and import prices.

The second question related to the potential gains and losses from pursuing aggregate as opposed to country-level analysis of such relationships. As discussed in the early part of the chapter, the value of area-wide analysis is enhanced if there is a similarity in parameters across the national equations, a high positive correlation between the independent variables and a negative correlation between the residuals from the national equations. As already indicated, the evidence on the common parameters was mixed, with it being possible to impose a restriction on the unemployment gap parameter. All the other unit labour cost and price variables as well as the constant showed marked differences across countries. It is also noteworthy that for most of the independent variables we found evidence of positive and statistically significant cross-country correlations. Overall there did not appear to be evidence of strong correlation – either positive or negative – in the residuals from the national equations. In addition, to shed further light on this second question we estimated an aggregate unit labour cost equation and compared the results with the aggregation of results from the national equations. Although the statistical properties of the area-wide equation were quite good overall, its standard error was slightly higher than the aggregated standard errors from the national equations, estimated both independently and as a system.

The third question was if, since the start of EMU, country-based or area-wide analysis had been used to forecast aggregate unit labour cost growth, which would have performed better? We found that if the Phillips curves developed in this chapter had been used, then this variable would have been slightly better predicted if the national approach had been adopted and the results aggregated. However, the gains from the disaggregate approach tended to disappear as the forecast horizon lengthened. One caveat here is that, if a constant rather than the time-varying NAIRU computed by the OECD is assumed, the relative forecast performance of the area-wide approach deteriorates further.

Overall, our results point to some limited advantages from estimating wage–price Phillips curves at the national level rather than conducting the analysis at the area-wide level. Most notably the standard errors and the 1-period-ahead out-of-sample forecasts from the aggregated national equations are found to be lower than those from the area-wide equation. However, the differences between the forecast errors disappear at longer horizons (3–4 periods ahead). Furthermore, some support for adopting an area-wide approach in Phillips-curves-based analysis stems from the fact that it proved possible to impose a common coefficient on the unemployment gap across countries and that there is some positive correlation in the movements of some of the national independent variables.

These results are open to different interpretations. In support of the aggregate approach, it could be argued that the key finding is the common unemployment coefficient. The other coefficients – on lagged prices – reflect expectations formation and the properties of the inflation process, which clearly differed markedly across countries in the past. Given the move to monetary union, we may expect a tendency towards a common inflation process and convergence of expectations formation. In other words, the coefficients on lagged inflation may become more similar across countries over time. Therefore the relative position of the aggregate approach may improve over time. Alternatively it could be argued that the simple models used in the chapter do not do justice to the more sophisticated, detailed type of analysis which could be carried out at the national level. Indeed, one of the key advantages of national as opposed to aggregate analysis may lie in the possibility of taking account of country-specific features in the specification of the Phillips curves, rather than adopting a common specification as we do here. Hence the results may provide only a lower-bound estimate of the likely superiority of bottom-up versus top-down approaches to area-wide labour market analysis. Nevertheless, our results suggest that if major advantages in undertaking national analysis do exist, they are likely to arise from the ability to develop country-specific structures for the Phillips curves and not from aggregation biases that emerge when a common structure is used.

NOTES

1. The authors' affiliations are, respectively, Banca d'Italia and the European Central Bank. The opinions expressed are those of the authors and are not necessarily those of the Banca d'Italia or the European Central Bank.
2. This chapter was presented as a paper at the 3rd ECB Labour Market Workshop, held in Frankfurt, 10–11 December 2001. We thank, without implicating, Olivier de Bandt, Michael Burda, Gabriel Fagan, Dennis Snower and other participants in the workshop for helpful comments and suggestions.
3. For a detailed explanation of the implications of the assumption of long-run homogeneity, see Fabiani and Mestre (2000).

4. Using the package available in the FAME software.
5. As a first attempt we tried to model the Phillips curve by computing the unemployment gap on the basis of the national unemployment rate, as in the other countries. This variable however performed very poorly, in line with the claim often made in the literature on the subject, that the strong regional segmentation of the Italian labour market implies that unemployment in the northern regions is the main factor affecting the bargaining process and hence the determination of wages in Italy (see also Fabiani at al., 1997, Turner and Seghezza, 1999).
6. For the main methods of constructing consistent aggregate data from disaggregate ones, see Fagan and Henry (1998).
7. It should be noted that these correlations relate to the variables as used in the equation. In their raw form the correlation coefficients are generally much higher – in fact in the case of wages and the consumers' expenditure deflator they range from 0.96 to 0.99.
8. This was the longest period for which data were available for all countries.
9. Another approach would have been to implement a seemingly unrelated regression estimation (SURE). However, for such an approach to have been worth while there would need to have been a clear sign that there was a correlation in the residuals from the national equations.
10. When running the n-steps-ahead forecasts, we used autoregressive processes (with four lags and a constant) to generate subsequent observations for the regressors (inflation, unemployment, the NAIRU and the change in the import deflator).
11. The Theil's U-statistic is a unit-free measure computed as the ratio of the root mean square error to the root mean square error of the 'naïve' forecast of no change in the dependent variable. A value of zero implies no forecast error.
12. The constant NAIRU then forms a part of the constant.
13. Full results using the constant NAIRU are available upon request from the authors.

REFERENCES

Dedola, L., E. Gaiotti and L. Silipo (2001), 'Money demand in the euro area: do national differences matter?', *Temi di Discussione*, Bank of Italy Working Paper No. 405.

Fabiani, S. and R. Mestre (2000), *Alternative Estimates of the NAIRU in the Euro Area: Estimates and Assessment*, ECB Working Paper No. 17.

Fabiani, S. and R. Mestre (2001), *A System Approach for Measuring the Euro Area NAIRU*, ECB Working Paper No 65.

Fagan, G. and J. Henry (1998), 'Long run money demand in the EU: evidence from area-wide aggregates', *Empirical Economics*, **23**, 483–506.

Gordon, R. (1997), 'The time-varying NAIRU and its implications for economic policy', *Journal of Economic Perspectives*, **11** (1), 11–32.

Grunfeld, Y. and Z. Griliches (1960), 'Is aggregation necessarily bad?', *The Review of Economics and Statistics*, **17**, 1–13.

Hansen, B.E. (1994), 'Testing for parameter instability in linear models', in N.R. Ericsson and J.S. Irons (eds), *Testing Exogeneity*, Oxford: Oxford University Press.

Morgan, J. and A. Mourougane (2001), *What can Changes in Structural Factors Tell us about Unemployment in Europe*, ECB Working Paper No. 81.

OECD (2000), 'Could aggregation be misleading?', in *EMU One Year on*, Paris: OECD.

Staiger, D., J.H. Stock and M.W. Watson (1997), 'The NAIRU, unemployment and monetary policy', *Journal of Economic Perspectives*, **11** (1), 33–49.

Turner, D. and E. Seghezza (1999), *Testing for a Common OECD Phillips Curve*, OECD Economics Department Working Paper No. 219.

9. Wage flexibility in Britain: Some micro and macro evidence

Mark E. Schweitzer[*]

INTRODUCTION

The flexibility of wages is a commonly cited reason for weaker inflation pressures in the 1990s, but the concept is generally left imprecise. Notably the microeconomic and macroeconomic concepts of wage flexibility are very distinct, though potentially related. Macroeconomic flexibility is conventionally defined as a larger wage response for a given unemployment rate in a Phillips curve, based on the elimination of factors contributing to sluggish wage adjustment (like micro-level wage rigidities). Microeconomic flexibility is conventionally defined as a lack of evidence for wage rigidities, notably a lack of a spike in wage change distributions at zero. The abundance of zero wage changes presumably reflects some hindrance in the accuracy and speed of wage adjustment.

This chapter uses a very detailed British data source (the New Earnings Survey) that allows micro and macro measures of wage rigidities to be calculated. In addition, because the data span 1975 to 2000, the time pattern of the micro- and macro-flexibility measures can be compared. For each test (macro- or microeconometric), we will also address whether the evidence has shifted over time. This is a very limited form of agreement between macro and micro definitions of wage flexibility, but even this is a challenge for wage flexibility measures.

For many policy issues establishing the current status of the economy is critical, although the history is interesting as the source of conventional views. To keep the analysis simple we evaluate whether there has been a one-time shift in the parameters of interest.

This permanent change in wage-setting patterns can be motivated by a variety of factors, although two stand out. The institutional arrangements for employment in the UK have clearly changed.[1] Evidence from the Workplace Employee Relations Survey (Cully et al., 2000) results clearly document the decline of private sector unions and substantial shifts in work patterns, like flexible hours and the rise of the service sector.[2] The other factor that cannot be ignored in wage-setting is the change in the UK's monetary policy arrangements. The form of wage contracts might have changed in response to the low and stable inflation rates of the late 1990s. Separating these factors is beyond the scope of this chapter, because either might have substantial and uncertain lagged effects on the wage-setting process.

Since this chapter compares alternative definitions of wage flexibility, the existing literature is reviewed throughout. A substantial part of this chapter involves showing what these alternatives reveal in a consistent data set for Great Britain. Many of our results are only new for the UK or update existing work, but comparing the results in a consistent data set does expose the importance of some methodological differences. In addition, the 'facts' of the UK labour market are open to interpretation and the existing results have not always agreed.

One area where this chapter offers a new approach is the exploration of real wage rigidities from a microeconomic perspective. This research was driven by the fact that spikes were evident in the distribution at points well above zero, the focus of the nominal rigidities literature. A modified Kahn (1997) approach reveals that these spikes and distributional anomalies around the inflation rate are statistically significant.

The chapter will next describe the data before going on to the macro evidence and micro evidence on pay rigidities.

THE NEW EARNINGS SURVEY PANEL DATA SET

The New Earnings Survey panel data set[3] is an exceptional source of information on wages. The survey covers a random 1 per cent sample of British workers based on two digits of their National Insurance (NI) number. Because NI numbers do not change and are always used when income is reported to the tax authorities, individuals can be followed if they change employers and residences within Britain. This feature makes the data set preferable to household-based panel data sets, where following individuals who change addresses can be difficult or is not attempted.

The survey is sent to the employers of these individuals, who are instructed to report the identified individuals' current earnings each April. In addition, employers report on several key pay determinants for the relevant pay period: the hours of work on which the pay is based, the number of paid overtime hours, whether pay was reduced due to absence and whether any bonuses were paid. Also, the firm reports whether the individual's 'job' has changed since the previous year. The individual's job may change in the firm without a new occupation code or a change of firms, so wage changes can be analysed for persons continuing in the same position within a firm. These features enable calculation of an unusually pure measure of base pay, free from several of the common sources of error.

Employers also report the individuals' sex, age, occupation, industry, place of work and whether a collective agreement or a wage council covers their pay. The occupation and industry codes change over the sample period. Helpfully, in the year of the largest change to the occupation coding system (1995) individuals' occupations were coded in both the old and new scheme. To construct consistent occupation codes, these were matched at the three-digit level and aggregated on both sides until the resulting codes were the most likely correspondence to both the old and the new codes. In most cases, the vast majority of individuals within a code do not change their constructed 'consistent' code when the new coding scheme is put into effect.

Despite the straightforward design of the survey, there is a tendency to undercount low-wage workers and workers in smaller firms. This tendency has been documented in Stuttard and Jenkins (2001). Under-sampling occurs in part because individuals whose wages are below a threshold are excluded from the tax system and thus no address is provided for their employer. Also, despite the ability to follow workers using tax records, a sizeable fraction of surveys are returned uncompleted because the employee no longer works for that organization. Overall, about 24 per cent of the potential records are not available, with the largest categories being a change of employer (8.7 per cent), survey not returned (5.8 per cent) and out of scope (3.7 per cent).[4]

These data losses are not likely to alter the qualitative results of this analysis. There may be a tendency for low-wage workers to be more likely to be exposed to wage rigidities, if their industries tend to small wage increases. Alternatively, low-wage workers and those who change employers may be more likely to have substantial wage changes because they are earlier in their careers or are changing contracts. To the extent that wage-setting behaviours are present for groups that are surveyed, the primary loss will be in getting the level wage rigidities wrong. Trends should be robust because the sample losses do not vary much over time.

MACRO EVIDENCE ON WAGE FLEXIBILITY

The simplest characterization of the macroeconomic wage-setting behaviour is a wage curve or wage equation. Theoretical models show where some of the key macroeconomic influences enter into wage-setting, but they do not particularly restrict the form of the relationship that is estimated. This leaves the literature primarily based on empirical relationships. The literature on whether the best estimate of the wage response to unemployment is a wage curve or a Phillips curve is extensive, but not conclusive in that both functional forms are still estimated.[5] At a micro level most of the tests are directly focused on wage changes, as wage levels are determined by a wide variety of idiosyncratic factors that are largely unchanged from year to year and which are accounted for in the previous year's wage.

Figure 9.1 shows the relationship between claimant count unemployment rates and wages changes in Great Britain. The wage rate shown controls for change in the composition of the workforce over time, following the approach of Bell, Nickell and Quintini (2000), hereafter referred to as BNQ.[6] The graph shows periods, for example 1980 to 1985, when the traditional Phillips curve relationship appears to hold. The prolonged period of the current expansion when the inflation rate was steady or dropping in tandem with falling unemployment is more difficult to account for. This is the period of time where an increasing degree of wage flexibility may be a potential explanation for the breakdown of the Phillips relationship.

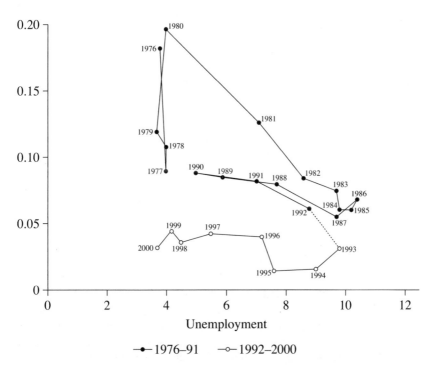

Source: Author's calculations from 2001 NES panel data set. Wage rate is adjusted for human capital differences.

Figure 9.1   Adjusted wages and unemployment: Great Britain

Wage Equations, Wage Curves and All That

Wage inflation and the unemployment rate show considerable variation across regions in the UK, which allows regional variation to refine the estimation of models of wage inflation. In *Wage Equations, Wage Curves, and All That*, Bell, Nickell and Quintini (2000) measure flexibility in the context of regressions of regional wages and/or wage changes on regional unemployment rates and panel regression controls. Their paper is focused on comparing alternative specifications of the relationship between wages and unemployment. The BNQ paper is highly relevant for establishing the UK baseline because their estimates show the value of applying regional estimates, are very recent (through 1996) and use the same data source (NES Panel).

The approach to adjusting the regional wages throughout this chapter follows that of BNQ. A model of wages is estimated using individual-level data on the workers' characteristics with a set of region cross-year effects, which become our adjusted mean wage figures for the region.

$$w_{ijt} = \alpha_{jt} + \gamma X_{it} + \varepsilon_{it}$$

where w_{ijt} is individual i's in region j wage level at time t, α_{jt} accounts for regional pay differences in each year, and X_{it} are the individuals' observed characteristics.[7] The coefficients on the region cross-time intercepts are the average wage rates after controlling for human capital.

Second-stage regressions use the α_{jt} estimated in the first stage as their dependent variables. The control variables are the lagged dependent variable, regional unemployment rates and general panel controls for time and region. In its most detailed form the wage curve regression is as follows:

$$\alpha_{jt} = \beta_1 \alpha_{jt-1} + \beta_2 \ln u_{jt} + \delta_j \mathbf{D}_j + \delta_t \mathbf{D}_t + \delta_{2j}(\mathbf{D}_t \cdot t) + \upsilon_{jt}$$

where u_{jt} is the region j claimant count unemployment rate, $\mathbf{D}_j$ and $\mathbf{D}_t$ are vectors of dummy variables for regions and time. The last term is a vector of region specific time trends, to account for steady changes between regions. With these controls, no additional explanatory power is gained by including variables that vary only between regions or across time, as this variation can be fully absorbed by the fixed effects. For example, there would be no difference in the R^2 or coefficients of interest if national inflation rates or productivity growth were added as controls in this regression. This regression repeated as a wage change simply imposes $\beta_1 = -1$ and moves the α_{jt-1} term over to the left-hand side of the equation.

$$\omega_{jt} \equiv \alpha_{ij} - \alpha_{jt-1} = \beta_2 \ln u_{jt} + \delta_j \mathbf{D}_j + \delta_t \mathbf{D}_t + \delta_{2jt}(\mathbf{D}_t \cdot t) + \upsilon_{jt}$$

Table 9.1   Adjusted regional wages and unemployment

	Log wage rate		Log wage changes	
Lagged regional log wage	0.7942	0.9150		
	(0.0617)	(0.0317)		
ln(unemployment rate)	–0.0143	–0.0058	–0.0079	–0.0073
	(0.0051)	(0.0042)	(0.0050)	(0.0043)
Region dummies	$p = 0.00$	$p = 0.01$	$p = 0.46$	$p = 0.39$
Region trends	$p = 0.15$		$p = 0.00$	
Time dummies	$p = 0.00$	$p = 0.00$	$p = 0.00$	$p = 0.00$
N	10	10	10	10
NT	250	250	250	250
R^2	0.9999	0.9999	0.9847	0.9842

Source: Author's calculations using 2001 NES panel data set.

Our estimates extend the data set through 2000 and include both male and female earners. Not surprisingly the results are close to BNQ's findings for men. Table 9.1 shows baseline regressions for a few of the specifications tested in BNQ.[8] In all cases, the standard errors have been adjusted for contemporaneously correlated errors across panels. The log unemployment rate has a negative coefficient in all of these regressions, but it is not always significant. The coefficient on the log of the unemployment rate is somewhat lower in these estimates than in BNQ, but the overall conclusions are similar. Their preferred specification is with a lagged dependent variable and regional trends. This specification shows the clearest relationship between unemployment and wages in our estimates as well.

The wage curve (levels) specification rejects (at a 5 per cent significance level) a coefficient of 1 on the lagged dependent variable favouring the wage curve specification. We are not focusing on this issue, so we favour the wage curve specification only because it seems to be statistically more precise on the relationship between regional wages and unemployment rates. None the less, wage equations (the specification with wage changes as the dependent variable) are also estimated to make the differences between BNQ and Staiger, Stock and Watson's (2001) approach more clearly delineated.

Both the region and time dummy variables are doing a substantial amount of work in these regressions. Both are generally significant at the 1 per cent level, which indicates the importance that general controls have in identifying this relationship. The controls for regional trends sometimes reduce the significance of the fixed regional dummies, but it is logical to include the intercept shifters as a baseline when trend variation is seen. In any case, regional trends help make the unemployment/wage relationship statistically significant. This could be due to substantial regional productivity trends that are evident in the UK data, which will be more directly explored in the next section.

In the wage curve (or wage equation) framework, wages are said to have become more flexible if their response to unemployment increases. They test whether the responsiveness of wages to unemployment is larger in the second half of their sample (1988 to 1996) and find evidence that wages are more flexible in the later portion of the sample.

Given the minor differences between our results and BNQ's results reported in Table 9.1, the results of these wage flexibility tests might appear to be a foregone conclusion. This is not the case, as the flexibility estimators put a lot of emphasis on the time variation provided by the added four years in our sample: a period of low inflation rates and unemployment declines. Table 9.2 shows results of break-point regressions on wage levels and changes including regional trends. The indicators of a change in flexibility are generally statistically significant, but the sign of the interaction indicates that labour markets have become less flexible. Wage responses to unemployment are unambiguously lower when the later period is from 1992 to 2000 in any of the specifications suggested Phillips curves shown earlier.

While 1992 (the beginning of the expansion) is a logical point to break the sample based on Figure 9.1, it is still arbitrary and may be the source of the difference between our results and those reported in BNQ. Figure 9.2 shows the full set of results of moving the potential break-point in the data from 1981 to 1996. This figure shows the parameters estimated in a sequence of regressions following Table 9.2 (column 1) with alternative dates for the change in

Table 9.2   Adjusted regional wages and unemployment

	Log wage rate	Log wage change
Lagged regional log wage	0.7707	
	(0.0573)	
ln(unemployment rate)	–0.0131	–0.0065
	(0.0044)	(0.0047)
Post 1992*	0.0170	0.0121
ln(unemployment rate)	(0.0048)	(0.0056)
N	10	10
NT	250	250
R^2	0.9999	0.9850

Source: Author's calculations using 2001 NES panel data set.

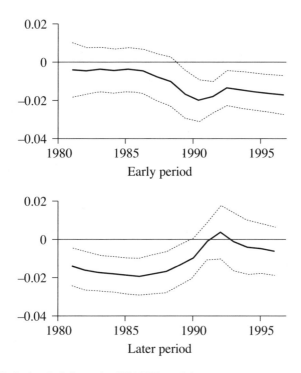

Source: Author's calculations using 2001 NES panel data set.

Figure 9.2 Coefficient stability in BNQ model: alternative break-points

wage-setting patterns. The left-hand panel shows the expected response to unemployment rates in earlier portions of the data, defined by the year of the break shown on the x-axis. The right-hand panel shows the response after the date of the break. The standard error bands shown are for 95 per cent confidence ranges. Choosing an earlier break-point in the data yields coefficients that are more negative in the later period than in the early data. This result is reversed for any break-point after 1988.

One possible explanation for this result is that productivity gains in some regions have offset the anticipated wage response in a pattern not picked up by the regional trend terms. Of course, it is also possible that there are insufficient data available for the current expansion to identify the response of detailed wages to unemployment. Tentatively, 1991 stands out as the point where wage-setting changes might have had an impact on the wage curve, but this change is not consistent with the standard macroeconomic definition of greater wage flexibility.

Building in Productivity Growth and Inflation

The general panel controls used in BNQ suggest some factors that could be controlled for: notably productivity and inflation. Simply adding these controls to the regressions often makes the results more confusing due to the fact that these other controls are likely to have substantial errors-in-variable problems. Smoothing the series can help to solve these problems, which is part of the approach followed by Staiger, Stock and Watson (2001), hereafter referred to as SSW.

SSW use panel regression on US states to estimate a US Phillips curve.[9] Their approach is also suitable for evaluating when the labour market might be more flexible. Their implicit measure of the NAIRU should respond to the wage structure becoming more flexible. Compared to BNQ, the underlying motivation is similar, but these authors impose more restrictions on the functional form of the relationship by starting with real unit labour costs. Their primary analysis is based on the following form:

$$\omega_{jt} - \rho_{it} - \pi_{jt} = \beta u_{jt-1} + \delta_j D_j + \delta_t D_t + \upsilon_{jt}$$

where ω is the nominal wage, deflated by current productivity growth (ρ) and inflation (π). Note that the regional trend is dropped from the specification, because the primary reason for including a trend – regional productivity patterns – is now directly accounted for.

Table 9.3 shows panel estimates for SSW-style wage equations across ten British regions. There are several ways in which these estimates might differ

Table 9.3   Wage growth beyond inflation and productivity growth

	Regional productivity growth		UK productivity growth	
Unemployment rate	–0.25	–0.21	–0.18	–0.18
	(0.07)	(0.05)	(0.04)	(0.04)
Second half of sample*			0.21	0.02
Unemployment rate			(0.05)	(0.04)
Region dummies	$p = 0.00$	$p = 0.02$	$p = 0.01$	$p = 0.06$
Time dummies	$p = 0.00$	$p = 0.00$	$p = 0.00$	$p = 0.00$
N	10	10	10	10
NT	240	240	250	250
R^2	0.93	0.93	0.96	0.96

Source: Author's calculations using 2001 NES panel data set.

substantially from the US estimates other than the substantive differences between the US and UK labour markets. Because we have detailed claimant count information by region, the unemployment rate is not affected by the sampling variation of the Current Population Survey-based measures, which are highly variable in small states. We do not smooth these figures, as we are confident that they accurately reflect conditions within each region. On the other hand productivity figures are difficult to calculate for UK regions and do vary substantially from period to period. We smooth these estimates using a Hodrick–Prescott filter, which yields a smooth, time-varying estimate similar to the Kalman filter used in SSW.

As a check on the importance of regional productivity figures, these regressions are also run using wages adjusted for the smoothed, national trend in productivity growth. These calculations are the best parallel with BNQ, because the time dummies in BNQ would absorb national productivity figures even when they are excluded. The coefficient on unemployment will be different primarily because (as in SSW) the unemployment rate is not entered in logs. Finally, subtracting these time-varying aspects of the model from the dependent variable, rather than including an estimate of them in the explained variation, lowers the R^2.

The coefficient on the unemployment rate (regional claimant count) is negative and significant: –0.25 with regional productivity adjustment and –0.17 with national productivity adjustment. The coefficient is larger primarily due to the unemployment rate being entered (untransformed) in levels, but these estimates also have relatively smaller standard errors compared to earlier estimates. The reasonably tight standard errors for the specification with regional productivity are encouraging, given the noisiness of the underlying regional productivity data. On the basis of the strength and reliability of the wage response to unemployment, this has to be the favoured specification, with a t-statistic of 3.8. Compared to the earlier BNQ estimates this is quite high. This is primarily due to the change in functional form because the estimates based on UK productivity growth that should, other than the functional form, be quite similar to the BNQ estimates.

Including regional productivity figures in the SSW estimation reveals a major break in the relationship between wages and unemployment; after 1992 the estimated relationship is essentially zero. The estimated coefficient prior to 1992 is slightly smaller than the full sample result, rather than larger as we might have anticipated if the long sample were simply an average of a larger figure and zero. This result is economically and statistically insignificant when national productivity figures are applied, implying that regional productivity patterns are important to this result.

The robustness of this result to alternative dates is assessed in Figure 9.3. The coefficients on the first half of the period unemployment term are always

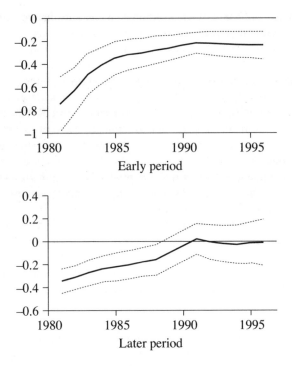

Early period

Later period

Source: Author's calculations using 2001 NES panel data set.

Figure 9.3   Coefficient stability in SSW model: alternative break-points

negative and statistically significant, but there is a clear trend towards a less negative relationship as more recent data are added to the early sample. The later period estimates also rise until about 1990, when the coefficient is essentially zero. Compared to Figure 9.2, based on the BNQ approach, the BNQ estimates are more likely to find a statistically insignificant early period coefficient on unemployment, while the SSW estimates find an even more negative estimate using only the first few years of data. The estimates are that the SSW specification generally results in smaller standard errors relative to the coefficients, but having specific regional productivity trends clearly matters. This break is not evident in Table 9.3 without the regional productivity trends. This lack of break-point when national productivity figures are used was true regardless of the dating of the potential break-point.

Both of the results based on BNQ and SSW are consistent with a changed labour market in recent years, but these changes are inconsistent with increased responsiveness of wages to unemployment rates. Overall, the macroeconometric evidence, while seemingly indicating that something has changed, is not particularly informative about the nature of the change.

MICRO EVIDENCE OF WAGE RIGIDITIES

The micro perspective begins with a notional wage change that an employer might desire for a particular job within their firm. This model follows Altonji and Deveraux (1999). These notional wages respond to the macroeconomic factors highlighted in the model above, but would in addition be expected to vary quite substantially from person to person within the firm. Defining a notional wage change helps to clarify how wages might be less than fully flexible at the individual level. Let notional wages be

$$w_{it}^* = x_{it}\beta + \alpha_i + \varepsilon_{it}$$

where x_{it} refers generally to controls particular to the individual, and α_t is included to account for aggregate factors (like the unemployment rate and productivity growth) in the notional wage contract. The error term ε_{it} accounts for individual heterogeneity in every time period. Conceptually this is desired wage variability and not an error in recording or an error by the firm.[10]

With the notional wage defined, restricted wages follow in a transparent manner depending on the form of the restriction. Altonji and Deveraux (1999) contemplate nominal rigidities of particular form. If the notional wage change is less then zero, but more than $-\chi$, then a constrained wage change of zero is realized. If the notional wage change is less than $-\chi$, then the firm actually pays according to the schedule, where w_{it}^0 is the realized wage based on the notional wage of w_{it}^*:

$$w_{it}^0 - w_{it-1}^0 = x_{it}\beta + \alpha_t - w_{it-1}^0 + \varepsilon_{it} \quad \text{if} \quad 0 \leq x_{it}\beta + \alpha_t + \varepsilon_{it} - w_{it-1}^0$$

$$w_{it}^0 - w_{it-1}^0 = 0 \quad \text{if} \quad -\chi < x_{it}\beta + \alpha_t + \varepsilon_{it} - w_{it-1}^0 < 0$$

$$w_{it}^0 - w_{it-1}^0 = x_{it}\beta + \alpha_t - w_{it-1}^0 + \varepsilon_{it} \quad \text{if} \quad x_{it}\beta + \alpha_t + \varepsilon_{it} - w_{it-1}^0 \leq -\chi$$

The χ in this equation is a free parameter to account for workers and firms agreeing that an extreme event has occurred, which requires a reduction in wages. It could be well below zero. Unemployment might occur if the wage were constrained – depending on how the firm is modelled – but should not occur when the notional wage is paid.

Altonji and Deveraux (1999) further augment this specification with an error term for the measurement of wages. This is an important issue because there is the potential for error in most micro-based data sources, and the identification of wage rigidities ultimately depends on the existence of spikes or reduction of observation below zero, which are both sensitive to the existence of errors. Reporting errors will typically reduce the size of the spike and increase the fraction below zero unless they are correlated across years.[11] In Swiss social security data similar to NES, Fehr and Goette (2000), using the Altonji and Deveraux (1999) estimator, ascribe most of the negative wage change observations to errors. The NES data ought to be fairly reliable, but it is certainly worth analysing some of the identifiable sources of error and being careful to use techniques that are not overly sensitive to errors.

Altonji and Deveraux (1999) focus solely on downward nominal rigidities, but it is not difficult to extend this set-up to real wage rigidities. A lower and an upper boundary need to established, which we will identify by ϕ and γ.

$$w_{it}^0 - w_{it-1}^0 = x_{it}\beta + \alpha_t - w_{it-1}^0 + \varepsilon_{it} \quad \text{if} \quad \gamma \leq x_{it}\beta + \alpha_t + \varepsilon_{it} - w_{it-1}^0$$

$$w_{it}^0 - w_{it-1}^0 = r, -\phi \leq r \leq \gamma \qquad \text{if} \quad -\phi < x_{it}\beta + \alpha_t + \varepsilon_{it} - w_{it-1}^0 < \gamma$$

$$w_{it}^0 - w_{it-1}^0 = x_{it}\beta + \alpha_t - w_{it-1}^0 + \varepsilon_{it} \quad \text{if} \quad x_{it}\beta + \alpha_t + \varepsilon_{it} - w_{it-1}^0 \leq -\phi$$

An optimizing model of why firms might deviate from the notional wage change can be found in MacLeod and Malcomson (1993). The firm's acceptance of restrictions on wage changes is supported by information and renegotiation costs, which could allow either nominal or potentially real rigidities to exist. Furthermore, a model allowing for two types of contracts (for example, nominal and real rigidities) could be patterned on the MacLeod and Malcomson model.

Distributions

Before moving on to statistical tests, it is useful to see what the data suggest as the key points where restrictions occur. Figure 9.4 shows the distribution of hourly wages changes for men continuing in the same job, excluding overtime pay and unusual hours. The bars shown in Figure 9.4 are one percentage point wide.[12] The prominence of the spike at zero varies from year to year, but is always present and clearly larger in low inflation periods. In 1994, the fraction of the workforce with no wage change reached over 6 per cent. Interestingly, the spike at no wage change is just as evident in the 1970s and it is quite high relative to the bars to the right and left of zero. This type of information can be useful in identifying nominal rigidities. It may indicate that wage rigidities were just as common or even more common in the 1970s, but the high inflation rates made this form of rigidity less relevant.[13]

There may be similar tendencies to have wage changes only above the inflation rate, which result in either a spike or a clustering of observations just

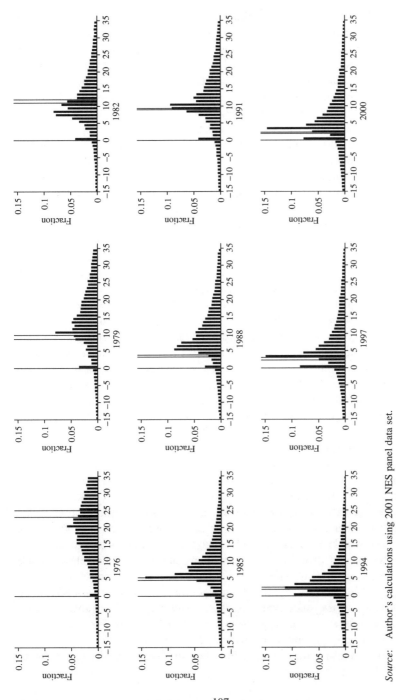

Source: Author's calculations using 2001 NES panel data set.

Figure 9.4   Wage change distributions

to the right of the relevant inflation rate. Defining the relevant inflation rate when wage changes may have been agreed upon any time in the last year makes this form of rigidity the hardest to identify. The vertical lines in these figures are the inflation rates from December to December in the previous year, and February to February. The variety of possible inflation reference points and complicated possible responses will make this more difficult to evaluate. In any case the spike just above the inflation rate in 1979 or 1985 in Figure 9.4 is potentially indicative of this form of rigidity. The figure for 1982 offers an interesting contrast, in that wages seem to be concentrated just below the inflation rate.

The other aspect of a rigidity, whether nominal or real, is that there ought to be less mass to the left of zero relative to the right, once the natural decline in frequencies away from the centre is accounted for. The evidence for this seems stronger for real rigidities than for nominal rigidities. The distribution in 1979 shows a substantial drop in mass left of the December and February inflation rates. On the other hand, the 1970s and early 1980s distributions that have many bars between the inflation rate and zero seem to be quite smooth through zero, once the spike has been excluded. It is, however, difficult to visually evaluate the fraction below zero or the inflation rate in these histograms, because it is difficult to guess how much the frequency should have declined due to being further from the median wage change.

None the less, the existence of the spike at zero is *prima facie* evidence of wage rigidity, but the nature and full extent of the rigidity is unclear. We would not expect to see rounding (as an error) in this data set large enough to generate this spike. It could be that firms do adjust pay rates less frequently than once a year, but this would still be wage rigidity, on an annual basis.

Kahn's Measures

Kahn (1997) offers an alternative approach to the issue of wage rigidities that doesn't require detailed functional form restrictions.[14] Using Kahn's method, estimates are based on deviations from the expected fraction of observations at a given amount left of the median in the histograms shown in Figure 9.4 associated with being at or near zero wage change. This is a general approach that relies on few distributional assumptions and is open to extension, but it may be susceptible to shifts in the form of the underlying notional wage change distribution. This weakness applies quite generally to microeconometric measures as this underlying distribution, no matter how is approximated, forms the basis for identifying the alternative in any micro approach. Kahn's method handles reporting errors in essentially the same way, by assuming that the distribution of errors changes little between years, so that it is approximately the same in the compared years.

Specifically, Kahn's test takes the other years' empirical distributions as the implicit comparison. Computing a histogram with a given window width (one percentage point in this and Kahn's original work), the fraction in the nth percentile to the left of the median is identified by r_1 to r_n. Using these values as the dependent variables, Kahn estimates a panel regression of these frequencies on n, and whether the observation is 1 or 2 per cent left of zero, zero wage change, or just above zero.

$$r_n = f(n, r_n \subset \Delta w > 0, r_n \subset \Delta w = 1, r_n \subset \Delta w = 2, r_n \subset \Delta w = -1, r_n \subset \Delta w = 0)$$

To simplify the specification, let $D0$ be a dummy variable that is 1 when the histogram range r_n includes zero wage change, that is, $r_n \subset \Delta w = 0$. Similar dummy variables are defined for percentage changes including 1, 2 and -1 and denoted $D1$, $D2$ and $DN1$ respectively. Finally, fixed effects, as a given amount less than the median, provide the estimates of typical wage change frequencies.

$$prop_{rt} = \alpha_r + \beta_1 DNEG_{rt} + \beta_2 D1_{rt} + \beta_3 D2_{rt} + \beta_4 DN1_{rt}$$
$$+ \gamma D0_{rt} + \mu_{rt}$$

All of the useful variation in this regression comes from these dummy variables moving through the distribution, so only r_n, where at one time one of these dummy variables is positive, are included in the regression.[15]

Because the Kahn approach uses variation in other years to define the baseline, we cannot estimate a degree of wage rigidity for each year, so instead we split the sample into two periods. This will indicate whether rigidities are becoming more or less pronounced relative to underlying distribution, although the timing of the change is left somewhat obscured. Ideally we would probably focus on the degree to which wage cuts are rare, but this measure may be prone to being falsely low if the distribution of reporting errors is symmetric. This follows because there will always be more mass in the true distribution above zero than below with or without wage rigidities, because the median wage change is always likely to be above zero in the UK due to inflation and productivity growth. The size of the spike is also susceptible to being reduced by errors, but if only some reports are in error the spike should still be recognizable.

This approach reveals statistically significant nominal wage rigidities in the hourly wage change distributions. The test results shown in Table 9.4 are based on the data revealed in Figure 9.4. The level of the nominal rigidity is lower than Kahn finds in the Panel Study of Income Dynamics (PSID), measured by the coefficient on the dummy variable for including a nominal zero wage change ($D0$). She typically gets coefficients well above one for her

*Table 9.4	Kahn measure: frequency of percentage pay changes*

	Full Sample	1976–91	1992–2001
Within zero band	1.26	0.75	2.24
	(0.10)	(0.14)	(0.11)
Nominal cut	−0.49	−0.43	−1.08
	(0.06)	(0.09)	(0.12)
Within +1% band	−0.71	−0.46	−1.21
	(0.10)	(0.14)	(0.11)
Within +2% band	−0.53	−0.51	−0.48
	(0.10)	(0.14)	(0.12)
Within −1% band	−0.17	−0.05	0.03
	(0.10)	(0.15)	(0.08)
N	24	24	23
NT	600	384	207
R^2 (within)	0.408	0.207	0.903

Source:	Author's calculations using 2001 NES panel data set.

all worker estimates. This may be due to the nature of either the wage data and how it is collected or the institutions in place.

When the sample is split, we find much stronger evidence of nominal wage rigidities in the period from 1992 to 2000, based on the coefficients on the dummy variable for including zero wage change in the observation ($D0$) which is more than doubled in the later period. Recalling that the zero spikes were far larger after 1992 in Figure 9.4, this may not be surprising, although much of the added height of those spikes was due to being closer to the median. It still suggests an increase in wage rigidities, rather than a reduction.

The regressions also reveal that there are statistically significant reductions in the frequency of wage cuts (based on the coefficients on *DNEG*). Bars less than zero are about a half percentage point lower than would be predicted based on their distance from the median. When the sample is split, this effect is again more than twice as strong in the later period.

Extending the early and late period break analysis to the Kahn measures results in Figure 9.5. The conclusion that nominal rigidities (at zero) have not declined in the later period is robust to any split in the sample up to 1993. After that the results change dramatically to reveal much-reduced evidence of nominal rigidity. Unfortunately, this could be an artefact of the limited data available to identify the underlying wage distribution.

This result seems to counter the conclusions of either Smith (2000) or Nickell and Quintini (2000), as both papers conclude that nominal rigidities

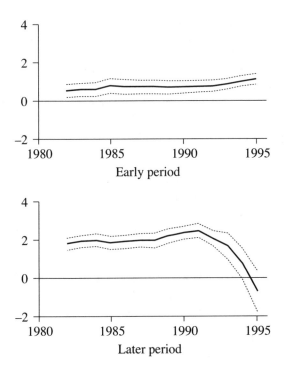

Source: Author's calculations using 2001 NES panel data set.

Figure 9.5 Coefficient stability at nominal zero: alternative break-points

are always insignificant in UK data. One critical difference in this conclusion is the use of a tighter testing strategy. These previous studies were more focused on how large the spike was relative to the prevailing view of wage-setting that argues that wage cuts are uncommon. Thus the standard was lower on showing some flexibility in UK wage-setting patterns. We wish to establish whether patterns have changed and needed a tighter standard. That said, it remains to be shown using the Kahn approach what level of rigidities are economically significant. 'Small' nominal rigidities may or may not be important.

Real Wage Rigidities

An interesting feature in Figure 9.4 is the evidence of spikes, or at least a collection of observations, around the inflation rate. While real rigidities have been discussed in the literature as one of the key differences between the US and European labour markets, the nominal wage rigidities literature has avoided exploring part of the distribution above zero. This is in part because papers want to connect to the theoretical literature on sources of monetary non-neutrality, but it has also been because these features are harder to define.

Extending Kahn's methodology to real wage rigidities involves two major complications. First, the reference value of inflation is not known and, second, wage responses around the inflation rate might be more diffuse, and thus harder to identify. Indeed, spikes and bumps in wage change distribution around the inflation rate have not been as evident as those at nominal zero. To account for the first issue, we estimate the model for both December or February inflation rates. The data shown in Figure 9.4 suggest that the second may not be a problem in this data set, although the effects do vary from year to year.

To the Kahn nominal wage rigidity measures we add dummy variables for wage changes including the inflation rate, negative real wage changes, and for being one or two percentage points up from these values or one percentage point below the inflation rate. This specification parallels the earlier implementation and is run simultaneously with the nominal controls, because in a low inflation period more than one effect could occur at wages a given distance from the median. Specifically, the linear estimation equation becomes

$$\text{prop}_{rt} = \alpha_r + \beta_1 DNEG_{rt} + \beta_2 D1_{rt} + \beta_3 D2_{rt} + \beta_4 DN1_{rt} + \gamma_1 D0_{rt}$$
$$+ \beta_5 DRNEG_{rt} + \beta_6 DR1_{rt} + \beta_7 DR2_{rt} + \beta_8 DRN1_{rt} + \gamma_2 RD0_{rt} + \mu_{rt}$$

At the outset, it is not obvious that it will cover most of the cases where wages bunch near inflation rates seen in Figure 9.4, but it is a reasonable place to start. Running counter to this approach is the fact that in some years the apparent concentrations around inflation moved above or below the rate. This technique will struggle to find a real-wage setting pattern if these moves are too common.

The full sample estimates show statistically significant evidence of real rigidities, based on the coefficients on *DR0*. Table 9.5 shows estimates using the February inflation rate, but results using the December inflation rate were similar. Interestingly, the scale of these estimates is similar to those accounting only for nominal rigidities. This is also true for the coefficients on negative real wage changes (*DRNEG*) and these coefficients will apply to a larger fraction of wages, particularly in the high inflation years. The coefficients around the inflation rate do not fit with the menu cost story, which collects small deviations at round figures, that was evident in the nominal estimates. Instead, these nearby wage change proportions (*DR1*, *DR2*, and *DRN1*) tend to show increases (when statistically significant), which is consistent with different time frames on inflation being used, as these deviations will tend to be small in most years.

Splitting the sample yields a similar picture in the early and late periods. The evidence does not support a reduction in wage rigidities, as evidenced by the

Table 9.5   Kahn-style tests for real rigidities

	Full sample Linear	1976–91 Linear	1992–2001 Linear
Within zero band	1.46	0.79	2.07
	(0.13)	(0.15)	(0.20)
Nominal cut	–0.34	–0.40	–1.33
	(0.08)	(0.09)	(0.22)
Within +1% band	–0.46	–0.40	–1.36
	(0.13)	(0.15)	(0.19)
Within +2% band	–0.29	–0.43	–1.35
	(0.13)	(0.14)	(0.18)
Within –1% band	–0.13	–0.04	0.02
	(0.13)	(0.15)	(0.16)
At inflation rate	1.74	0.78	1.14
	(0.14)	(0.15)	(0.22)
Real cut	0.12	–0.19	–1.58
	(0.12)	(0.12)	(0.25)
1% above inflation rate	1.15	0.42	0.51
	(0.14)	(0.15)	(0.19)
2% above inflation rate	0.59	0.46	–0.18
	(0.13)	(0.15)	(0.16)
1% below inflation rate	–0.03	0.01	0.32
	(0.14)	(0.15)	(0.18)
N	37	37	37
NT	925	592	333
R^2 (within)	0.339	0.214	0.747

Source: Author's calculations using 2001 NES panel data set.

rising coefficient on wage changes, *DR0*. Comparing across the full range of possible splitting points (in Figure 9.6) shows that these estimates are generally higher in the later period. The coefficients for bars near zero real wage change are also typically negative, along with the coefficient on negative real wage changes. In the linear specification the other boosted categories are nominal zero and just below the inflation rate. Nominal zero frequencies are actually little changed from the Table 9.4 results, suggesting that the apparent rise in nominal rigidities in the later period was associated with a reduction of real wage rigidities. Generally, including real wage controls did not substantially alter the nominal-only estimates. Together, these tables show little movement towards a more flexible labour market, while nominal rigidities may have increased.

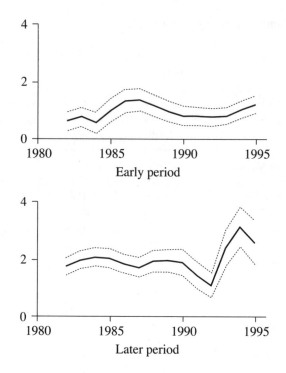

Early period

Later period

Source: Author's calculations using 2001 NES panel data set.

Figure 9.6   Coefficient stability at real zero: alternative break-points

Real wage rigidities potentially represent a large wedge between notional wages and the actual outcomes, when inflation is positive. This characterization is weakened in part because the evidence for reduced real wage cuts is sometimes small or insignificant in Table 9.5 when the estimates of the effect at the inflation rate are large. This may not be critical, though, as nominal wage cuts are reduced and these would all be real wage cuts. A more structural approach is required to better untangle the evidence on real wage rigidities, but these estimates are suggestive of some real wage rigidities.

CONCLUSION

This chapter has sought to collect both macroeconomic and microeconomic evidence on pay flexibility from a consistent source, the New Earnings Survey Panel data set. Regional wage rates do not appear to be more responsive to regional unemployment levels in the 1990s. This is true both for estimates based on the approach of Bell, Nickell and Quintini (2000) and for those of Staiger, Stock and Watson (2001). None the less, these estimates do seem to reveal some important changes in wage adjustment. Estimates focusing on the 1990s reveal no statistically significant aggregate wage response to regional unemployment levels. The overarching conclusion is that the macroeconomic tests leave much to explain, but the estimates have revealed some patterns that are worth trying to reconcile with other sources of evidence. Both sets of estimates suggest focusing on the beginning of the 1990s.

The microeconomic evidence reveals clear evidence of nominal wage rigidities. These rigidities are just as evident in the later data, indeed stronger until 1993. The sharp turn in 1993 is worrisome, because the Kahn approach may need more data than remains to define the underlying change distribution. The prolonged evidence of nominal rigidities is a surprise when compared with the view that the UK labour market has gradually become more flexible. The nominal wage rigidity coefficients are somewhat smaller than Kahn showed in PSID for the USA over the full sample period, but the values for current estimates are similar. The issue for any estimates of rigidities is what effect they have on employment. It is beyond the scope of this chapter to say whether these rigidities are economically meaningful, but they are statistically significant. Indeed, one interpretation of the continued rigidities while the Phillips curve estimates have shifted is that the two concepts are largely unrelated. At this point, this conclusion is probably premature, although these results do point to the need for a better reconciliation of micro wage rigidities and unemployment patterns. The NES data are suitable for a parametric analysis of rigidities and the costs they impose along the lines of Altonji and Deveraux (1999), which might help to pursue these issues.

Finally this chapter revealed a significant pattern of real wage rigidities. Some noticeable clustering around the inflation rate is evident in the raw wage change distributions. The Kahn (1997) approach is extended to explore the parts of the wage change histogram around the inflation rate. The estimated level of real wage rigidities is steady or even rising in the 1990s. Of course, the disruption caused by real wage rigidities would probably be lower with low inflation rates.

These results leave the correspondence between alternative wage flexibility measures puzzling, but it does point to the critical gap that exists between micro and macro definitions. The evidence from the Phillips curves suggests that changes have occurred that might have helped to keep wage inflation down. Two directions have been suggested by this research. The macro approach pointed to the importance of productivity differences, suggesting that a better model of notional wages in the micro approach might be informative. It also became clear that the micro approach needs to be formulated so that the cost of rigidity can be evaluated, whether it is nominal or real.

NOTES

* Federal Reserve Bank of Cleveland, Research Department, Cleveland, Ohio, 44120, USA. This research was completed by the author while on secondment at the Bank of England. The views expressed are those of the author and do not necessarily reflect the views of the Bank of England, the Federal Reserve Bank of Cleveland or the Federal Reserve System. The reported results are preliminary and based on a confidential data source. Nigel Stuttard, Alex Clifton-Fearnside, Brian Bell, Steve Nickell, Mike Joyce, Maria Guadalupe, Lorenz Goette, Richard Barwell and the ECB Labour Market Workshop participants are all thanked for their help in this project.

1. See for example Clegg (1979) and Kessler and Bayliss (1995).
2. Cully et al. (1999). See Faggio and Nickel (2002) for an exploration of the effects of unionization rates on macro wage flexibility measures.
3. The New Earnings Survey is crown copyright and used with the permission of the Office of National Statistics. More details on the design and coverage rates in each year can be found in annual result books ONS (1975–2000).
4. These figures were drawn from 1996 New Earning Survey notes, but were not unusual. Major 'out-of-sample' groups are pensioners, non-salaried directors, working for spouse, working outside the UK.
5. The macroeconomic estimates most closely follow Bell, Nickell and Quintini (2000) and Staiger, Stock and Watson (2001). Bell et al. (2000) estimate both forms but favour a flexible form of the wage curve (with lagged wages entering with a coefficient less than one). Staiger et al. (2001) favour estimates in changes, although they consider some alternatives that are consistent with wage curves.
6. A first stage, regression wages on age, age squared, eight occupation dummy variables, ten industries, ten regions and years dummy variables is run. The coefficients on the time dummies represent the average wage rates after controlling for human capital. This estimate is differenced to yield the reported wage inflation measure.
7. This regression is conceptually quite close to that used in BNQ (2000). The first stage regression becomes wages on age, age squared, eight occupation dummy variables, ten industries, and ten regions interacted with year dummy variables. The differences are mainly due to coding differences in the occupations.
8. Results were also calculated for a male only sample (like in BNQ) and were similar enough to make them repetitive.
9. SSW use these estimates to produce a time-varying estimate of the NAIRU, which would also be possible here. The results would likely follow Greenslade et al. (2001), who have shown that aggregate Kalman filter estimates for the UK yield evidence of a declining NAIRU.
10. Groshen and Schweitzer (1999) estimate the size of firm errors and treat a rising relationship with inflation as evidence of a 'sand' effect of inflation in labour markets. This would complicate this model as inflation rose.
11. Smith (2000) finds that the spike is potentially boosted by measurement error in a household survey where many observations are rounded and thus more likely to be unchanged between years.
12. The microeconomic model of wage rigidities is fundamentally ambivalent on what rate of pay is relevant, yet this can matter quite a lot to the measurement of wage rigidities. When we compared three different definitions of wages available in the NES, we found that the qualitative features of the wage change distributions include spikes at zero, and the inflation rates were largely unchanged. An appendix describing these results is available from the author.

13. While not shown, 1999 does not stand out from other nearby years. It is true that the distribution has more mass just to the right of the inflation than either 1998 or 2000, but the difference is small and unlikely to disrupt any of the tests proposed below.

14. There is a literature of tracking moments of the distribution of wage changes, beginning with McLaughlin (1994). Summary measures of wage flexibility, for example skewness or the more sophisticated measures offered by Lebow, Stockton and Wascher (1995) and McLaughlin (1999), were also explored. Unfortunately, these measures failed to offer a consistent interpretation of the UK data.

15. Kahn's (1997) proportional estimator accounts for the non-linear restrictions implied by estimation of a density, but significantly complicates estimation and the extension of the model. The results for the proportional model of nominal rigidities were very similar to the linear model.

REFERENCES

Altonji, J.G. and P.J. Deveraux (1999), *The Extent and Consequences of Downward Nominal Wage Rigidity*, NBER Working Paper No. 7236.

Bell, B., S. Nickell and G. Quintini (2000), *Wage Equations, Wage Curves, and All That*, Centre for Economic Performance Discussion Paper, 0427.

Clegg, H.A. (1979), *The Changing System of Industrial Relations in Great Britain*, London: Basil Blackwell.

Cully, M., S. Woodland, A. O'Reilly and G. Dix (2000), *Britain at Work: As Depicted by the 1998 Workplace Employee Relations Survey*, London: Routledge.

Faggio, G. and S. Nickell (2002), 'The Responsiveness of Wages to Labour Market Conditions', manuscript.

Fehr, E. and L. Goette (2000), *The Robustness and Real Consequences of Downward Nominal Wage Rigidity*, University of Zurich Institute for Empirical Research in Economics Working Paper No. 44.

Greenslade, J., R. Pierse and J. Saleheen (2001), *A Kalman Filter Approach to Estimating the UK NAIRU*, London: Bank of England.

Groshen, E. and M. Schweitzer (1999), 'Identifying inflation's grease and sand effects in the labour market', in M. Feldstein (ed.), *NBER Report Series, The Costs and Benefits of Price Stability*, Chicago and London: University of Chicago Press, pp. 273–308.

Kahn, S. (1997), 'Evidence of nominal wage stickiness from microdata', *American Economic Review*, **87** (5), 993–1008.

Kessler, S. and F. Bayliss (1995), *Contemporary British Industrial Relations*, Basingstoke, Hampshire: Macmillan Press.

Lebow, D., D. Stockton and W. Wascher (1995), *Inflation, Nominal Wage Rigidity, and Efficiency of Labor Markets*, Finance and Economics Discussion Series No. 95–45, Board of Governors of the Federal Reserve System.

MacLeod, W.B. and J.M. Malcomson (1993), 'Investments, holdup, and the form of the market contracts, *American Economic Review*, **83** (4), 811–37.

McLaughlin, K.J. (1994), 'Rigid wages?', *Journal of Monetary Economics*, **34** (3), 383–414.

McLaughlin, K.J. (1999), 'Are nominal wage changes skewed away from wage cuts?', *Federal Reserve Bank of St. Louis Review. Proceedings from the 23rd Annual Economic Policy Conference*, May, 117–36.

Nickell, S. and G. Quintini (2001), *Nominal Rigidity and the Rate of Inflation*, Centre for Economic Performance Discussion Paper 0489.

Office of National Statistics (1975–2000), *New Earning Survey*, various issues.

Smith, J. (2000), 'Nominal rigidity in the UK', *Economic Journal*, **110**, 176–95.

Staiger, D., J.H. Stock and M.W. Watson (2001), *Prices, Wages and the U.S. NAIRU in the 1990s*, NBER Working Paper No. 8320.

Stuttard, N. and J. Jenkins (2001), 'Measuring low pay in the new earnings survey and the LFS', *Labour Market Trends*, January, 55–66.

10. Centralized bargaining and reorganized work: Are they compatible?

Assar Lindbeck and Dennis J. Snower[*]

1 INTRODUCTION

A large and growing literature documents the widespread reorganization of work within firms in advanced market economies. The evidence, as summarized in Section 2, indicates that the new breakthroughs in information and production technologies have made it profitable for firms to flatten the hierarchies of control and responsibility and to allow for greater decentralization of decision-making. In the traditional firms, work was divided into well-defined families of tasks, each often performed in a different department, such as the production, marketing, sales, accounting and product development departments. Production workers were often assigned highly specialized and monotonous tasks. Labour, like capital equipment, was treated as a single-purpose input; and this, in fact, is also the way labour and capital are depicted in mainstream production theory. In the contemporary reorganization of work, by contrast, firms use labour in more flexible and versatile ways. Workers increasingly combine different tasks in wide varieties of ways to suit the new production technologies, workers' preferences for more varied work, and customers' varied needs. Recent evidence suggests that the new forms of work are often organized around small, customer-oriented teams rather than large functional departments, with considerable discretion for both teams and individual workers.

We will call the traditional organization of work, with substantial specialization by task and centralization of responsibilities, a 'Tayloristic' organization. The recently emerging work organization, characterized by multitasking and decentralization of work responsibilities, will be called 'holistic'. In this context, we will interpret job rotation and multitasking widely, to include not only the pursuit of several traditional occupational tasks, but also communication with other employees and customers, participation in consultative groups and so on.

199

To some extent, the resulting breakdown of occupational barriers amounts to a reversal of a trend that began with the Industrial Revolution, in which productivity improvements were exploited through increasing specialization of work.[1] But it is important to note that reduced task specialization among workers does not necessarily imply reduced specialization in production among firms. Quite the contrary, job rotation and multitasking often occur simultaneously with a downsizing process that involves a narrower focus on a firm's 'core competencies' in production.

This chapter examines the implications of this reorganization of work for centralized wage bargaining. Our analysis suggests that when work is reorganized, the efficiency cost of centralized wage bargaining rises, since it prevents firms from offering their employees the incentives to perform the appropriate mix of tasks. The intuition underlying this result may be summarized as follows.

Although the content of centralized bargaining arrangements varies across countries,[2] those conducting such bargaining are everywhere forced to apply highly standardized principles for wage-setting. The reason is that they have very little, if any, information about conditions in individual firms. A very common form of such standardization is that central negotiators often strive towards 'equal pay for equal work', which means paying different employees the same (or similar) amounts for the same tasks. Centralized wage bargaining of this type may not be severely inefficient when different workers do different tasks, particularly if workers within an occupation have similar productivity. But once work is restructured to promote multitasking and employees' decentralized choices among tasks, the practice may become very inefficient indeed.

The source of the inefficiency is to be found in the complementarities among the multiple tasks performed by individual employees. Such complementarities are a primary motive for multitasking. For example, insights gained on one position on the production line may be put to use on other positions on the line. Similarly, the knowledge an employee acquires in one production team may be useful when the employee moves to another team. In a similar vein, experiences on production work may be put to use in quality control, information about customer preferences gained through selling may be useful in employee training, and knowledge acquired through product repairs may be applied to production work or even product development. When different employees combine different sets of complementary tasks, there is no reason to believe that the marginal product of one employee's time at a particular task should be similar to the marginal product of another employee's time at that task, even if the two employees have the same abilities. For instance, there is no reason why time spent with customers should affect the productivity of a customer service employee in the same way as it affects the productivity of a production worker or a trainer of new recruits. The same principle holds, though to a lesser degree, even when different employees perform the same set of tasks, but in different proportions.

Consequently the restructured firms have an incentive to offer different workers different wages at the same tasks. Beyond that, firms have an incentive to reward workers for learning how to use their experience gained at one set of tasks to enhance their performance at another set of tasks. But it is precisely these practices that centralized bargaining inhibits. Thus we argue that the reorganization from occupational specialization to multitasking raises the efficiency costs of centralized bargaining and thereby gives employers and employees growing incentives to choose decentralized bargaining arrangements instead.

Beyond that, we argue that the above inefficiency cannot be avoided by reforming the nature of the centralized wage bargaining process. In particular, suppose that centralized bargainers stopped imposing wage uniformity on the traditional occupational categories and, instead tried imposing it on the new occupational clusters that emerge under multitasking. In practice this would be an insuperably difficult task, since the switch to multitasking is likely to make work more idiosyncratic in terms of task assignments among employees, both within most reorganized firms and across such firms. The problem is magnified by the firms' need to assign multiple tasks not just on the basis of workers' abilities at these tasks, but also with regard to their judgement, initiative, creativity and social competence. And in so far as workers differ in terms of these latter attributes, even when they are of equal ability at particular tasks, it will be efficient to allocate different task clusters to workers of equal ability.

But even if centralized wage bargaining could be reformed along the lines above, it would still be inefficient for the reorganized work for the following reason. Under multitasking, wages have a dual role: they influence both the number of people employed and their time allocations across tasks. Thus, to maximize profits firms need to give their employees sufficiently large diversity of wage signals to perform this dual role. Imposing wage uniformity within occupational clusters restricts this diversity. Thus, even if the centrally determined wages were to induce efficient levels of employment, they will not in general ensure that the time allocations across tasks are efficient as well.

In these ways our analysis provides a rationale for the trend towards more decentralized wage bargaining, as described in Section 2.

The literature emphasizing the advantages of centralized wage bargaining occupies a position analogous to the centralized price-setting literature half a century ago. There it was argued that centralized price-fixing in product markets is desirable, since the central planner is able to internalize various externalities operative among firms acting in isolation.[3] Over the past decades, however, the influence of this central planning literature has gradually waned, as economists have come to appreciate the difficulties of centralized price-setting when products, technologies and tastes are highly heterogeneous. This chapter suggests that as the contemporary reorganization of work makes jobs more heterogeneous, centralized wage-setting becomes more difficult as well. Information about workers' productivities at heterogeneous task clusters is becoming as hard to centralize as information about the marginal revenues and costs of producing different products. As labour markets become more like product markets in terms of their heterogeneity, we argue that the inefficiencies of centralized wage bargaining are becoming similar to the inefficiencies of centralized price fixing. In this respect, our analysis suggests that Hayek's objections to centralized pricing of goods and services now apply increasingly to the labour market as well.[4]

The chapter is organized as follows. Section 2 provides a summary of the evidence on the reorganization of work and the decentralization of wage bargaining. Section 3 presents a simple model of how the move from occupational specialization towards multitasking raises the efficiency cost of centralized bargaining. Section 4 provides some extensions. Section 5 concludes.

2   AN OVERVIEW OF THE EVIDENCE

The contemporary reorganization of work was first described and analysed in a sizeable literature in management and business administration.[5] Various aspects of the reorganization process have also been examined in the economics literature.[6] The process is a gradual one, proceeding unevenly among firms and countries. Until recently, the evidence of these organizational developments has been based on a large number of case studies. The quantitative importance of the process, therefore, has been uncertain. However, more systematic and representative studies are now available. Comprehensive studies for Japan established long ago the emergence of new types of work organization, sometimes baptized 'The Toyota model' (for example Aoki, 1990). Recent studies for the USA and Europe have documented that reorganization of work is a wide-ranging phenomenon in these parts of the world as well. For instance, a representative study by Osterman (1994) documents the development in US manufacturing establishments (with 50 or more employees). The conclusion is that 55 per cent of the establishments were using work teams, 43 per cent work rotation, 34 per cent 'total quality management' (TQM) and 41 per cent quality circles; only 21 per cent had none of these features.[7] There is also evidence that these organizational forms are new phenomena. About half of the observed arrangements were introduced fewer than five years before the survey year of 1992.[8]

The most comprehensive documentation of the quantitative importance of the shifts to more flexible work organization apparently pertains to the Nordic countries (NUTEK, 1996, 1999). These studies indicate that the majority of establishments (with more than 50 employees) in all Nordic countries – more specifically, 68–75 per cent of these establishments – moved to more flexible organization of work during the 1990s (NUTEK, 1999, ch. 4).[9] The most important elements of these reorganizations are delegation of responsibility to production workers, organized development of human capital (training), as well as teamwork, job rotation and multitasking (reflected in an increase in the average number of tasks per employee).

For instance, daily planning of one's own work has been decentralized to individuals in 57 per cent of Swedish establishments and in 40 per cent of Finnish establishments and to work teams in 38 and 25 per cent, respectively (NUTEK, 1999, ch. 2). The figures for quality control and weekly planning of one's own work are somewhat lower, and for customer relations and maintenance considerably lower.[10] Internal information circulation within firms is also reported to have increased. Within the teams, informal work rotation (multitasking) is usual. Moreover, formally planned work rotation is recorded in about a fifth of the studied firms. Another finding is that the education level among the employees is higher in reorganized firms than in traditional firms. Employee participation in decision-making within firms seems also to have increased in the other major West European countries (OECD, 1996, ch. 6). Indeed, in a systematic questionnaire study among managers in this part of the world, four out of five firms report that they have taken steps in this direction (European Foundation, 1997).

In this chapter we argue that the above reorganization of work gives a rationale for decentralization in wage-setting. There is indeed a trend in this direction, which has also been widely documented,[11] though it has taken different forms in different countries. The move towards decentralized bargaining agreements has been particularly pronounced in countries that previously had highly centralized bargaining, namely the Nordic countries. These also happen to be the countries in which the reorganization of work seems recently to have gone the furthest (European Foundation, 1997, NUTEK, 1999).[12] For example, over the 1980s and 1990s wage bargaining arrangements in Denmark and Sweden became increasingly fragmented, as these countries moved from a highly centralized system[13] towards industry-level bargaining. Whereas plant-level bargaining has always been important in these countries (and was responsible for wage drift under the centralized bargaining regime), the centralized bargaining agreements became smaller in scope and influence with the passage of time.[14] Germany's formal bargaining structure has remained largely unchanged over the past two decades, but it has nevertheless witnessed a gradual rise in the importance of plant- and workshop-level bargaining since the beginning of the 1980s, regarding both wages and the organization of work.[15] A similar trend has been witnessed in Italy,[16] which abandoned its Scala Mobile in the 1980s. In both Germany and Italy, the scope of national bargaining agreements has shrunk, concentrating increasingly on working hour targets and general conditions of employment, while leaving wage agreements, work organization and job classifications increasingly to local negotiations.

The UK has witnessed a marked rise in single-employer agreements at the expense of multi-employer contracts[17] and a rise in the number of agreements negotiated below the company level (for example the plant, division or profit-center level) since the start of the Thatcher era.[18] The USA has also experienced a drop in multi-employer agreements in favour of company- and plant-level bargaining,[19] accompanied by a decline in pattern bargaining.[20] As in other countries, the local negotiations have focused increasingly on work organization and remuneration schemes.[21]

Even though the timing of reorganization of work happens to coincide with the shifts to more decentralized wage bargaining, the latter trend may also have been driven by other factors. For example Freeman and Gibbons (1993) argue that the decentralization trend is due, in part, to rising volatility in local labour market conditions. Numerous observers have suggested that the decline of centralized bargaining is due to falling union density and rising management power. But this cannot be the whole story since local unions frequently support the move towards decentralization.[22]

Numerous case studies suggest that changes in the organization of work have played a critical role in the decline of centralized bargaining.[23] To the best of our knowledge, however, no attempt appears to have been made thus far to provide a theory of how this could happen. This chapter seeks to do so.

3   MULTITASKING WITH DIFFERENT TASK PROPORTIONS

We begin with a particularly simple demonstration of how the switch from task specialization to multitasking raises the efficiency cost of centralized bargaining. For this purpose, we assume that different employees perform the same set of tasks, but in different proportions. Section 3 will then extend this analysis to show how this efficiency problem of centralized bargaining can occur under the more prevalent form of multitasking, namely when different employees perform different sets of overlapping tasks.

Production and Labour Services

Consider a firm that produces an output q through two tasks (1 and 2), and employs two types of workers, who differ in terms of their comparative advantage at these tasks: type-1 workers are comparatively better at task 1 and type-2 workers are comparatively better at task 2 (as formalized below).

Let λ_i, $i = 1,2$ be the total labour services that these two types of workers provide at task i. The production function, relating these labour services to the firm's output, is

$$q = f(\lambda_1, \lambda_2) \tag{10.1}$$

where $(\partial f/\partial \lambda_1)$, $(\partial f/\partial \lambda_2) > 0$ and $(\partial^2 f/\partial \lambda_1^2)$, $(\partial^2 f/\partial \lambda_2^2) < 0$

The determinants of these labour services are defined as follows:

1. Let τ be the fraction[24] of a type-1 worker's time devoted to task 1, and $(1 - \tau)$ be the fraction devoted to task 2. Similarly let T be the fraction of the type-2 worker's time spent at task 2, and $(1 - T)$ be the fraction spent at task 1.
2. Let e_1 and e_2 be the type-1 worker's labour endowment at tasks 1 and 2, respectively (that is, the efficiency units of labour provided by that worker at these tasks). Similarly, let E_1 and E_2 be the type-2 worker's labour endowment at tasks 1 and 2, respectively.
3. Finally, let n and N be the number of type-1 and type-2 workers employed, respectively.

(Observe that the variables pertaining to type-1 workers are in lower case, whereas those pertaining to type-2 workers are in upper case.) The type-1 workers have a comparative advantage at task 1 (relative to worker 2 at task 1) in the sense that $(e_1/e_2) > (E_1/E_2)$, for any given $\tau = T$.

Then the labour services provided at the two tasks may be expressed as

$$\begin{aligned} \lambda_1 &= e_1 \tau n + E_1 (1-T) N \\ \lambda_2 &= e_2 (1-\tau) n + E_2 T N \end{aligned} \tag{10.2}$$

Along the lines of Lindbeck and Snower (2000), we assume that each worker's labour endowment (e_i and E_i, $i = 1,2$) at a particular task is a function of two factors: (i) the 'return to specialization', whereby a worker's productivity at a task rises with experience at that task; and (ii) an 'informational task complementarity', whereby the worker's productivity at a task depends on the information gained from the experience acquired at another task.[25] Although these two factors may not be easy to separate in practice, it is conceptually convenient to represent them by two separate variables.

For the type-1 worker, let s_i, $i = 1,2$ be the returns to specialization at task i, and let c_i, $i = 1,2$ be the informational task complementarities running to task

i (that is, the rise in the worker's productivity at task i achieved by gaining information about the other task). We assume that the type-1 worker's returns to specialization at a task depend positively on the fraction of time spent at that task (*ceteris paribus*):

$$s_1 = s_1 (\tau) \text{ and } s_2 = s_2 (1-\tau) \qquad (10.3a)$$

where $s_1', s_2' > 0$.

Regarding the informational task complementarities, we assume that the greater the fraction of time that a type-1 worker spends at one task (*ceteris paribus*), the greater will be the worker's productivity at the other task:

$$c_1 = c_1 (1 - \tau) \text{ and } c_2 = c_2 (\tau) \qquad (10.3b)$$

where $c_1', c_2' > 0$.

Then a type-1 worker's labour endowment may be expressed in terms of the returns to specialization and the informational task complementarity:

$$e_1 = e_1 (s_1, c_1) \text{ and } e_2 = e_2 (s_2, c_2) \qquad (10.3c)$$

where $(\partial e_i / \partial s_i) > 0$ and $(\partial e_i / \partial c_i) > 0$, $i = 1, 2$.

For the type-2 worker, along the same lines, the returns to specialization at the two tasks are

$$S_1 = S_1 (1-T) \text{ and } S_2 = S_2 (T) \qquad (10.4a)$$

where $S_1', S_2' > 0$; and the informational task complementarities are

$$C_1 = C_1 (T) \text{ and } C_2 = C_2 (1-T) \qquad (10.4b)$$

where $C_1', C_2' > 0$. Thus the type-2 worker's labour endowment may be expressed as

$$E_1 = E_1(S_1, C_1) \text{ and } E_2 = E_2(S_2, C_2) \qquad (10.4c)$$

where $(\partial E_i / \partial S_i) > 0$ and $(\partial E_i / \partial C_i) > 0$, $i = 1, 2$.

By (10.2)–(10.4c), the labour services λ_1 and λ_2 may be expressed in terms of the number of workers employed and their time allocation between tasks:[26] $\lambda_1 = \lambda_1 (\tau, T; n, N)$ and $\lambda_2 = \lambda_2 (\tau, T; n, N)$. Thus the firm's production function (10.1) may also be expressed in terms of these arguments:

$$q = q (\tau, T; n, N) \qquad (10.1')$$

Wages and Labour Costs

An important aspect of multitasking, documented in the recent empirical literature, is that employees often have discretion over the proportions in which different tasks are performed. In practice, employers generally determine the range of tasks that each of their employees perform, while the employees often have some latitude in deciding the task mix.[27] This aspect is a significant source of decentralization of decision-making within restructured enterprises. Employees often have a significant amount of tacit, local information that cannot be readily transmitted to management. To exploit this information, the employees often have some control over how to mix the tasks within their remit. Beyond that, task mixing is usually difficult to monitor, and thus managers often have little alternative but to leave some of the decision-making to the employees. Managers can, however, influence their employees' decisions through wage incentives. These wage incentives may be distorted through centralized wage bargaining. It is this wage-setting problem to which we now turn.

Suppose that in the absence of centralized bargaining, the firm can offer (at least implicitly[28]) a different wage to each worker at each task: each type-1 worker receives the real wages w_1 and w_2 at tasks 1 and 2, respectively; and each type-2 worker receives the real wages W_1 and W_2 at these tasks. Then the firm's labour costs are

$$\kappa = w_1 \tau n + w_2(1-\tau)n + W_1(1-T)N + W_2TN \qquad (10.5)$$

Given these wages, each worker decides on his time allocation between the two tasks. For simplicity, let the utility function of each type-1 worker be

$$u = y + v(\tau) \qquad (10.6a)$$

where $y = w_1\tau + w_2(1-\tau)$ is the worker's wage income[29] and $v(\tau) < 0$ is the disutility of work. The worker has 'specialist preferences' when $v'(\tau) > 0$ for $0 \le \tau \le 1$, so that the worker's utility rises as he allocates more time to the task at which he has a comparative advantage. On the other hand, the worker has 'versatile preferences' when, for some $\tau = \tau^0$ (a constant, $0 < \tau^0 < 1$), $v'(\tau) > 0$ for $\tau \le \tau^0$ and $v'(\tau) < 0$ for $\tau \ge \tau^0$. Here the worker's most preferred time allocation is $\tau = \tau^0$, involving multitasking, and utility falls as the time allocation diverges from this most preferred allocation.

The prevailing wages w_1 and w_2 are predetermined when the workers make their time allocation decisions. The first-order condition for the type-1 worker's utility maximization is

$$\frac{du}{d\tau} = (w_1 - w_2) + v'(\tau) \geq 0, \quad \frac{du}{d\tau} (1-\tau) = 0 \qquad (10.6b)$$

Similarly, the utility function of each type-2 worker is

$$U = Y + V(T) \qquad (10.7a)$$

where $Y = W_1(1-T) + W_2 (T)$ is the worker's wage income. The first-order condition for this worker's utility maximization is

$$\frac{dU}{dT} = (W_2 - W_1) + V'(T) \geq 0, \quad \frac{dU}{dT} (1-T) = 0 \qquad (10.7b)$$

For simplicity, the firm is assumed to know the workers' reaction functions (10.6b) and (10.7b) when setting wages. We now proceed to the firm's decision-making problem.

Profit Maximization and the Organization of Work

The firm offers the wages w_1, w_2, W_1, and W_2 that elicit the profit-maximizing time allocations[30] τ^* and T^*. In addition, the firm makes the profit-maximizing employment decisions n* and N*. The firm's decision-making problem may therefore be expressed as maximizing profit[31] $\pi = q - \kappa$ with respect to the wages w_1, w_2, W_1 and W_2 and the employment levels n^* and N^*, subject to the production function (10.1), the labour services described by (10.2)–(10.4c), the labour cost function (10.5), and the workers' reaction functions (10.6b) and (10.7b). To maximize profit, the firm finds the lowest feasible wages necessary to induce the workers to offer the profit-maximizing time allocations τ^* and T^*. Thus the reaction functions (10.6b) and (10.7b) hold as equalities:

$$w_1 - w_2 = -v'(\tau) \text{ and } W_2 - W_1 = -V'(T) \qquad (10.8)$$

Furthermore, the firm sets these wages at the minimum levels necessary to induce the workers to work. Suppose that workers' utility from not working is zero. Then the type-1 and type-2 workers' reservation wages (at which the worker is indifferent between providing a time unit of labour and providing none) are defined as[32]

$$w_1\tau + w_2 (1-\tau) + v(\tau) = 0$$
$$W_2T + W_1 (1-T) + V(T) = 0 \qquad (10.9)$$

Substituting (10.8) and (10.9) into the firm's costs function (10.5), we obtain

$$\kappa = -v(\tau)n - V(T)N \tag{10.5'}$$

Then the firm's problem may be restated as follows:[33]

$$\underset{\tau,T;n,N}{\text{Maximize}}\ \pi = q(\tau,\ T;\ n,\ N) + v(\tau)n + V(T)N \tag{10.10}$$

To avoid trivial solutions, we assume that the profit-maximizing employment levels n and N are positive.[34] Then the first-order conditions are

$$\frac{\partial \pi}{\partial n} = \frac{\partial q}{\partial n} + v(\tau) = 0, \qquad \frac{\partial \pi}{\partial N} = \frac{\partial q}{\partial N} + V(T) = 0 \tag{10.11a}$$

$$\frac{\partial \pi}{\partial \tau} = \frac{\partial q}{\partial \tau} + v'(\tau)\,n \geq 0 \quad \text{and} \quad \frac{\partial \pi}{\partial \tau}(1-\tau) = 0 \tag{10.11b}$$

$$\frac{\partial \pi}{\partial T} = \frac{\partial q}{\partial T} + V'(T)\,N \geq 0 \quad \text{and} \quad \frac{\partial \pi}{\partial T}(1-T) = 0 \tag{10.11c}$$

It is easy to see that these profit-maximizing decisions are efficient. The efficient outcome is one that permits the employer and the employees to maximize output minus the associated disutility of work: $q(\tau,T;n,N) + v(\tau)n + V(T)N$. This is equivalent to maximizing profit, by (10.10).

We define a Tayloristic organization of work as one in which workers specialize by task. By contrast, we let a 'holistic' work organization be one in which workers engage in multitasking, with the freedom to choose their task allocation in response to wage incentives.[35] When profit is maximized at a corner point of the feasible time allocations:

$$\tau^* = T^* = 1 \tag{10.12a}$$

Here workers specialize completely in accordance with their comparative advantage, and the organization of work will be Tayloristic. On the other hand, when profit is maximized in the interior region of the feasible time allocations:

$$0 < \tau^*, T^* < 1 \tag{10.12b}$$

so that workers engage in multitasking, there is a holistic organization of work.

Our model identifies four major determinants of the organization of work:

1. *The return to specialization versus the return to informational task complementarities*: As τ rises from zero to unity, the type-1 worker's return to specialization (s) at task 1 rises, but the informational task complementarity (c) falls. Analogously for the type-2 worker. The greater the decline in the informational task complementarity relative to the rise in the return to specialization, the greater the incentive to establish a holistic work organization.

2. *The technological task complementarity versus substitutability*: As τ rises from zero to unity, there are diminishing returns to labour at task 1 $(\partial^2 f/\partial\lambda_1^2) < 0$. On the other hand, there may be a 'technological task complementarity', so that the two tasks are Edgeworth complements in the production function, $\partial^2 f/(\partial\lambda_1\partial\lambda_2) > 0$. Then a rise in the type-1 worker's time allocation τ, while reducing the marginal product of task 1, raises the marginal product of task 2; and analogously for the type-2 worker. The greater the technological task complementarity relative to the rate of diminishing returns, the greater the incentive for holistic work organization.[36]

3. *Specialist versus versatile endowments of workers*: If type-1 workers' endowments are versatile (that is, their comparative advantage at task 1 is small), then, as τ approaches unity, the output foregone at task 2 rises relative to the extra output generated through task 1. Analogously for the type-2 workers. Thus, the more versatile the workers' endowments, the greater the incentive for a holistic work organization.

4. *Specialist versus versatile preferences of workers*: If type-1 workers have versatile preferences, then, as τ approaches unity, the wage cost of these workers eventually rises. (The reason is that when preferences are versatile, $v(\tau)$ achieves a maximum when the time allocation τ is in the interior of the feasible region: $\tau = \tau^o, 0 \le \tau^o \le 1$.) Analogously for the type-2 workers. The more versatile are the workers' preferences (that is, the closer to $\frac{1}{2}$ and the further from 1 their time allocations τ^o and T^o lie), the greater the incentive for a holistic work organization.

Figures 10.1(a) and 10.1(b) illustrate the first-order condition (10.11b) in a Tayloristic and a holistic organization, respectively.[37] Observe that in the Tayloristic organization, the marginal product $\partial f/\partial\tau$ declines slowly relative to the marginal cost $\partial\kappa/\partial\tau$, and thus the optimal organization of work involves complete specialization: $\tau^* = 1$. In the holistic organization, by contrast, the marginal product declines rapidly relative to the marginal cost, and thus the profit-maximizing time allocation τ^* lies in the interior of the feasible region $0 < \tau \le 1$.

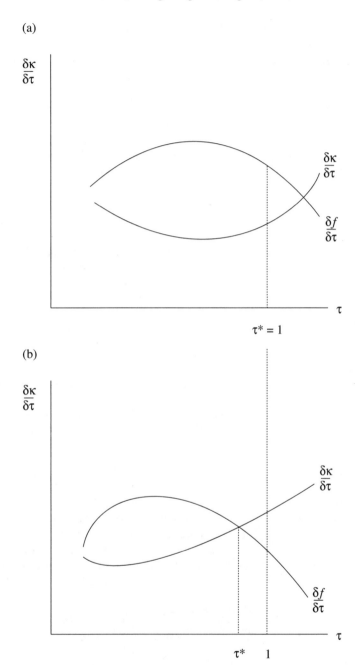

Figure 10.1   The profit-maximizing organization of work

The recent literature on the business organization (discussed above) suggests that the reorganization of work from Tayloristic to holistic lines is driven significantly by changes in production and information technologies that make tasks more complementary to one another. Changes in human capital that make workers more versatile and give them preferences favouring versatile work reinforce this process. In terms of Figure 10.1, these developments imply that the marginal product curve $\partial f/\partial \tau$ becomes more steeply downward-sloping and the marginal cost $\partial \kappa/\partial \tau$ becomes more steeply upward-sloping with the passage of time. As result, the profit-maximizing allocation of hours between the two tasks shifts from specialization (in Figure 10.1a) to multitasking (in Figure 10.1b).

The Influence of Centralized Bargaining

As noted, a salient characteristic of centralized wage bargaining is that it imposes some uniformity of wages across workers at given tasks. To make this point starkly in the context of our analysis, let us simply assume that centralized bargaining imposes the following constraint on wage setting:[38]

$$w_1 = W_1 \text{ and } w_2 = W_2 \qquad (10.13)$$

that is, the wage of both workers at task 1 is the same, and similarly for task 2.

When work is organized along Tayloristic lines ($\tau^* = T^* = 1$), the centralized bargaining constraint (10.13) need not be inefficient. By (10.9), the efficient and profit-maximizing wages under this form of organization is

$$w_1 = -v(1) \text{ and } W_2 = -V(1) \qquad (10.14)$$

If the centrally bargained wages are set at these levels, the resulting employment and work organization will be efficient and profit-maximizing.

On the other hand, if profit-maximizing organization of work is holistic – with $\tau^* = \tau^o$ and $T^* = T^o$, where $0 < \tau^o, T^o < 1$ – the situation is radically different. Now, by (10.8) and (10.9), the efficient and profit-maximizing wages are

$$w_1^o = -v'(\tau^o)(1-\tau^o) - v(\tau^o)$$
$$W_1^o = V'(T^o) T - V(T^o) \qquad (10.15a)$$

for task-1 work, and

$$w_2^o = v'(\tau^o) \, \tau^o - v(\tau^o)$$
$$W_2^o = -V'(T^o) \, (1-T^o) - V(T^o) \qquad (10.15b)$$

for task-2 work. Here centralized bargaining will generally be inefficient, since there is no reason why w_1^o should be equal to W_1^o, and why w_2^o should be equal to W_2^o, thereby satisfying the centralized bargaining constraint (10.13).

The intuitive reason is straightforward. Since workers differ in their abilities and preferences with respect to the two tasks, holistic firms need four independent wage instruments (w_1, w_2, W_1 and W_2) to induce the two types of workers to allocate their work time optimally across the two tasks. By imposing uniformity of wages across workers at given tasks, centralized bargaining grants firms two independent wage instruments, one for each task. In general, this constraint will prevent holistic firms from achieving the efficient and profit-maximizing allocation of labour resources. This problem does not arise for Tayloristic firms: when workers specialize by task, the firm needs only two independent wage instruments to achieve the optimal allocation.

Following similar lines to the analysis above, it can be shown that the switch from task specialization to multitasking raises the efficiency cost of centralized bargaining when different employees perform different sets of overlapping tasks.

4 EXTENSIONS

The model of Section 3 is very restrictive; it is merely a simple analytical device for showing why centralized bargaining becomes inefficient when work is reorganized with emphasis on multitasking and decentralization of some work-related decisions. We now extend our analysis in two important ways to indicate the robustness of our result.

Is Centralized Bargaining Reformable?

The efficiency problem of Section 3 arose because the skill categories of traditional centralized bargaining do not correspond to the skill categories of holistic firms. Wage uniformity imposed on traditional occupations is bound to be inefficient when work no longer falls within the traditional occupational boundaries. Is it then possible to reform the centralized wage bargaining so as to avoid this problem of inefficiency? In particular, suppose that centralized wage bargaining were to abandon the traditional occupational categories, and were instead to impose uniformity within the new occupational clusters. Would efficiency be assured?

We argue that the answer is no. To see why, let us return to our analytical framework above and ask how the wage categories of centralized bargaining could be optimally aligned to the new holistic task clusters. Under the Tayloristic organization of work, the occupational categories are divided by task: the type-1 worker has occupation 1 by virtue of performing task 1, and the type-2 worker has occupation 2 by virtue of performing task 2. But under the holistic work organization, workers perform two clusters of tasks: the type-1 worker performs both tasks in one specific proportion ('proportion 1'), while the type-2 worker performs them in another proportion ('proportion 2'). If centralized bargaining categories were to align themselves perfectly to this change in the occupational mix, then the central bargainers would adopt proportions 1 and 2 as the new occupational categories and impose some uniformity of wages with respect to these categories. Within the framework of our analysis, this means that type-1 multitaskers would get one wage and type-2 multitaskers would get another. Expressed starkly, the new centralized bargaining constraint would then become

$$w_1 = w_2 \text{ and } W_1 = W_2 \tag{10.13'}$$

However, equations (10.15a) and (10.15b) indicate that this new centralized bargaining constraint is also inefficient, provided that both types of workers are not completely versatile, that is, provided that $\tau^o \neq T^o \neq \frac{1}{2}$.

The intuitive reason for the inefficiency is straightforward. In a Tayloristic firm, wages have only one function for the firm: they determine the number of people employed in each occupational category. In order to maximize profits in our model, the firm needs to set these wages at their reservation wage levels: $w_1 = -v(1)$ and $W_2 = -V(1)$, by equation (10.14). (In other words, wages are as low as possible without inducing workers to quit.) In a holistic firm, by contrast, wages have two functions: they determine the number of people employed and their division of time among their tasks. Thus, to maximize its profit, the holistic firm needs two wage instruments for each type of worker:

1. It needs to pay the reservation wage combination in order to achieve the profit-maximizing employment level. For the type-1 worker, by (10.9), $w_1\tau^o + w_2 (1-\tau^o) = v(\tau^o)$, so that the employment level n of type-1 workers is set so that $(\partial\pi/\partial n) = (\partial q/\partial n) + v'(\tau^o)$, by (10.11a). Similarly for the type-2 worker.
2. In addition, the firm needs to pay the wage differential that will enable it to achieve the profit-maximizing time allocation between tasks. For the type-1 worker, the wage differential needs to be $(w_1-w_2) = v'(\tau^o)$, by (10.6b),[39] in order to induce the worker to set his time allocation τ so that $(\partial\pi/\partial\tau) = (\partial q/\partial\tau)n + v'(\tau)n = 0$, by (10.11b).[40] And similarly for the type-2 worker.

But the centralized bargaining constraint (10.13′) gives the firm only one wage instrument for each type of worker. Thus this constraint is inefficient. For the type-1 worker, if the wage $w_1 = w_2$ enables the firm to achieve the profit-maximizing employment level, this wage is bound to induce the workers to choose a non-profit-maximizing time allocation.[41] In short, if centralized bargaining imposes uniformity of wages within each occupational cluster, it may induce firms to employ the efficient number of people or it may induce the workers to allocate their time efficiently across their tasks, but in general it cannot do both.

Beyond that, it is worth noting that our model understates the difficulty for centralized wage bargaining to adjust to the move from Tayloristic to holistic organizations of work. Since our model contains just two tasks and two types of workers, it is easy to identify the change in occupational classification required of centralized bargaining. In practice, firms perform a large number of heterogeneous tasks through the services of a large number of heterogeneous workers. Under these circumstances, the move from Tayloristic to holistic organizations of work may involve a vast increase in the number of occupational clusters.

The importance of this heterogeneity comes out even more forcefully when we consider that the efficient formation of occupational clusters within a firm depends, in practice, not only on the technological and informational task complementarities and the employees' skills at the available tasks. It also depends on the employees' social competence, judgement, initiative and creativity – attributes which do not fall within the domain of any particular task. Since employees of equal productive ability at a particular combination of tasks often differ in terms of these attributes, firms may find it profitable and efficient to allocate different task combinations to workers of equal productive ability.

Besides, as noted, the move from Tayloristic to holistic organizations also commonly involves the firm in switching from large functional departments (for example sales, production, finance and market departments) to smaller customer-oriented teams, producing more differentiated products that are designed specifically for the firm's particular customers. Consequently, the task composition of the holistic occupational clusters is likely to vary from one firm to another.

Given the increase in the number of occupational clusters within firms and the more varied composition of these clusters across firms, centralized wage bargaining may be expected to have trouble establishing occupational categories within which wage uniformity can be imposed without a threat a to efficiency and profitability.

Incentives for Intertask Learning

Thus far, we have assumed that when workers perform multiple tasks, the informational task complementarities can be reaped automatically. In practice, of course, a worker's mere performance of multiple tasks usually does not guarantee that this worker uses the experience gained at one job to improve performance at another job. For this purpose the worker generally needs to engage in a cognitive process that is generally (a) difficult for the employer to monitor and (b) costly to the employee in terms of effort, concentration and initiative.

The employers' motivation to provide incentives for their employees to engage in this learning process is analogous to their motivation to discourage shirking in the efficiency wage theory. In both cases there is asymmetric information about employees' productivities and employers can use remuneration as an incentive device. In the moral hazard model of Shapiro and Stiglitz (1984), for example, employees receive a wage above the market-clearing wage, provided that they are not caught shirking. Similarly, when workers are assigned multiple tasks, they may be offered a bonus for using their experience at one task to enhance their productivity at the other tasks. This bonus is paid only if they are not caught shirking, now interpreted as the mindless performance of multiple tasks that yields no informational task complementarities.

To capture this idea in a particularly simple way, let us modify the model of Section 3 so as to make informational task complementarities dependent on work effort. Specifically let ω denote the worker's effort to use his experience at one task in performing the other task. Then, for simplicity let us express the informational task complementarities as follows:

$$c_1 = c_1 (\omega (1-\tau)) \text{ and } c_2 = c_2 (\omega \tau) \tag{10.3b$'$}$$

where $c_1 \bar{\omega} (1 - \tau)) > C_1 (0)$ for $\tau < 1$ and $C_2 (\bar{\omega}\tau) > C_2 (0)$ for $\tau > 0$. In other words, when the worker expends no intertask effort ($\omega = 0$), then there are no informational task complementarities. We assume that intertask effort is a discrete variable: $\omega = (0, \bar{\omega})$, where $\bar{\omega}$ is a positive constant. When $\omega = 0$, the worker shirks; when $\omega = \bar{\omega}$, he does not.

We modify the worker's utility function in the following simple way to include intertask effort:

$$u = (y + b) + v(\tau) - \omega \tag{10.6a$'$}$$

We assume that the firm is unable to monitor the effort level ω directly, but is able to influence it through a bonus payment. Let b be the bonus that the worker receives if he is not caught shirking. Thus if the worker does not shirk, his utility is $u_n = (y + b) + v(\tau) - \bar{\omega}$. If he does shirk, he faces a probability θ of being detected, in which case he does not receive the bonus b. With probability $(1 - \theta)$ he is not detected and receives b. His associated utility from shirking is

$$u_s = (1-\theta)[(y + b) + v(\tau)] + \theta[y + v(\tau)].$$

If the firm sets the bonus as low as possible without inducing the worker to shirk, the wage will be given by the 'no shirking constraint': $u_n = u_s$, which implies that

$$b = \frac{\bar{\omega}}{\theta} \qquad (10.16a)$$

Similarly, for the type-2 worker, let the informational task complementarities be given by

$$C_1 = C_1(\Omega\, T) \quad \text{and} \quad C_2 = C_2(\Omega\, (1 - T)) \qquad (10.4b')$$

where Ω is the worker's intertask effort $\Omega = (0, \bar{\Omega})$, C'_1, $C'_2 > 0$ and $C_1(0) = C_2(0) = 0$. Moreover, let the type-2 worker's utility be $U = (Y + B) + V(T) - \Omega$, where B is the type-2 worker's bonus. Then his no-shirking constraint is

$$B = \frac{\bar{\Omega}}{\theta} \qquad (10.16b)$$

Suppose that the firm's production function (10.1), the returns to specialization (10.3a) and (10.4a), the informational task complementarities (10.3b') and (10.4b'), the labour endowment functions (10.3c) and (10.4c), the detection probability θ, and the effort disutilities $\bar{\omega}$ and $\bar{\Omega}$ are such that it is profit-maximizing for the firm to adopt a holistic organization of work. Along the same lines as in Section 3, it can be shown that if this outcome is profit-maximizing, it is also efficient.

However, this outcome is unlikely to arise under centralized wage bargaining, for two reasons. First, intertask bonuses generally violate the rule of 'equal pay for equal work'. Different workers will generally receive different bonuses for a particular task, provided that they use their experience from that task differently in the performance of other tasks. (On this account, the profit-maximizing bonus b will generally differ from the bonus B.) Second, centralized wage bargaining assigns wages to tasks, not bonuses to intertask learning. The negotiators of the centralized bargaining agreements usually do not have enough information to set such bonuses, since informational task complementarities tend to be highly idiosyncratic across enterprises. The reason is that workers at different enterprises often perform different combinations of tasks, and even when they perform the same sets of tasks, differences in production technologies, customer attributes, opportunities for innovation and team dynamics would still give rise to different opportunities for the cross-task use of information.

These issues are irrelevant when work is organized along Tayloristic lines, for then informational task complementarities are non-existent. But when work is holistic, these issues become important, for then centralized wage bargaining may prevent firms and their employees from achieving efficient production–employment outcomes. For instance, suppose that centralized bargaining imposed the constraint $b = B = 0$ in the analysis above. Then, by (10.16a) and (10.16b), workers would provide no intertask effort: $\omega = \Omega = 0$. Thus there are no informational task complementarities: $c_1 = c_2 = 0$ and $C_1 = C_2 = 0$.

In the absence of informational task complementarities, there will be less multitasking than would otherwise have taken place. In other words, if $\tilde{\tau}$ and $\tilde{T}$ are the time allocations in the absence of informational task complementarities, τ^* and T^* are the profit-maximizing time allocations in the presence of informational task complementarities, then $\tilde{\tau} > \tau^*$ and $\tilde{T} > T^*$. Since the outcome (τ^*, T^*) is profit-maximizing and efficient, the outcome $(\tilde{\tau}, \tilde{T})$ is inefficient.

5   CONCLUDING REMARKS

Centralized bargaining has been acclaimed as a device that enables employers and employees to internalize a variety of externalities.[42] But over the 1980s and 1990s, country after country relinquished these benefits as bargaining agreements were made at more local levels. This chapter provides a new theoretical explanation for why this happened – one that fits well with the wide body of evidence that the decentralization of wage bargaining went hand in hand with changes in the organization of work.

We have argued that the trend away from occupational specialization towards multitasking has increased the efficiency cost of centralized bargaining. The underlying reason suggested by our analysis is that the reorganization from Tayloristic to holistic work can lead to a vast increase in the informational requirements for efficient wage-setting. When workers are specialized by occupation and when the members of each occupational group have similar productivity and willingness to work, the central bargainers require little information to set wages efficiently. All that is required are estimates of productivity and the reservation wage for each occupation. But once workers engage in multitasking, much more information is required for efficient wage-setting. In general, the efficient set of wage incentives will vary from one combination of tasks to another. They depend on the constellation of complementarities among these tasks and the effort workers must expend to exploit these complementarities. Only the employers and employees at each establishment have any hope of possessing such detailed, heterogeneous, establishment-specific pieces of information. Central bargainers simply cannot acquire and assimilate this information, much as central planners are unable to get all the relevant cost and revenue information to determine the efficient prices of vast arrays of goods and services.

In the absence of detailed information about task complementarities, the negotiators in centralized wage bargaining have little choice but to set wages schematically, such as prescribing one wage (or a range of wages) for every broadly defined group of tasks. However, multitasking makes this practice patently inefficient, since workers' productivities at any task can vary widely, depending on the other tasks they are performing. The traditional way for centralized wage bargaining to permit some local flexibility is to allow for wage drift, but once this drift becomes large, it undermines the operability of centralized bargaining. For then the central bargainers can retain their clout only if they can distinguish between 'justifiable' wage drift in response to, say, genuine task complementarities and 'unjustifiable' drift resulting from local rent-seeking. But to make such a distinction, the central bargainers would need the detailed information about complementarities and effort that is beyond their reach.

Our analysis suggests that the trend towards multiskilling may be driven by advances in information and production technologies that augment the informational and technological task complementarities, improved education that makes workers more versatile across occupational pursuits, and a swing in worker preferences away from Tayloristic jobs and towards holistic work. As such, this reorganizational trend is an efficient response to changes in preferences, technologies and endowments of physical and human capital. However, the 'same wage for the same job' rule of centralized bargaining impedes this trend, and thereby imposes an ever larger cost on society. In this way our analysis provides a rationale for the decline of centralized bargaining in many industrialized countries. To the extent that centralized wage bargaining has been used in many European countries to compress the wage distribution, our analysis leads us to expect that decentralization of wage decisions will lead to widening wage differentials in these countries.

NOTES

* Reprinted from European Economic Review, Vol. 45, No. 10, Lindbeck, A. and Snower, D.J., 'Centralized bargaining and reorganized work: Are they compatible?', pp 1851–1875, 2001, with permission from Elsevier Science. The authors are indebted for useful comments by Mike Orszag and Gylfi Zoega as well as two anonymous referees.

1. This is of course just a general tendency, to which exceptions are not uncommon. Indeed,

specialization of work may have continued to increase in some fields, such as research and advanced medicine.

2. At one extreme, Austria and the Nordic countries have traditionally had highly centralized wage bargaining processes. In other countries, such as France, Germany, Italy and the Netherlands, the important wage-setting decisions tend to be made at the industry level.
3. See for example Lange (1938).
4. See for example von Hayek (1940).
5. See for example Appelbaum and Bott (1994), Hammer and Champy (1993), Pfeiffer (1994), Wikstrom and Norman (1994) and Womack, Jones and Roos (1991).
6. See for instance Carmichael et al. (1993), Holmstrom and Milgrom (1994), Kremer and Maskin (1995), Lindbeck and Snower (1996, 2000), Milgrom and Roberts (1990), Mitchell, Lewin and Lawler III (1990), Piore and Sabel (1984) and Yang and Borland (1991).
7. For firms in which at least 50 per cent of the workforce was engaged in such activities, the corresponding percentage figures are 41, 27, 24, 27 and 36.
8. Forty-nine per cent of the teams, 38 per cent of the job rotation practices, 71 per cent of TQM programmes and 68 per cent of problem-solving groups or quality circles were introduced in the period 1986–92. These results are broadly consistent with a study of a sample of large firms by Lawler, Mohrman and Ledford (1992), according to which 66 per cent of the firms in the sample have quality circles, 47 per cent have self-managed work teams and 64 per cent TQM.
9. If workplaces with 10–49 employees are included, the proportion of reorganized work places decreases by about 20 percentage points.
10. For customer relations the corresponding figure in Sweden (Finland) is 36 (19) per cent in the case of individuals, and 13 (7) per cent in the case of teams. For maintenance the figure for Sweden (Finland) is 28 (10) per cent in the case of individuals and 23 (9) per cent in the case of teams.
11. Katz (1993) and European Industrial Relations Review (1992) give good accounts of this development.
12. Today we can only speculate about the reasons for this. One may be that the Nordic countries have rather even and fairly high levels of general education. Another conceivable reason may be that unions and firms are accustomed to close cooperation, in particular at the firm level.
13. In this centralized system the employers' confederation SAF and the blue-collar union confederation LO negotiated wages and other issues until the early 1980s, providing a lead for subsequent sectoral negotiations.
14. For example EIRR (1992).
15. For example Streeck (1984) and Windolf (1989).
16. EIRR (1992), Locke (1992), Windolf (1989).
17. Brown (1981), Marginson et al. (1988), Millward et al. (1992).
18. Brown and Walsh (1991), IRRR (1989), Marginson et al. (1988).
19. Katz and Kochan (1992) and Turner (1991).
20. Budd (1992), Katz and Meltz (1989).
21. Cutcher-Gershenfeld (1991), Eaton and Voos (1992).
22. See for example Katz (1993).
23. For instance Katz (1993), Locke (1992) and Turner (1991). Empirical studies also suggest that much more complex remuneration systems are used in reorganized firms than in traditional firms. For instance, there is a much higher frequency of various types of ability pay and performance pay, such as pays for qualification and bonus for individual attitude, team bonus for output and profit sharing (European Foundation, 1997, ch. 10, and NUTEK, 1999, ch. 3).
24. To focus attention on the distinction between specialization of work and multitasking, we make the simplifying assumption that each worker's available working time is given (normalized to unity) and we will examine how this time is divided between the two available tasks. Extending our analysis to the case in which the workers' total available time is endogenously determined as well does not substantively affect our qualitative conclusions, provided that workers' utilities decline with total hours of work performed.

25. For example, workers often function better within a production team if they have experience not only of their particular task, but also those of other team members, as well as tasks of other teams. Another example is that the information about customer preferences that a worker gains at the task of marketing can generate information that is useful in product design or in the provision of ancillary services.

26. Note that the labour services (λ_i, $I = 1, 2$) depend on the time allocations (τ and T), the productivities (e_j and E_j, $j = 1, 2$) and the number of type-1 and type-2 workers employed. The productivities in turn depend on the time allocations [by (10.3a)–(10.3c) and (10.4a)–(10.4c)]. Consequently, the labour services are a function simply of the time allocations and the number of workers employed.

27. Alternatively, employers may determine the task mix that each employee is to perform, but the employee determines his effort level at each task, in response to wage incentives (as addressed in Section 4). Yet another possibility is that the employees are in a better position than the employer to identify the most profitable task mix (from the range of designated tasks set by the employer) as the profit opportunities arise, while the employer evaluates the employees' performance *ex post*. In that event it may be profitable for the employer to award 'flexibility bonuses'. (Lindbeck and Snower, 2000, analyse the organization of work when the firm determines its employees' task mix unilaterally.)

28. Explicitly, the firm may offer each worker a single wage which depends on the task mix that worker performs. This is of course analytically equivalent to offering workers different wages for different tasks.

29. The inclusion of non-wage income would not affect the conclusions of our analysis, since utility is linear in income and thus there is no income effect.

30. By implication, the organization of work is determined on the basis of profit-maximizing principles. At the cost of some expositional simplicity, but without affecting the qualitative conclusions of our analysis, the organization of work could alternatively be portrayed as the outcome of a Nash bargain between the firm and its employees. The latter is perhaps more closely in line with the process or organizational change in various OECD countries. (For evidence see, for example, Katz, 1993.)

31. Since the wages w_1, w_2, W_1, and W_2 are functions of the time allocations τ and T, by equations (10.6b) and (10.7b) we can state the firm's profit-maximization problem in terms of the time allocations rather than the wages, even though the wages are actually the firm's choice variables.

32. If the wages are the outcome of a Nash bargain between the firm and each employee, the right-hand sides of these equations are positive constant (that is, the positive level of utility each employee receives as a result of the bargain).

33. Instead of finding the profit-maximizing wages w_1, w_2, W_1, and W_2, we frame the problem in terms of the profit-maximizing time allocations τ^* and T^* elicited by these wages.

34. Since the aim of this analysis is to depict the organization of work, the focus of our analysis is on the profit-maximizing time allocations τ and T, and thus no insights are gained from taking account of the non-negativity constraints on n and N.

35. Whereas this chapter concentrates on the intrapersonal allocation of time across complementary tasks, much of the existing literature on specialization of work focuses on the interpersonal coordination of workers performing complementary tasks. (See for instance Becker and Murphy, 1992; Bolton and Dewatripont, 1994; Krugman, 1987; and Stigler, 1951.)

36. If instead there is a technological task substitutability ($\partial^2 f/(\partial\lambda_1 \partial\lambda_2) < 0$), this feature reinforces the diminishing returns in providing an incentive for a Tayloristic work organization.

37. Analogous figures could of course be drawn for worker 2.

38. Alternatively, we could portray this function of centralized bargaining as setting lower and upper bounds on the dispersion of wages across workers at given tasks. Provided that these constraints are binding, this extension would not affect the qualitative conclusions of our analysis.

39. When the firm maximizes profit, the first inequality of equation (10.6b) holds as equality.

40. Under profit maximization, the first inequality of equation (10.11b) holds as equality.
41. And vice versa: if the wage induces the optimal time allocation, it is bound to lead to a suboptimal employment level.
42. See for example Calmfors and Driffill (1988).

REFERENCES

Aoki, M. (1990), 'A new paradigm of work organization and coordination?', in S. Marglin (ed.), *The Golden Age of Capitalism*, Helsinki: Wider Institute, pp. 267–315.

Appelbaum, E. and R. Bott (1944), *The New American Workplace*, Ithaca, NY: ILR Press.

Becker, G.S. and K.M. Murphy (1992), 'The division of labor, coordination costs and knowledge', *Quarterly Journal of Economics*, **107** (4), 1137–60.

Bolton, P. and M. Dewatripont (1994), 'The firm as a communication network', *Quarterly Journal of Economics*, **109** (4), 809–39.

Brown, W.A. (ed.) (1981), *The Changing Contours of British Industrial Relations: A Survey of Manufacturing Industry*, Oxford: Blackwell.

Brown, W.A. and J. Walsh (1991), 'Pay determination in Britain in the 1980s: the anatomy of decentralization', *Oxford Review of Economic Policy*, **7** (1), 44–59.

Budd, J.W. (1992), 'The determinants and extent of UAW pattern bargaining', *Industrial and Labor Relations Review*, **45** (3), 523–39.

Calmfors, L. and J. Driffill (1988), 'Bargaining structure, corporatism, and macroeconomic performance', *Economic Policy*, **6**, 14–61.

Carmichael, I., H. Horne and W.B. McLeod (1993), 'Multiskilling technical change and the Japanese firm', *Economic Journal*, **103**, 142–60.

Cutcher-Gershenfeld, J. (1991), 'The impact on economic perforce of a transformation in workplace relations', *Industrial and Labor Relations Review*, **44** (2), 241–60.

Eaton, A.E. and P.B. Voos (1992), 'Unions and contemporary innovations in work organization, compensation and employee participation', in L. Mishel and P.B. Voos (eds), *Unions and Economic Competitiveness*, Washington, DC: Economic Policy Institute, pp. 173–216.

European Foundation (1997), *New Forms of Work Organization: Can Europe Realise its Potential?*, Dublin.

European Industrial Relations Review (1992), *The Rise and Fall of Centralized Bargaining*, No. 220, April, pp. 20–22.

Freeman, R. and R. Gibbons (1993), *Getting Together and Breaking Apart: The Decline of Centralized Collective Bargaining*, Cambridge, MA: NBER Working Paper No. 4464.

Hammer, M. and J. Champy (1993), *Reengineering the Corporations*, New York: Harper Business.

von Hayek, F.A. (1940), 'Socialist calculation: the competitive solution', *Economica*, **7** (26), 125–49.

Holmstrom, B. and P. Milgrom (1994), 'The firm as an incentive system', *American Economic Review*, **84** (4), 972–91.

Industrial Relations Review and Report (1989), *Decentralized Bargaining in Practice: 1*, No. 454, pp. 5–10.

Katz, H.C. (1993), 'The decentralization of collective bargaining: a literature review and comparative analysis', *Industrial and Labor Relations Review*, **47** (1), 3–22.

Katz, H.C. and T.A. Kochan (1992), *An Introduction to Collective Bargaining and Industrial Relations*, New York: McGraw-Hill.

Katz, H.C. and N. Meltz (1989), 'Changing Work Practices and Productivity in the Auto Industry: A US–Canada Comparison', in *Proceedings of the 26th Conference of the Canadian Industrial Relations Association*, Quebec: University of Laval Press, pp. 384–96.

Kremer, M. and E. Maskin (1995), *Segregation and the Rise in Inequality*, mimeo.

Krugman, P.R. (1987), 'The narrow moving band, the Dutch disease, and the consequences of Mrs Thatcher: notes on trade in the presence of dynamic scale economics', *Journal of Development Economics*, **27**, 41–55.

Lange, O. (1938), 'On the economic theory of socialism', in R.E. Lippincott (ed.), *On the Economic Theory of Socialism*, Minneapolis: University of Minnesota Press, pp. 72–96.

Lawler, E., S. Mohrman and G. Ledford (1992), *Employee Involvement and Total Quality Management: Practices and Results in Fortune 1000 Companies*, San Francisco: Jossey-Bass.

Lindbeck, A. and D.J. Snower (1996), 'Reorganization of firms and labor market inequality', *American Economic Review, Papers and Proceedings*, **86** (2), 315–21.

Lindbeck, A. and D.J. Snower (2000), 'Multi-task learning and the reorganization of work', *Journal of Labor Economics*, **18** (3), 353–76.

Locke, R.M. (1992), 'The decline of the National Union in Italy: lessons for Comparative Industrial Relations Theory', *Industrial and Labor Relations Review*, **45** (2), 229–49.

Marginson, P. et al. (1988), *Beyond the Workplace: Managing Industrial Relations in Multi-Establishment Enterprises*, Oxford: Blackwell.

Milgrom, P. and J. Roberts (1990), 'The economics of modern manufacturing: technology, strategy and organization', *American Economic Review*, **80**(6), 511–28.

Millward, N. et al. (1992), *Workplace Industrial Relations in Transition*, Brookfield: Dartmouth University Press.

Mitchell, D.J.B., D. Lewin and E.E. Lawler III (1990), 'Alternative pay systems, firm performance, and productivity', in A.S. Blinder (ed.), *Paying for Productivity: A Look at the Evidence*, Washington, DC: The Brookings Institution.

NUTEK (1996), *Towards Flexible Organisations*, Stockholm: Swedish National Board for Industrial and Technical Development.

NUTEK (1999), *Flexibility Matters: Flexible Enterprises in the Nordic Countries*, Stockholm: Swedish National Board for Industrial and Technical Development.

OECD (1996), *Technology, Productivity and Job Creation*, Vol. 2, Analytical Report, Paris.

Osterman, P. (1994), 'How common is workplace transformation and who adopts it?', *Industrial and Labor Relations Review*, **47** (2), 173–89.

Pfeiffer, J. (1994), *Competitive Advantage through People*, Boston, MA: Harvard Business School Press.

Piore, M.J. and F. Sabel (1984), *The Second Industrial Divide: Possibilities for Prosperity*, New York: Basic Books.

Shapiro, C. and J.E. Stiglitz (1984), 'Equilibrium unemployment as a worker discipline device', *American Economic Review*, **74** (3), 433–44.

Stigler, G.J. (1951), 'The division of labor is limited by the extent of the market', *Journal of Political Economy*, **59**, 185–93.

Streeck, W. (1984), *Industrial Relations in West Germany: A Case Study of the Car Industry*, New York: St Martin's Press.

Turner, L. (1991), *Democracy at Work: Changing World Market and Future Unions*, Ithaca, NY: Cornell University Press.

Wikström, S. and R. Norman (1994), *Knowledge and Value*, London: Routledge.

Windolf, P. (1989), 'Productivity coalitions and the future of corporatism', *Industrial Relations*, **28** (Winter), 1–20.

Womack, J., D.J. Jones and D. Roos (1991), *The Machine that Changed the World*, New York: Harper Perennial.

Yang, Z. and J. Borland (1991), 'A microeconomic mechanism for economic growth', *Journal of Political Economy*, **99**, 460–82.

11. The impact of active labour market policies in Europe

Julian Morgan and Annabelle Mourougane[1]

INTRODUCTION

In recent years there has been a growing policy focus on active labour market policies (ALMPs).[2] The aim is generally to replace, or complement, other forms of labour market intervention such as unemployment benefits with 'active measures'. Such measures come in many different forms and include job brokering services, training and job creation. One unifying feature is that, in contrast to unemployment benefits, 'active' measures require significant activity on the part of the unemployed. This activity can either be in the form of an increased job search effort, participation in education or training schemes, or undertaking some form of employment. Such measures have the potential to impact on labour supply and in some cases also labour demand and thereby would be expected to have a bearing on wage pressures.

The aim of this chapter is to highlight the policy measures that are being undertaken in the EU, review the literature on the effectiveness of such interventions and draw some general conclusions on their likely impact on unemployment and wage formation. With this aim, this chapter begins with a discussion of a conceptual framework, including a typology and brief description of the main types of policies that are classified as ALMPs. This is followed by an analysis of the extent to which such policies are used in Europe, drawing on aggregate statistics and descriptive information on current policy initiatives. Next, there is a review of theoretical considerations and finally an examination of the empirical evidence which draws on both macro- and microeconomic studies.

CONCEPTUAL FRAMEWORK

A distinction is often made between 'active' and 'passive' measures. Passive measures are generally defined as relating to welfare payments made to people of working age who are not in employment, for which no work or activity is required, beyond an obligation actively to seek work. This heading would embrace unemployment insurance, unemployment assistance and some forms of early retirement payments. By contrast, a key feature of active measures is that they normally require some activity on the part of the unemployed person. However, ALMPs take many different forms and the degree of activity required can vary significantly. To order our analysis we use a typology similar to that used by Fay (1996), whereby ALMPs are classified into five different types:

1. *Job search assistance (JSA)* – this includes job clubs, individual counselling and measures to encourage the motivation of job seekers. In addition, JSA is often linked by the public employment services (PES) with the monitoring of active job search on the part of the unemployed, which can be a condition for the receipt of some social security benefits.
2. *Training* – this includes both formal classroom training and on-the-job training gained while in employment.
3. *Subsidies to employment* – essentially demand-side measures with subsidies to encourage the employment of certain types of workers – generally the long-term unemployed. Such subsidies can be paid either to the employer or to the employee in the form of 'in-work benefits'.
4. *Direct job creation* – measures, such as public works, where the unemployed are usually directly recruited by the state to engage in non-market activities.
5. *Supporting entrepreneurship* – aid to the unemployed starting enterprises, such as subsidies to help cover the initial costs of setting up and running a business.

THE USE OF ACTIVE LABOUR MARKET MEASURES

Table 11.1 gives details of total labour market spending, passive and active labour market spending drawing on statistics from the OECD *Employment Outlook*.[3] This shows that between 1985 and 2000 total labour market spending in the EU[4] amounted to around 2.5–2.8 per cent of GDP compared with 0.4–0.7 per cent in the USA. Typically, around 30–50 per cent of this spending related to active measures in both the USA and the EU. Sweden has traditionally tended to be the keenest advocate of ALMPs, and in 1985, expenditures on such policies were more than twice the EU average. However, the differences between Sweden and the rest of the EU have narrowed somewhat in recent years.

In most EU countries there was an increase in active labour market spending between 1985 and 2000. In contrast, spending on passive measures has

Table 11.1 Structure of public expenditure in labour market programmes (as a percentage of GDP)

	AUT	BEL	GER	DNK	ESP	FIN	FRA	UKM	GRC
1985									
Total	1.2	4.7	2.2	–	3.1	2.2	3.0	2.9	0.5
Passive measures	0.9	3.4	1.4	–	2.8	1.3	2.4	2.2	0.4
Unemployment compensation	0.8	2.5	0.3	–	1.4	–	2.8	0.9	1.2
Active measures	0.3	1.3	0.8	–	0.3	0.9	0.7	0.8	0.2
PES and administration	0.1	0.2	0.2	–	0.1	0.1	0.1	0.2	0.1
Labour market training	0.1	0.2	0.2	–	0.1	0.1	0.3	0.1	0.0
Youth measures	0.0	0.0	0.0	–	0.0	0.3	0.2	0.3	0.0
Subsidized employment	0.0	0.8	0.2	–	0.2	0.4	0.1	0.2	0.1
of which: subsidized to regular employment	0.0	0.0	0.1	–	0.1	0.1	0.0	–	0.0
direct job creation	0.0	0.8	0.1	–	0.1	0.4	–	0.2	0.0
sub. to entrepreneurship	–	–	–	–	0.0	–	0.0	0.0	–
Measures for disabled	0.0	0.2	0.2	–	0.0	0.1	0.1	0.0	–
1990									
Total	1.3	3.8	2.1	5.4	3.1	2.1	2.6	1.6	0.8
Passive measures	1.0	2.6	1.1	4.3	2.3	1.1	1.8	1.0	0.5
Unemployment compensation	0.8	1.9	1.1	3.1	2.3	0.6	1.3	1.0	0.5
Active measures	0.3	1.2	1.0	1.1	0.8	1.0	0.8	0.6	0.4
PES and administration	0.1	0.2	0.2	0.1	0.1	0.1	0.1	0.2	0.1
Labour market training	0.1	0.2	0.4	0.3	0.2	0.3	0.3	0.2	0.2
Youth measures	0.0	–	0.0	0.3	0.1	0.1	0.2	0.2	0.0
Subsidized employment	0.1	0.7	0.2	0.3	0.4	0.5	0.1	0.0	0.1
of which: subsidized to regular employment	0.0	0.1	0.1	0.0	0.1	0.0	0.1	–	0.1
direct job creation	0.0	0.6	0.1	0.2	0.1	0.4	0.0	–	–
sub. to entrepreneurship	–	0.0	–	0.1	0.2	0.0	0.0	0.0	0.0
Measures for disabled	0.1	0.2	0.2	0.2	0.0	0.1	0.1	0.0	0.0

Table 11.1 continued

1999/2000

	AUT	BEL	GER	DNK	ESP	FIN	FRA	UKM	GRC
Total	1.6	3.7	3.1	4.5	2.2	3.3	3.1	0.9	0.8
Passive measures	1.1	2.3	1.9	3.0	1.3	2.2	1.8	0.6	0.5
Unemployment compensation	1.0	1.8	1.9	1.3	1.3	1.8	1.5	0.6	0.5
Active measures	0.5	1.4	1.2	1.5	0.9	1.1	1.4	0.4	0.3
PES and administration	0.1	0.2	0.2	0.1	0.1	0.1	0.2	0.1	0.1
Labour market training	0.2	0.3	0.3	0.8	0.2	0.4	0.3	0.1	0.2
Youth measures	0.0	–	0.1	0.1	0.1	0.2	0.4	0.2	0.1
Subsidized employment	0.1	0.8	0.3	0.2	0.4	0.3	0.4	0.0	–
of which: subsidized to regular employment	0.1	–	0.0	0.0	0.3	0.2	–	–	–
direct job creation	0.0	–	0.25	0.2	0.1	0.1	–	–	–
sub. to entrepreneurship	0.0	–	0.0	–	0.0	0.0	–	–	–
Measures for disabled	0.1	0.1	0.3	0.3	0.0	0.1	0.1	0.0	0.0

1985

	IRE	ITA	LUX	NET	POR	SWE	USA	EU
Total	4.9	–	1.4	4.6	–	3.0	–	2.8
Passive measures	3.4	–	0.9	3.4	–	0.9	–	2.1
Unemployment compensation	3.4	–	0.3	3.4	–	0.8	–	1.4
Active measures	1.5	–	0.5	1.3	–	2.1	–	0.8
PES and administration	0.2	–	0.0	0.3	–	0.3	–	0.2
Labour market training	0.6	–	–	0.1	–	0.5	–	0.2
Youth measures	0.5	–	0.1	0.0	–	0.2	–	0.1

Subsidized employment	0.2	–	0.1	0.1	–	0.4	–	0.2
of which: subsidized to regular employment	0.0	–	–	0.0	–	0.1	–	0.0
direct job creation	0.1	–	–	0.0	–	0.3	–	0.2
sub. to entrepreneurship	0.1	–	–	–	–	0.0	–	0.0
Measures for disabled	0.0	–	0.3	0.7	–	0.7	–	0.1
1990								
Total	4.0	–	0.9	3.7	1.0	2.6	0.7	2.4
Passive measures	2.6	–	0.6	2.4	0.4	0.9	0.4	1.5
Unemployment compensation	2.5	–	0.1	2.4	0.3	0.8	0.4	1.3
Active measures	1.4	–	0.3	1.3	0.6	1.7	0.2	0.9
PES and administration	0.1	–	0.0	0.3	0.1	0.2	0.06	0.2
Labour market training	0.5	–	0.0	0.2	0.1	0.5	0.09	0.3
Youth measures	0.4	–	0.1	0.1	0.3	0.1	0.03	0.1
Subsidized employment	0.3	–	0.1	0.0	0.1	0.1	0.01	0.2
of which: subsidized to regular employment	0.0	–	0.0	0.0	–	0.0	–	0.1
direct job creation	0.2	–	0.0	0.0	0.0	0.1	0.0	0.1
sub. to entrepreneurship	0.0	–	–	–	0.0	0.0	–	0.1
Measures for disabled	0.1	–	0.1	0.6	0.1	0.8	0.0	0.1
1999/2000								
Total	4.0	–	0.9	3.7	–	2.7	0.4	2.6
Passive measures	2.3	0.6	0.6	2.1	–	1.3	0.2	1.4
Unemployment compensation	2.2	0.6	0.4	2.1	–	1.3	0.2	1.3
Active measures	1.6	–	0.3	1.0	–	1.4	0.2	1.0
PES and administration	0.2	–	0.0	0.3	–	0.3	0.0	0.2
Labour market training	0.2	0.1	0.0	0.3	–	0.3	0.0	0.2
Youth measures	0.2	0.3	0.1	0.0	–	0.0	0.0	0.2

Table 11.1 continued

	IRE	ITA	LUX	NET	POR	SWE	USA	EU
Subsidized employment	0.9	0.3	0.1	0.4	–	0.3	0.0	0.3
of which: subsidized to regular employment	–	–	–	0.1	–	0.2	–	0.1
direct job creation	–	–	–	0.4	–	0.1	0.0	0.2
sub. to entrepreneurship	–	–	–	–	–	0.1	–	0.0
Measures for disabled	0.1	–	0.0	0.6	–	0.5	0.0	0.2

Notes: latest year available is 2000 for most of the countries. The exceptions are:
1999 for BEL, FRA, UKM, ITA, JPN
1998 for CAN, GRC
1997 for LUX
1996 for IRE.
– means no data are avalaible.
The EU average is computed as a weighted average of countries for which data exist.

Source: OECD (2002).

tended to decline over this period in the majority of countries. Consequently, on average across the EU the share of labour market expenditures devoted to active rather than passive measures has risen, from 28 per cent in 1985 to 37 per cent in 1990 and 41 per cent in 1999/2000. This pattern of an increasing share of resources being devoted to active measures has been seen in all countries except Sweden and Finland (in addition there has been little change in Luxembourg). To some extent these two countries may be special cases as unemployment rose sharply in both during the early 1990s, thus automatically increasing passive expenditures on unemployment benefits.

However, it can be reasonably questioned whether the time profile of these data is informative due to the effects of the economic cycle. Both active and passive spending are affected by the cycle, but the effects on passive expenditures tend to be larger (see Martin and Grubb, 2001) and therefore fall more rapidly than expenditures on active measures in an upturn. Hence during an upturn, active measures will tend to assume a greater share of total expenditures. Nevertheless, given that the changes that we observe occur over a 15-year period, it seems reasonable to conclude that there has at least been some shift towards the greater use of active measures in Europe.

In terms of the categories of ALMPs, most spending was concentrated on subsidized employment in 1999/2000 (33 per cent of total active spending). The share of expenditures devoted to subsidized employment rose markedly during the 1990s, and there was a corresponding fall in the share of resources devoted to PES and training.[5] In relation to the latter, an important difference between countries is the extent to which the training is general in nature or more tailored to the requirements of firms and the market. In the 1980s and early 1990s, the Nordic countries tended to provide classroom training in government centres that used standardized materials and teaching methods. However, the emphasis has shifted, especially in Sweden, towards decentralized and firm-based training. In the UK, the structure is decentralized and participant characteristics and training content can be very different between localities, which suggests that the impact of training may vary substantially across individuals and programmes.

Some Examples of Active Labour Market Policies in the EU Countries

The increasing emphasis being placed on active labour market policies can be seen in the EU's European Employment Strategy. It was agreed at the Luxembourg Jobs Summit in November 1997 that a European Employment Strategy would be built on thematic priorities described in a set of 'Employment Guidelines'. Every year these Guidelines are translated into National Action Plans for Employment by member states. These plans are then analysed by the Commission and the Council, the results of which are presented in a document entitled the *Joint Employment Report* (JER). This report provides the basis for conclusions to be drawn and for a subsequent reshaping of the guidelines and country-specific recommendations for member states' employment policies. The 2002 Employment Guidelines specify three main areas for policy actions by member states. Guideline 1 stresses the need to tackle youth unemployment and to prevent long-term unemployment. Guideline 2 emphasizes the need for a more 'employment-friendly' approach relating to benefits, taxes and training systems. Finally, Guideline 6 stresses the need for active policies to develop job matching.[6]

It is beyond the scope of this chapter to give more than a brief summary of the wide range of ALMPs that are under way in EU countries (more information is provided in the JER for 2001). However, the main characteristics of the current policies are as follows:

- The range of measures on offer to the unemployed has become more diversified. Unemployed persons are offered a greater variety of individually tailored pathways to reintegration into the labour market. In many countries there is a growing emphasis on work experience programmes, employment incentives, on-the-job training, start-up and apprenticeship programmes instead of traditional labour market training. Measures are also more tailored to the needs of specific target groups, such as young people, older people and the unemployed with the greatest difficulties. In addition, programmes are more flexible (for example in Finland the duration of measures is tailored to the individual).
- There appears to be a general tendency to reform the PES along three dimensions. First, reform of the organizational structure of the PES by improving the coordination between passive and active measures, strengthening the infrastructure for vocational training, tailoring PES services to the needs and opportunities at regional and local level and improving the organizational and legislative framework for a nationwide implementation of the 'new start' strategy. Second, PES staff numbers have been increased in some countries and staff skills have been upgraded. Last, PES working methods have been improved, with the development of computer-based self-services, the methodology of individual case management and a stricter monitoring of job search behaviour of benefit recipients.
- There is a general trend of increasing cooperation with employers in the design of the active measures. Cooperation between the different actors (local PES, social assistance offices) has also been enhanced.

THEORETICAL CONSIDERATIONS

In this section we briefly review some theoretical considerations with respect to ALMPs. In doing so we draw heavily on the analysis set out by Calmfors (1994), which examines the effects of policies on employment and wage-setting.[7]

Beginning with *JSA*, this form of ALMP should encourage more active search behaviour on the part of the unemployed. The main direct effect of JSA comes through its effect on the matching process, which is expected to be unambiguously positive. This will tend to increase the effective labour supply, thereby easing wage pressures as there is less need for firms to offer higher wages to attract new recruits. In addition, JSA will make it easier and therefore less costly for firms to fill vacancies, leading to an increase in labour demand and thereby higher wages. Furthermore, JSA has the potential to increase competition within the labour market by making the unemployed more competitive with the employed.[8] This competitive effect, which weakens the bargaining power of the employed, would be expected to lead to a moderation of wage pressures. Taken together, the overall impact of JSA on employment should be positive, although the impact on wages is uncertain.

As has already been discussed, when PESs provide JSA they may also monitor the extent to which the unemployed are actively seeking work and thereby enforce eligibility criteria for some social security benefits. One consequence of this may be to reduce (recorded) labour force participation through what is known as the 'work-test' effect. When the PESs check the search effort of the unemployed, it may be the case that those who were not genuinely seeking work may opt to leave the unemployment register rather than increase their search effort. This reduces recorded unemployment and raises non-participation.

Training can be expected to have a number of effects. It may help improve the matching process if those receiving training become better suited to the available vacancies – what is known as the 'treatment effect'. This would make it less costly for firms to fill their vacancies and should lead to a pick-up in labour demand. However, while participants are receiving the training, they can reduce their search activity, at least temporarily (the so-called 'locking-in effect'). Clearly, the net impact of training on the matching process will depend on the balance of these two effects. Training programmes will also affect competition within the labour market, although once again the effect is ambiguous, with both treatment and locking-in effects. Once participants have received training they may well be better placed to compete with incumbents, but while they are being trained they are less likely to be providing a competitive effect. Another effect of training may be to reduce the welfare loss from becoming unemployed. This is particularly likely to be the case where such schemes offer higher remuneration than unemployment benefits. In addition, if schemes are successful, they should raise the employment prospects of the unemployed and/or reduce the wage loss following unemployment. While such a welfare improvement may in itself be desirable, it has the potential side effect of making those in employment less concerned about the possibility of becoming unemployed and therefore potentially more willing to push for higher wages. In most models of wage-setting a lower welfare loss from becoming unemployed is associated with a higher wage level.

In common with training, *subsidies to employment* should have the negative and positive impacts on matching and competition in the labour market from locking-in and treatment effects. However, there are two additional effects which particularly apply to employment creation – deadweight and substitution losses.[9] Deadweight losses occur when a person is enrolled on a scheme who would have found work in the absence of the scheme. The substitution (or displacement) effect arises because the jobs created have merely displaced jobs elsewhere because relative wages have changed. The main way to reduce these losses is to target schemes at those who are least likely to find employment without the scheme.[10]

In many ways the effects of *direct job creation* are quite similar to subsidies to employment, although there are a few notable differences. As with employment subsidies, direct job creation may be associated with negative locking-in and positive treatment effects, and also deadweight and substitution effects. One important drawback with direct job creation is that it would not be expected to provide an opportunity for participants to demonstrate their abilities to prospective employers, and the work undertaken may be less likely to be closely related to that undertaken in the regular jobs market. However, in principle substitution losses are less likely to occur with direct job creation than with subsidized private employment. This is because direct job creation organized by the government can be targeted on activities that would not otherwise have been undertaken.

By *supporting entrepreneurship*, it is possible that economic activity will be promoted that would not otherwise have occurred, perhaps due to market failures that mean that the unemployed do not have full access to financial markets. As well as providing employment to the formerly unemployed entrepreneur, these businesses may at some stage hire labour and therefore lead to a rise in labour demand. If these new businesses increase competition in the markets in which they operate, they may reduce the profitability of incumbent firms and hence reduce their willingness to pay higher wages. However, as with employment creation, there may be deadweight and substitution effects. Some of these businesses would have been set up even without support and the new businesses may simply displace existing businesses which do not receive a subsidy.

All forms of ALMPs may have an impact on labour force participation. ALMPs may help to maintain labour force participation by reducing the risks that the long-term unemployed and other groups of outsiders leave the labour force. While this should raise employment, it may well lead to a rise in recorded unemployment as labour force participation increased by more than employment. As a consequence, there will be more competition for the available jobs and subsequently downward pressures on the wages.

As Calmfors (1994) discusses, it is also important to consider how ALMPs interact with other existing institutions and policies impacting on the labour market (for example social security and tax policies). In addition there is the question of how they are financed. If ALMPs cost more than unemployment benefits, they may increase total public expenditure which must be financed through increased taxation. However, if ALMPs are very effective in reducing unemployment they may ultimately be self-financing or even reduce total spending. Either way, the impact on the government budget constraint should be taken into account. Any changes in taxation induced by such policies may have implications for labour demand or labour supply, depending on which taxes are affected and interactions within the labour market.

EMPIRICAL EVIDENCE

To order the available empirical evidence we shall distinguish between macroeconomic evaluations of broad measures of ALMPs and microeconomic evaluations of specific schemes. There is an important conceptual difference between trying to gauge the full macroeconomic effects after ALMPs have interacted with other labour market structures and institutions, and assessing the effect of a specific scheme on its participants. The macroeconomic effects are of primary interest if one wants to know whether these schemes can improve aggregate labour market outcomes, not least in leading to lower aggregate unemployment. The microeconomic effects are of interest if one wants to know the distributional effects and which types of interventions work better.

Macroeconomic Evaluations

There has been a considerable amount of cross-country macroeconomic analysis, and the seminal contribution in the area is by Layard et al. (1991), who estimated a cross-sectional equation for the institutional determinants of the unemployment rate averaged over the period 1983–88 for 20 OECD countries. This study – and the subsequent works in this vein – does not look solely at the effects of ALMPs but considers them as one of the institutions to be included in the analysis (in addition to trade unions, unemployment benefits, employment protection legislation and so on). Layard et al. (1991) found a significant role for expenditure on ALMPs per unemployed person (expressed as a percentage of output per person in 1987). The results indicated that higher levels of expenditure on ALMPs were associated with lower levels of unemployment over this period.

Nickell and Layard (1999) reworked the earlier results to cover two periods, 1983–88 and 1989–1994, and found a similar result. In the Nickell and Layard (1999) paper, the authors also tested the impact of labour market institutions on long-term and short-term unemployment separately. They found that the ALMPs' variable was a statistically significant determinant of long-term unemployment, but was not a significant determinant for short-term unemployment. The authors also examined the impact of ALMPs on various measures of total labour input, such as employment to population ratios and total hours worked, but found no significant effects.

In the spirit of Layard et al. (1991) other papers have examined different aspects of the role of ALMPs. For example, a paper by Forslund and Krueger (1994) undertook a similar analysis using data from 1983–88 and 1993 and found evidence of parameter instability in the ALMPs' terms. When using data for 1993, the ALMPs' terms were found to be positively associated with the unemployment rate. Using the same measure of ALMPs, Blanchard and Wolfers (2000) analysed the role of economic shocks and institutions. In regressions with measures of institutions and time effects, expenditure on ALMPs appears to be associated with lower unemployment. However, once the role of economic shocks is allowed for the ALMPs' variable generally becomes insignificant.

A study by Scarpetta (1996) for 17 countries contained a more pronounced time-series dimension as annual data were used for the period 1983–93 (although many of the independent variables had no time-series dimension). He found that the estimated impacts of ALMPs on the unemployment rate were generally small and in some cases not statistically significant. However, the results were strongly influenced by the presence of Sweden in the sample. Excluding this country would yield a larger and more significant effect from ALMPs. This work has been updated by Elmeskov et al. (1998) with similar results.

Looking instead at the impact on the Beveridge curve, Jackman et al. (1990) examine the impact of ALMPs for a pooled sample of 14 OECD countries using data for the 1970s and 1980s. They take the unemployment rate as the dependent variable and regress this on two measures of ALMPs (the expenditure per unemployed person and dummies for the existence of ALMPs) along with the vacancy rate, the replacement rate, duration of benefits and an index of corporatism. In general, the authors find a clear negative relationship between the variables capturing ALMPs and the unemployment rate.

In relation to country-specific studies, reflecting the fact that the Nordic countries, and most notably Sweden, have been pioneers of ALMPs, a large volume of research has been conducted on these countries. Skedinger (1995) examined the effect of ALMPs that are targeted at young people (that is, those under 25) in Sweden for the period 1970–91. In particular, he looked at the impact of these measures – quantified by the number of participants – on total regular youth employment using a VAR specification that also includes the unemployment rate to control for the business cycle. Skedinger found very significant displacement effects whereby, at least initially, increases in programme participation are more than offset by falls in non-scheme employment. Using various methods (including a non-parametric matching approach), Larsson (2000) estimates the direct effect of two Swedish programmes for youths in the first half of the 1990s: youth practice and labour market training. She found either zero or negative effects from both programmes in the short run, while long-run effects are zero or slightly positive.

A recently introduced major package of measures in the UK called the 'New Deal for Young People' (NDYP)[11] is the subject of ongoing macro and micro evaluations. The initial evaluations of the scheme have been positive, and Riley and Young (2000) estimate that, as of March 2000, it had reduced youth unemployment by 40 000 and reduced long-term youth unemployment by around 45 000. The scheme was also estimated to have raised UK national income by around £0.5 billion (around 0.05 per cent of GDP).

Lalive et al. (2000) find that after participation in ALMP, the likelihood of transition into work increases for Swiss women (suggestive of positive treatment effects) but not for men. However, the probability of moving from unemployment to employment is also strongly reduced for both sexes during the programmes (suggestive of negative locking-in effects). Johansson (2002) examines the impact of Swedish labour market programmes on labour force participation. She finds that these programmes have relatively large, albeit temporary, positive effects on labour force participation. The results indicate that such programmes can prevent outflows from the labour force during downturns and thereby exert a countercyclical effect on the participation rate.

Calmfors et al. (2002) argue that the problem of simultaneity bias in many of the above studies may be quite serious. This is because the measure used is typically ALMP spending per unemployed person as a proportion of GDP which, as discussed earlier, is likely to be inversely related to unemployment. Interestingly, if steps are taken to address the simultaneity problem, this tends to have a major bearing on the results, and as Calmfors et al. (2002) note: 'the results of ALMPs tend to become less favourable'. As has already been mentioned, a more limited number of studies examine the impact of ALMPs on wages. Heylen (1993) examined the impact of ALMPs on an index of real wage flexibility. Using a cross-sectional OECD data set, he regressed this index on a number of institutional variables[12] and five measures of ALMPs based on expenditure on different categories of schemes and the ratio of active to passive expenditures. The author finds that expenditure on PES measures and training have strong impacts on wage flexibility, while other expenditures, such as public sector job creation and wage subsidies, did not. A study by Calmfors and Nymoen (1990) estimated wage equations for the Nordic countries and examined the impact of two measures of ALMPs (the share of the labour force participating in ALMPs and the share of participants in ALMPs in total unemployment). They found that for three of the four countries (Sweden, Denmark and Finland) the ALMPs' measures were actually associated with higher wage pressures, although there were high standard errors attached to these results.

A notable study by Calmfors and Forslund (1991) looked at the impact of ALMPs on real wages in Sweden for the period 1960–86. In line with the notion that ALMPs may lead to a reduced welfare loss from unemployment, the authors found that such policies have a strong and significant role in driving up wages.[13] The effect is so large that an increase in scheme participation is likely to be more than offset by a decrease in non-scheme employment.

However, the effects of ALMPs on wage formation in Sweden have been revisited by Forslund and Kolm (2000) using data for the 1990s. They find that, according to most of their estimates, ALMPs do not seem to contribute significantly to increased wage pressure. Calmfors et al. (2002) reviewed the more recent evidence and concluded that the impact of ALMPs on wages is 'unclear'. In relation to the UK, Anderton and Soteri (1996) examined the impact of ALMPs through their effects on real wages, disaggregated by both industry and region. Youth training programmes are found to have increased wages in one sector (distribution).

Microeconomic Evaluations of Specific Schemes

An enormous amount of work has been undertaken evaluating the effects of specific schemes. Thorough surveys of this literature have already been undertaken, notably by Fay (1996) and Meager and Evans (1997), although these surveys are not always fully in agreement on the main findings of this literature. There is little merit in repeating this survey work, so in this section we begin by reviewing and where appropriate contrasting the findings of these two comprehensive survey papers and then build upon these using the results of more recent work. One issue that we do not address in detail is that of the evaluation methodology, which has a critical bearing on the findings of the evaluation studies. These questions are covered in the two aforementioned survey articles and a volume by Schmid et al. (1996).[14] It is also worth pointing out that there is very little evidence of the 'long-run' impact of the examined programmes, most of the studies focus only on the short-run outcomes (typically for one or two years at most after participation in the programme).

Turning first to *JSA*, Fay (1996) notes that it appears to help most groups of the unemployed, but seems most effective for women and single parents. He suggests that such measures provide the lowest-cost interventions with the largest relative payoffs. However, while the benefits appear to be widespread, such schemes do not necessarily help large numbers of people and the longer-term impacts are uncertain. While recognizing that JSA appears cost-effective and can play a useful role, Meager and Evans (1997) are somewhat more sceptical about whether the positive assessment made by Fay (1996) can be justified by the evaluation evidence. They argue that the employment effects of such measures tend to be small or non-existent. The evidence from the USA seems to support the view that JSA can offer tangible, albeit small, benefits. The US literature is reviewed by Stanley et al. (1998), who conclude that JSA helps the unemployed return to work and saves government money, but that the impact on earnings tends to be moderate at best.

As has already been discussed, when providing JSA, the PESs can have the additional role of implementing benefit eligibility criteria. A particular difficulty with identifying the effects of changes in JSA interventions is that they have often been introduced along with changes in benefit administration, usually to put greater pressure on the unemployed to search more intensively. Sweeney and McMahon (1998) examined the impact of a change in unemployment benefit administration in the UK with the introduction of the Job Seeker's Allowance in October 1996. This allowance reduced the period of entitlement for unemployment insurance from 12 to six months, included a range of measures to encourage more successful job search, and increased checks on claimants to ensure that they fulfilled eligibility criteria. Following its introduction there was a marked fall in unemployment claimants – the majority of which was thought due to the removal of employed or inactive claimants rather than an increase in the number of people entering employment. This highlights the importance of the work-test effect discussed in the theoretical section. However, when programme participation and continuing entitlement to unemployment benefit are linked, there is a risk of reducing the incentives to take up a regular job and inducing cycles of unemployment and programme participation. To minimize these risks, Martin and Grubb (2001) suggest closely associating the management of referrals to ALMPs with the regular placement function of the PES.

Fay (1996) concludes that *training* appears to help women re-entrants into the labour market but not youths (unless combined with other programmes), prime-age men and older workers with low initial education. He also concludes that such training works best when it is targeted at specific groups and that it is important that courses 'signal' strong labour market relevance and that they are of high quality. One danger that Fay (1996) envisages is that training measures may simply encourage greater reporting of existing training by firms rather than actually increasing its volume. Meager and Evans (1997) suggest that although many studies have shown that training makes little difference to the employment (or earnings) chances of participants, some caution should be exercised before drawing very negative conclusions. Payoffs to training and skill acquisition are likely to be long-term and may be larger than indicated by the short-term impacts. Meager and Evans (1997) also suggest that training of the long-term unemployed is likely to have a greater effect when it is customized to the needs of employers rather than being more general in nature.

A number of recent studies have pointed to positive impacts from some training schemes. Holm (2002) finds a positive and significant effect of training in Denmark. He argues that the apparent negative effect of training, which has been found in other studies, is due to selection bias and once this has been accounted for, a positive effect of the training programme appears. Work on France by Fougère et al. (2000) finds that schemes aimed at unemployed young persons have no effect on post-training wages or employment probabilities unless they have a large training content. Heckman et al. (1999) indicate that some public training programmes for disadvantaged groups in the USA have led to improvements in terms of earnings and the rate of exit from unemployment for participants, the latter being the most important effect. However, the estimated earning gains were not sufficient to lift people out of poverty.

A number of other studies have emphasized the benefits that training schemes can provide by allowing participants to demonstrate their abilities to the firms providing the training. Main and Shelly (1990) and Mealli et al. (1996) show that those who complete a UK Youth Training Scheme have significantly higher employment rates than those who leave early. Carling and Richardson (2001) examine the relative efficiency of eight Swedish labour market programmes in reducing unemployment duration. They find that participants who receive training and subsidized work experience provided by firms have better outcomes than those who receive classroom vocational training. Their work indicates that the more regular work that participants are allowed to undertake, the better the programme performs. Carling and Richardson (2001) suggest that their findings may be, at least in part, due to the fact that such 'on-the-job' experience provides participants with an opportunity to show their competence to prospective employers (also suggested by Upward, 2000, for the UK). Nevertheless, for the most part, the recent work in the Swedish context has not led to favourable assessment of training programmes. Calmfors et al. (2002) provides an up-to-date review of the evidence on training programmes in Sweden. They find marked differences between evaluations undertaken in the 1980s and the 1990s. Earlier evaluations, particularly those from the first half of the 1980s, generally indicate positive effects of training on participants' employment and/or incomes. In contrast, evaluations of training programmes undertaken in the 1990s often find insignificant or negative effects, although there are some exceptions.

Fay (1996) found that *employment subsidies* seem to work best for the long-term unemployed and women re-entrants. Once again, they do not seem suitable for youths unless combined with other programmes. Fay (1996) also noted that such policies require careful targeting and controls to avoid large deadweight losses and substitution effects and the possibility that firms may use such schemes to permanently subsidize their workforce. Meager and Evans (1997) concluded that subsidies to employment had a high cost per participant and most notably per net job created. They also noted that such measures often had high deadweight effects. Some studies had also reported significant substitution effects. Nevertheless they felt that there was a role for such subsidies targeted at the most disadvantaged groups – such as the long-term unemployed – for whom other measures had not worked.

A large volume of work has been undertaken examining the magnitude of displacement effects from ALMPs in Sweden. This work, which is reviewed by Calmfors et al. (2002), finds that employment subsidies can have very large displacement effects, as between 39 and 84 per cent of the jobs created by such schemes are offset by a decline in regular employment. In general, the closer a labour market programme is to the regular labour market, the larger are such displacement effects. Gerfin and Lechner (2001) find positive effects of a wage subsidy for temporary jobs in the regular labour market that would otherwise not be taken up by the unemployed.

A form of effective employment subsidy that has become more popular in recent years is 'earned income tax credits'. These are in-work benefits in the form of an income supplement, often targeted at certain groups such as low-income families with children. They are typically means-tested according to family income and vary in line with family size and, unlike ALMPs, they are usually paid indefinitely. Blundell and Meghir (2002) consider the relative merits of ALMPs that involve wage subsidies together with improved job matching as compared with an alternative policy of earned income tax credits. They observe that indefinite means-tested tax credit programmes may generate incentives to reduce human capital accumulation and may thus lead participants to become dependent on the programme. They suggest that a possible way of addressing this problem is to simultaneously encourage training, for example as in the UK's New Deal programme.

According to Fay (1996), *direct job creation* appears to help only the severely disadvantaged labour market groups who might otherwise face very significant barriers to gaining employment. Direct job creation typically provides few long-run benefits and usually involves jobs with low marginal products. Meager and Evans (1997) found the evidence on the success of such measures to be 'very mixed'. They noted pessimistic conclusions being drawn for many countries with long-established and large-scale direct job creation schemes, but nevertheless some schemes in some countries have been given more positive assessments. They argue, *inter alia*, that the more successful schemes are those that offer work activities similar to those found in the open labour market, offer training and other support to participants, are targeted towards the long-term unemployed and do not make participation a condition of continued receipt of benefits.

Eichler and Lechner (2002) find a significant reduction in the probability of unemployment for those engaged in public employment programmes in East Germany in the period following participation. This finding is fairly robust to several different specifications and to the use of different sub-populations. Calmfors et al. (2002) find displacement effects for direct job creation to be much lower than for other forms of employment subsidy. In addition they find that such programmes appear to work better when they are closer to regular employment.

An important issue is whether direct job creation can provide a pathway to regular employment. A study by the OECD (2002) suggests that job creation programmes interrupt long-term unemployment but generate repeated spells of short-term unemployment instead. In the same vein, Martin and Grubb (2001) conclude in their survey that direct job creation has been of little success in helping unemployed get permanent jobs in the open labour market.

Meager and Evans (1997) and Fay (1996) conclude that *aid to the unem-ployed starting enterprises* can only help a limited number of people and that deadweight and displacement losses are high. A number of more recent stud-ies have examined the effects of self-employment grants in Sweden. Carling and Gustafson (1999) compare the effects of self-employment grants and recruitment subsidies on employment duration. They find that the former led to significantly better employment results than the latter. Similarly, Carling and Richardson (2001) also find comparatively positive effects for such schemes in reducing unemployment durations. At the same time, a couple of studies (Okeke, 1999, and Okeke and Spånt Enbuske, 2001) find that self-employment grants have no impact on enterprise survival rates, although they may increase the probability of the self-employed earning a living through their enterprises.

CONCLUSIONS

This chapter has highlighted how expenditures on active labour market policies have been rising in Europe and have steadily assumed a larger share of total labour market spending. As indicated by the 2001 JER, recent policy initiatives have become increasingly diversified, incorporating a number of different elements and frequently involving programmes tailored to the needs of individuals. In addition, policies are being increasingly targeted towards certain groups, such as younger and older workers. There is also an increased involvement of employers in the design of new policies.

Expenditure on public employment services accounted for around 16 per cent of active labour market expenditure in the EU in 2000. According to the 2001 JER, there appears to be a general tendency to reform the organization and administration of these services. In general, both the theoretical and empirical literature is supportive of the effects of JSA. The theoretical analysis indicates that it is likely to have a positive impact on employment, although the impact on wages is uncertain. The empirical evidence suggest that JSA interventions are effective and represent good value for money but are ultimately only able to play a modest role in reducing unemployment.

Significant resources are devoted to training (around 24 per cent of the EU total in 2000), although the share of resources available for this category has declined in recent years as other categories have assumed increased importance. According to the 2001 JER, training is increasingly likely to be undertaken 'on the job' rather than in the classroom, with an increased emphasis on ICT training. The theoretical evidence on the effects of training on both the matching process and competition in the labour market is ambiguous and depends on the balance between positive treatment and negative locking-in effects, and the impact on the welfare loss from unemployment. Although a significant share of the empirical evidence is quite pessimistic about the effectiveness of training schemes in the short term (especially for youths), some studies have suggested that they can play a useful role when closely aligned to the needs of the labour market in the form of on-the-job training. Schemes also tend to be more effective when provided by a future potential employer.

A large part of the growth in expenditure on active measures has been devoted to forms of subsidized employment and direct job creation, which accounted for around 28 per cent of spending in the EU in 2000. According to the 2001 JER, the increased emphasis on targeted subsidized work is continuing in current policy initiatives. Despite the increased policy efforts in this area, such interventions attract, at best, only mixed support from the theoretical and empirical economic literature, although there is backing for the increased use of targeting towards certain groups in the labour market, such as the long-term unemployed. Of the two forms of employment creation, subsidized employment attracts more support than direct employment creation.

Comprehensive figures for the use of measures to support entrepreneurship are not available, although for those countries where data are available, it is clear that these measures account for a comparatively small share of the resources available. The theoretical evidence suggests that measures to support entrepreneurship can raise employment directly and indirectly through competitive effects. However, such policies are also potentially vulnerable to deadweight and substitution losses. There is some empirical support for such schemes, but it is recognized that such interventions can help only a very limited number of people.

NOTES

1. The authors are affiliated to the European Central Bank (ECB) and the Organization for Economic Cooperation and Development (OECD), respectively, although the work was begun while the latter was still employed by the ECB. The views expressed are those of the authors and do not necessarily reflect those of the institutions to which they are affiliated. The authors are grateful to Ignazio Angeloni, Gabriel Fagan, Peter Hoeller, Dennis Snower and Melanie Ward-Warmedinger for helpful comments and suggestions on earlier drafts while retaining responsibility for all remaining errors.
2. For instance, *The OECD Jobs Study* (OECD, 1995) recommended a stronger emphasis on active rather than passive labour market policies. Recommendations in relation to active labour market policies can be found in the EU's Employment Guidelines (Council decision of 18 February 2002 on guidelines for Member States' employment policies for the year 2002 [2002/177/EC]).
3. The statistics that we use have certain drawbacks. For instance, they do not provide information on the number of people actually benefiting from such expenditure, the quality of the expenditure, the average length of time spent on the programme or information on how many times participants have attended the programmes. Moreover, spending on some types of ALMPs may change automatically in line with changes in unemployment (or long-term unemployment). Therefore changes in expenditures within the economic cycle cannot be assumed to represent deliberate policy innovations. A further problem is that there is not a perfect correspondence between the categorizing used in the OECD and the typology described in the previous section. It should be noted that the OECD data set only includes public spending and therefore does not cover private sector spending on training. Not all forms of public spending are included (for example some by sub-national levels of government) and many tax subsidies and exemptions for training are not covered. The passive measures are also probably markedly underestimated, given the large number of people in early retirement or disability schemes.
4. EU data have been computed as the weighted average using countries for which data are available.
5. However, it should be noted that private provision of JSA has grown rapidly in some EU countries – see, for instance, Storrie (2002).
6. Previously there was a quantitative target for active measures involving education, training or similar measures offered to the unemployed. However, recently, the EC appears to focus more on the 'dimension of effectiveness and efficiency' rather than on the numbers of beneficiaries (see 2002 Draft JER).
7. Such policies can also be assessed in relation to the Beveridge curve – see, for instance, ECB (2002).

8. For example, in 'insider–outsider' models where insiders have the dominant influence on wage-setting, JSA may help outsiders compete more effectively with insiders – Lindbeck and Snower (1988).
9. See for instance Haveman and Hollister (1991).
10. Orszag and Snower (1999) argue that there may be important differences between the short- and long-term effects of employment subsidies. They illustrate this with a simple model of the effects of 'employment vouchers', which are taken to cover a wide variety of policy instruments including tax breaks and grants to support employment. As the authors discuss, such policies are likely to raise both the rate at which people are hired from unemployment (the hiring rate) and the rate at which people who are currently in work lose their jobs (the firing rate). On the assumption that such policy interventions provide a proportionately larger stimulus to the hiring rate than the firing rate, Orszag and Snower (1999) show that the long-run employment effects of such subsidies will be greater than the short-run effects.
11. The NDYP aims to cut youth unemployment by helping the young long-term unemployed to improve their job search and, for those who do not find work offering work, experience and/or training. The main innovations of the NDYP were on the one hand that its support was intended to be tailored to the individual needs of its participants and on the other hand that young people who did not actively participate in the programme faced the sanction of losing their unemployment assistance.
12. Namely an index of the degree of centralization of wage bargaining (and the square of this index to pick up non-linear effects), a measure of institutional sclerosis, the replacement ratio, the duration of unemployment benefits, union density and the frequency of temporary layoffs.
13. This finding is consistent with a number of other studies published around the same time. Calmfors et al. (2002) provide a brief review of these studies.
14. There can be important differences in how programmes are designed and implemented, and participants often receive a variety of different services making it hard to distinguish the effects of differing types of interventions. Certain features of schemes may affect an individual's decision to participate in training (for example in Sweden and the UK, participation in training is a condition for receiving unemployment benefits). Programme administrators often have considerable discretion over whom they admit into government training programmes (for example, in the USA, but also in Austria, Denmark, Germany and the UK), which raises the possibility of a 'selection' bias on the basis of some (unobserved) characteristics of the participants. This can make it difficult to compare outcomes between scheme participants and non-participants. In some countries (for example Finland) there is an incentive to provide public sector ALMPs jobs as they are paying for social assistance but not for subsidies to this type of work. In this context the genuine effect of ALMPs might be biased, though difficult to take up in empirical works.

REFERENCES

Anderton, R. and S. Soteri (1996), *Wage Determination and Active Labour Market Programmes*, NIESR Discussion Paper No. 96.

Blanchard, O. and J. Wolfers (2000), 'The role of shocks and institutions in the rise of European unemployment: the aggregate evidence', *The Economic Journal*, **110**, C1–33.

Blundell, R. and C. Meghir (2002), *Active Labour Market Policy vs Employment Tax Credits: Lessons from Recent UK Reforms*, IFAU Working Paper 2002:1.

Calmfors, L. (1994), 'Active labour market policy and unemployment: a framework for analysis of crucial design features', *OECD Economic Studies*, **22** (Spring), 7–47.

Calmfors, L. and A. Forslund (1991), 'Real wage determination and labour market policies: the Swedish experience', *The Economic Journal*, **101**, 1130–48.

Calmfors, L. and R. Nymoen (1990), 'Nordic employment', *Economic Policy*, **5**, 398–448 .

Calmfors, L., A. Forslund and M. Hemström (2002), *Does Active Labour Market Policy Work? Lessons from the Swedish Experiences*, IFAU Working Paper No. 4.

Carling, K. and L. Gustafson (1999), *Self-Employment Grants vs Subsidized Employment: Is there a Difference in the Re-Unemployment Risk?*, IFAU Working Paper 1999:6.

Carling, K. and K. Richardson (2001), *The Relative Efficiency of Labor Market Programs: Swedish Experience from the 1990s*, IFAU Working Paper 2001:2.

ECB (2002), *Labour Market Mismatches in Euro Area Countries*, ECB Occasional Paper, Frankfurt.

Eichler, M. and M. Lechner (2002), 'An evaluation of public employment programmes in the East German State of Sachsen-Anhalt', *Labour Economics*, **9**, 143–86.

Elmeskov, J., J.P. Martin and S. Scarpetta (1998), 'Key lessons for labour market reforms: evidence from OECD countries experiences', *Swedish Economic Policy Review*, **5** (2), 205–52.

European Commission (2001), *Joint Employment Report*, Brussels.

European Commission (2002), *Joint Employment Report*, draft, Brussels.

Fay, R.G. (1996), *Enhancing the Effectiveness of Active Labour Market Policies: Evidence from Programme Evaluations in OECD Countries*, OECD Labour and Social Policy Occasional Paper No. 18.

Forslund, A. and A. Kolm (2000), *Active Labour Market Policies and Real-Wage Determination – Swedish Evidence*, IFAU Working Paper No. 7.

Forslund, A. and A. Krueger (1994), *An Evaluation of the Swedish Active Labor Market Policy: New and Received Wisdom*, NBER Working Paper No. 4802.

Fougère, D., F. Kramarz and T. Magnac (2000), 'Youth employment policies in France', *European Economic Review*, **44**, 928–42.

Gerfin, M. and M. Lechner (2001), *A Microeconometric Evaluation of Active Labour Market Policy in Switzerland*, Centre for Economic Policy Research Working Paper No. 2993.

Haveman, R. and R. Hollister (1991), 'Direct job creation: Economic evaluation and lessons for the United States and Western Europe', in A. Björklund, R. Haveman, R. Hollister and B. Holmlund (eds), *Labour Market Policy and Unemployment Insurance, FIEF Studies in Labour Market and Economic Policy*, Oxford, New York, Toronto and Melbourne: Oxford University Press, Clarendon Press, pp. 5–65.

Heckman J., R. Lalonde and J. Smith (1999), 'The economics and econometrics of active labor market programs', in O. Ashenfelter and D. Card (eds), *Handbook of Labor Economics, Vol. 3A*, Amsterdam, New York and Oxford: Elsevier Science, North-Holland, pp. 1865–2097.

Heylen, F. (1993), 'Labour market structures, labour market policy and wage formation in the OECD', *Labour*, **7**, 25–51.

Holm, A. (2002), 'The effect of training on search durations: a random effects approach', *Labour Economics*, **9**, 433–50.

Jackman, R., C. Pissarides and S. Savouri (1990), 'Labour market policies and unemployment in the OECD', *Economic Policy*, **11**, 450–90.

Johansson, K. (2002), *Labor Market Programs, the Discouraged-Worker Effects and Labor Force Participation*, IFAU Working Paper 2002:9.

Lalive, R., J.C. van Ours and J. Zweimuller (2000), *The Impact of Active Labour Market Programs and Benefit Entitlements Rules on the Duration of Unemployment*, IEW Working Paper No. 41.

Larsson, L. (2000), *Evaluation of Swedish Youth Labour Market Programmes*, IFAU Working Paper Series 2000:1.

Layard, R., S. Nickell and R. Jackman (1991), *Unemployment*, Oxford and New York: Oxford University Press.

Lindbeck, A. and D. Snower (1988), *The Insider-Outsider Theory of Employment and Unemployment*, Cambridge, MA: MIT Press.

Main, B. and M. Shelly (1990), 'The effectiveness of YTS as a manpower policy', *Economica*, **57**, 495–514.

Martin, J.P. and D. Grubb (2001), *What Works and For Whom: A Review of OECD Countries' Experiences with Active Labour Market Policies*, IFAU Working Paper 2001:14.

Meager, N. and C. Evans (1997), *The Evaluation of Active Labour Market Policies for the Long-Term Unemployed*, Geneva: International Labour Organization.

Mealli, F., S. Pudney and J. Thomas (1996), 'Training duration and post-training outcomes – a duration limited competing risks model', *The Economic Journal*, **106**, 422–33.

Nickell, S. and R. Layard (1999), 'Labour market institutions and economic performance' in O.C. Ashenfelter and D. Card (eds), *Handbook of Labor Economics, Vol. 3C*, Amsterdam, New York and Oxford: Elsevier Science, North-Holland, pp. 3029–84.

OECD (1995), 'Labour adjustments and active labour market policies', in *The OECD Jobs Study: Evidence and Explanations*, Paris, pp. 63–112.

OECD (2002) *Employment Outlook*, Paris.

Okeke, S. (1999), *Starta Eget-Bidragets Effekter – Utvårdering av Företag Tre År Efter Start*, Ura 1999:12, Stockholm: National Labour Market Board.

Okeke, S. and A. Spånt Enbuske (2001), *Utvårdering av 1995 Års Nystartade Företag*, Ura 2001:2, Stockholm: National Labour Market Board.

Orszag, J.M. and D. Snower (1999), 'The effectiveness of employment vouchers: a simple approach', mimeo.

Riley, R. and G. Young (2000), 'New deal for young people: implications for employment and the public finances', NIESR mimeo.

Scarpetta, S. (1996), 'Assessing the role of labour market policies and institutional settings on unemployment: a cross country study', *OECD Economic Studies*, **26** (Spring), 43–98.

Schmid, G., J. O'Reilly and K. Shömann (1996), *International Handbook of Labour Market Policy and Evaluation*, Cheltenham, UK and Lyme, USA: Edward Elgar Publishing Ltd.

Skedinger, P. (1995), 'Employment policies and displacement in the youth labour market', *Swedish Economic Policy Review*, **2** (1), 135–71.

Stanley, M., L.F. Katz and A. Krueger (1998), *Developing Skills: What We Know About the Impacts of American Employment and Training Programmes on Employment, Earning and Educational Outcomes*, Malcom Wiener Center for Social Policy, Working Paper H–98–02, Harvard: John F. Kennedy School of Government, Harvard University.

Storrie, D. (2002), *Temporary Agency Work in the European Union*, European Foundation for the Improvement of Living and Working Conditions, Dublin.

Sweeney, K. and D. McMahon (1998), 'The effect of Jobseeker's Allowance on the claimant count', *Labour Market Trends*, April, 195–203.

Upward, R. (2002), 'Evaluating outcomes from the youth training scheme using matched firm-training data', *Oxford Bulletin of Economics and Statistics*, **64** (3), 277–306.

Index